THE MATTERING INSTINCT

THE
MATTERING
INSTINCT

HOW OUR DEEPEST
LONGING DRIVES US
AND DIVIDES US

**Rebecca Newberger
Goldstein**

Liveright Publishing Corporation

*A Division of W. W. Norton & Company
Independent Publishers Since 1923*

For information about permission to reproduce selections from this book,
write to Permissions, Liveright Publishing Corporation, a division of
W. W. Norton & Company, Inc., 500 Fifth Avenue, New York, NY 10110

For information about special discounts for bulk purchases, please contact
W. W. Norton Special Sales at specialsales@wwnorton.com or 800-233-4830

Manufacturing by Lakeside Book Company
Book design by Daniel Lagin
Production manager: Anna Oler

Library of Congress Cataloging-in-Publication Data is available.

ISBN 978-1-32409-685-6

Liveright Publishing Corporation, 500 Fifth Avenue, New York, NY 10110
www.wwnorton.com

W. W. Norton & Company Ltd., 15 Carlisle Street, London W1D 3BS

Authorized EU representative: EAS, Mustamäe tee 50, 10621 Tallinn, Estonia

10 9 8 7 6 5 4 3 2 1

For Solly and Kai,

who give me endless joy

We know that the real lesson to be taught is that the human person is precious and unique; but we seem unable to set it forth except in terms of ideology and abstraction.

—Iris Murdoch

CONTENTS

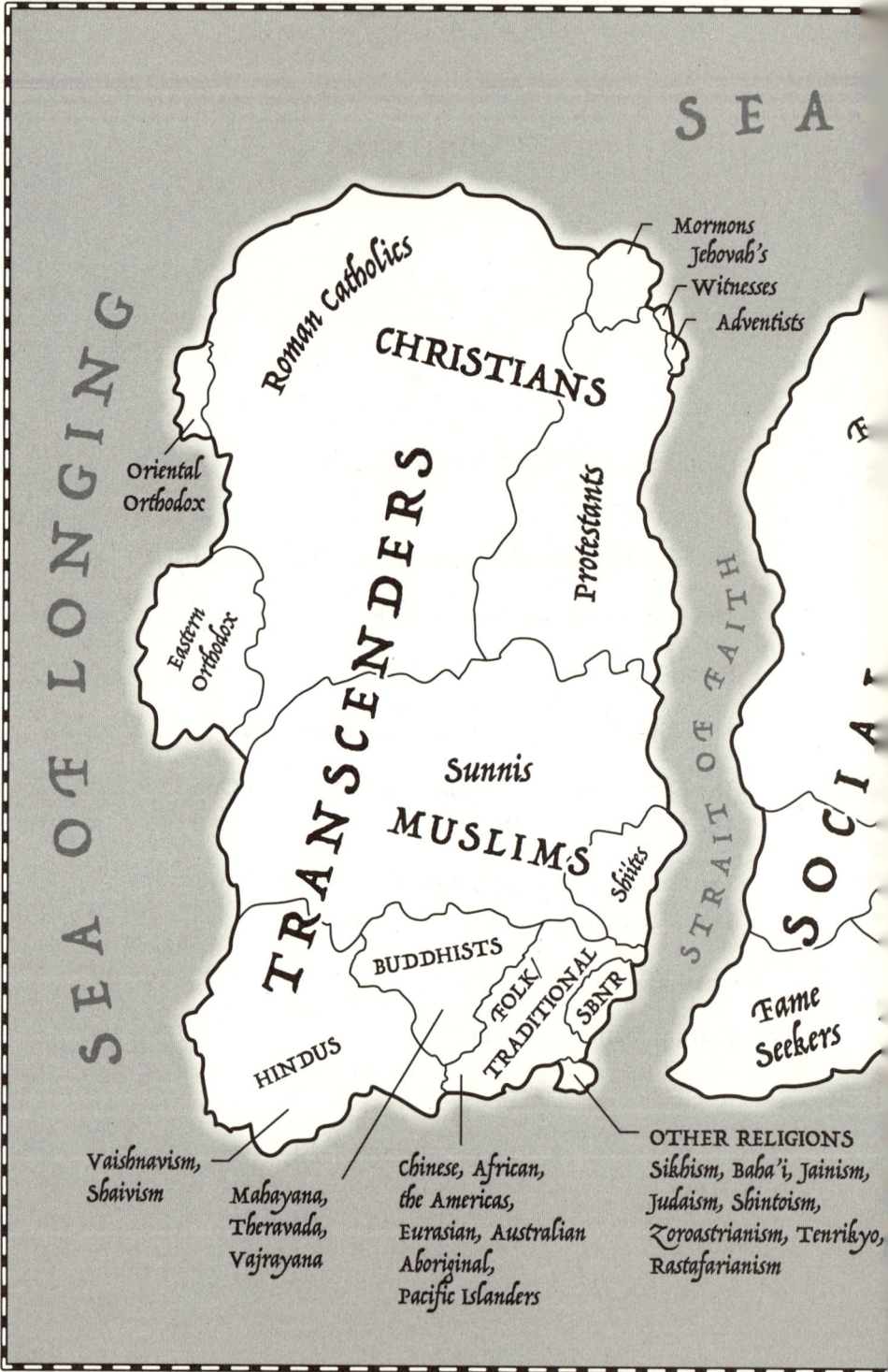

SEA

Mormons
Jehovah's
Witnesses
Adventists

Roman Catholics

CHRISTIANS

Oriental
Orthodox

Protestants

TRANSCENDERS

Eastern
orthodox

SEA OF LONGING

Sunnis

MUSLIMS

Shiites

STRAIT OF FAITH

SOCIA

BUDDHISTS

FOLK/
TRADITIONAL

SBNR

HINDUS

Fame
Seekers

Vaishnavism,
Shaivism

Mahayana,
Theravada,
Vajrayana

Chinese, African,
the Americas,
Eurasian, Australian
Aboriginal,
Pacific Islanders

OTHER RELIGIONS
Sikhism, Baha'i, Jainism,
Judaism, Shintoism,
Zoroastrianism, Tenrikyo,
Rastafarianism

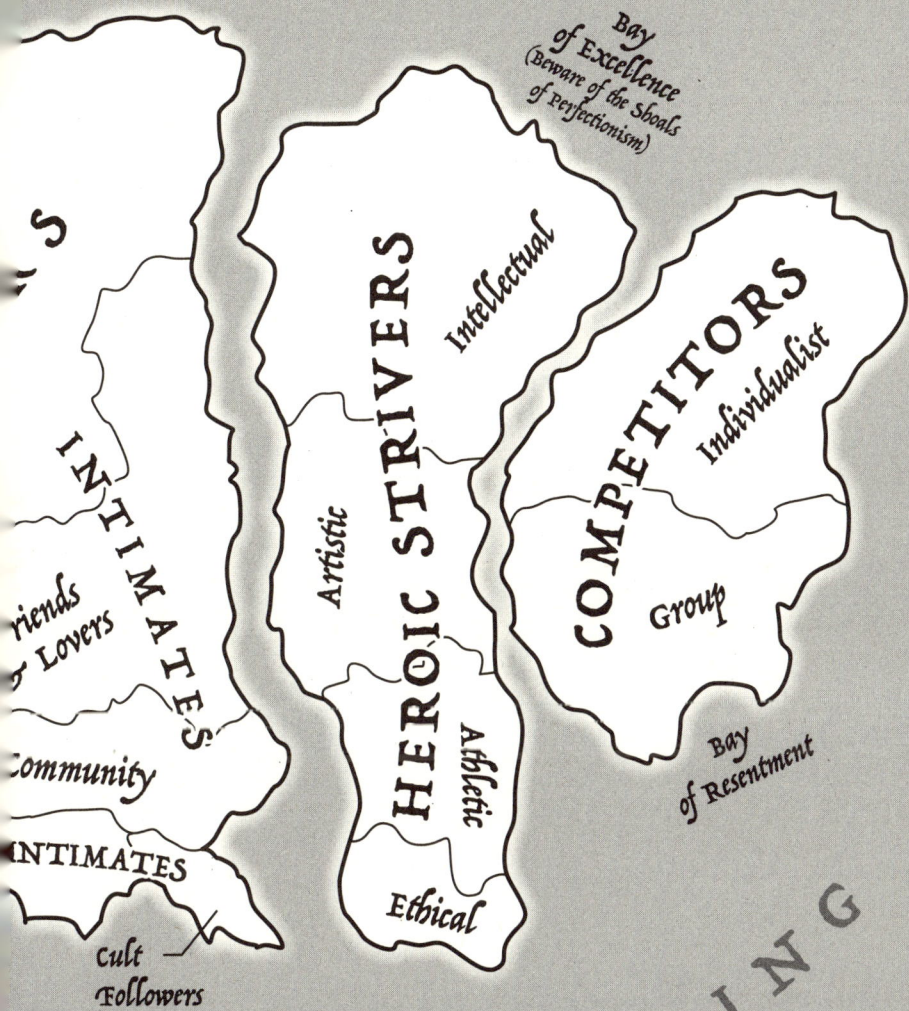

Explanatory note: The areas of the continents and regions are determined by estimations of the comparative percentage of inhabitants. No claim is being made as to which continents or regions matter more than others.

PREFACE

More than forty years ago I published my first book, *The Mind-Body Problem*, and that is how long I've been pursuing the theory laid out in this one.

Strangely, that first book was a novel. I say strangely since I was then a professor of philosophy, with a specialty in the philosophy of science. There is the kind of philosophy that takes novels seriously. Think Jean-Paul Sartre, Albert Camus, Simone de Beauvoir. But I was not that kind of philosopher. Though I loved reading novels, I had never entertained the intention of writing one until I found myself doing so. Its writing introduced me to a train of ideas I doubt I'd have otherwise pursued. These ideas, which were about mattering, seemed entirely separate from my training as a philosopher, but eventually, my storytelling and theorizing merged. Still, it remains strange to me that the philosophical ideas that have come to mean the most to me came about in such a roundabout way.

It was the editor of that first book who precipitated my

theorizing. After he'd read the first draft, he confessed that he didn't entirely understand my main character. "She's beautiful, smart, funny, and sexually desirable. So why is she always so unhappy?" I pondered the editor's question and out came my character's response, which was all about mattering. "To matter. Not to be as naught. Is there any will deeper than that?" she muses. This train of thought gave rise to the idea of the mattering map, which my character first introduces to explain what drew her to the man she eventually marries, a mathematical genius named Noam Himmel. "A person's location on [the mattering map] is determined by what matters to him, matters overwhelmingly, the kind of mattering that produces his perceptions of people, of himself and others: of who are the nobodies and who the somebodies, who the deprived and who the gifted, who the better-never-to-have-been-born and who the heroes. . . . And so at those Princeton parties, when we sat around sharing stories of our heroes, of those now gone, like Einstein, or those still with us, like Himmel, we would get high on love, on love for our idols and love for each other. For in loving our great men and women we unite ourselves not only with human excellence, but also with one another. Those who share my heroes are, in the deepest sense, *of my own kind*." It's only at the book's conclusion that she comes to understand how the mattering map explains her own unhappiness. In many regions of the mattering map, my smart, funny, and sexually desirable character would have every reason to be happy. Her problem was that she didn't reside in any of those regions.

What I'd said about mattering in that first book—most especially the idea of the mattering map—proved useful to some academic researchers in disparate fields. For example, the psychologist Ellyn Kaschak uses the mattering map in her writings, beginning in 1992 with *Engendered Lives: A New Psychology of Women's Experience*, and in 2009 the behavioral economists George Loewenstein and Karl Moene published an article entitled "How Mattering Maps Affect Behavior" in the *Harvard Business Review*. This suggested that the idea had wider applicability than I had first realized.

Over the years, I've spoken to many people about their own sense of mattering, gathering information about what the world feels like from within different regions of the mattering map—though not because I planned to write a book devoted to the subject. The subject of mattering, as it continued to develop in my mind, seemed too big and sprawling, calling for a systematic deduction from first premises in the style of my favorite philosopher, Baruch Spinoza, and thus too daunting. I kept talking to others about mattering only because it allowed me to connect with people quite different from myself and yielded such rich and startling revelations about human diversity. Some of the ideas leaked into books that I wrote on other topics. This was particularly true of my last book, *Plato at the Googleplex*, in which I hazarded a hypothesis as to why it was the ancient Greeks who invented Western philosophy.

One person took special notice: Martin Seligman, the founder of positive psychology, and in March 2018 he organized a three-day workshop on the topic of mattering. Present at the workshop were the psychologists Roy Baumeister, Gabriella Kellerman, Andrew Reece, Barry Schwartz, and David Yaden. A paper emerged from those three days: "Mattering as an Indicator of Organizational Health and Employee Success," authored by all those who attended the workshop, together with Alexi Robichaux.

More important, at least for me, was the interest these psychologists had in what I had to say about mattering—above all Marty, who after the workshop wrote, "There comes from time to time an idea from the discipline of philosophy so sensible that it lays bare the poverty of ideas in the discipline of psychology. Mattering is such an idea."

These lines were supposed to introduce another paper produced out of this workshop, whose first draft I was delegated to write. I soon realized that only a book would do.

WHY MATTERING MATTERS

This book is about a missing piece in the puzzle of understanding ourselves, one another, and our troubled times. It offers a new framework for analyzing what can go wrong both in our individual lives and in society and invites us to imagine how the flourishing of both can be enhanced.

It is about mattering. Every living thing is organically driven by a mandate that ensures it matters to itself—which is to say that it prioritizes its own surviving and thriving. In lifeforms as massive as blue whales and as scanty as a sliver of grass struggling up through a crack in the sidewalk, biology encodes the message of self-mattering.

But when it comes to humans, mattering takes on a different order of complexity. In us, the organic mandate of self-mattering engenders one of the most persistent forces in human motivation, which has us striving not only to survive and thrive but also striving after an existence that we deem to be meaningful in our own eyes. For us, and us alone, the organic mandate of self-mattering does not suffice. We need to convince ourselves that our own self-mattering is warranted, that we can provide a reason for it that extends beyond our being, trivially, ourselves—just as all things are, trivially, themselves. We long to demonstrate that the reason we *subjectively* feel that we matter is that we *objectively* do. This longing is what I am calling *the mattering instinct*, and I'll use the two expressions—the longing to matter and the mattering instinct—interchangeably, though the latter phrase stresses its genealogy.

So powerful is the longing to matter that people will sacrifice their lives for it, leaving behind statements that attest to the fact that what made them feel their lives worth living also made them feel their lives worth sacrificing. "Hold the cross high so I may see it through the flames!" Joan of Arc was reported to say as the fire beneath her was lit. "The unexamined life is not worth living," announced Socrates when sentenced to die rather than cease his philosophical way of life. "It is better to die for an idea that will live, than to live for an idea that will die," said the South African anti-apartheid activist Steve Biko, who died in police custody. "I may not get there with you," said Martin Luther King Jr. a day before his assassination. "But I want you to know tonight that we, as a people, will get to the Promised Land."

But it's not only the laudably heroic who hold mattering above life itself. We all do. We don't want to live if we become convinced that we don't, can't, will never truly matter. The paradigmatic words of the suicidally depressed are "I don't matter." It's no accident that the URL for the US Hotline for Suicide Prevention is https://youmatter.suicidepreventionlifeline.org.

THE BEST AND THE WORST IN US

What have we generated in our responses to the mattering instinct?

Nothing less than religion and philosophy, which have as their source the question of what it is that matters most in shaping a life that matters.

Nothing less than the arts, which have provided the source of mattering for some among us, so that Leonard Bernstein could write, "The key to the mystery of a great artist is that for reasons unknown, he will give away his energies and his life just to make sure that one note follows another . . . and leaves us with the feeling that something is right in the world," and Vincent van Gogh could write, "I can very well do without God, both in my life and in my painting, but I cannot, suffering as I am, do without something which is greater than I am, which is my life, the power to create."

Nothing less than the sciences, which have also provided the source of mattering for some among us, so that the planetary scientist Carolyn Porco could remark, "The story of all our scientific explorations to the celestial bodies that orbit our sun has been, at its heart, a story about longing—a longing to know ourselves, to understand us and know exactly where we are," and the theoretical physicist Henri Poincaré could write, "If nature were not beautiful, it would not be worth knowing, and if nature were not worth knowing, life would not be worth living."

Nothing less than the art of politics, devoted to different factions pursuing their own mattering, and the art of warfare, which Carl van Clausewitz famously defined as "the continuation of politics by other means."

Nothing less than the multitude of social distinctions by which some seek to demonstrate their mattering by diminishing the mattering of others, such as racism, sexism, classism, jingoism, elitism, ethnic biases, and other forms of mattering diminishment that we haven't yet gotten around to naming.

As we would expect from a motivation that lies at the core of our humanness, the longing to matter can bring out the best and the worst of us, while generating bottomless disputes as to what is the best and the worst of us. The instinct we so deeply share spawns the most fraught and irresoluble divides among us. At their worst, these divides can make us regard targeted others as hardly mattering at all. We don't need to look only to the horrors of history to witness what the worst looks like. A glance at today's headlines gives us ample examples.

In fact, amidst the kind of progress that can dazzle and daze us, most especially in the spheres of science and technology, there is also significant backsliding toward the worst to which we can be driven by our longing to matter.

And that is why it is crucial that we understand the mattering instinct—its role in every human life, and its potential to toxically warp or expansively modify the way we see ourselves and one another.

SOME KEY IDEAS

Every reader is owed an introduction that will give some inkling of what is to follow so that they can judge whether they're in the right place. Otherwise, it's like entering a doctor's waiting room not knowing whether you're about to see a cardiologist, a dermatologist, a proctologist, or a psychiatrist.

So here are the ideas that will be explored and defended in the pages to follow:

1. We are creatures *of matter* who *long to matter*.
2. To matter means, at its most basic level, to be deserving of attention.
3. The mattering instinct derives from the need to persuade ourselves that we are truly deserving of all the attention that we must give ourselves to pursue our lives. It is how creatures with our evolved capacity for self-reflection experience the laws of nature that have shaped us.
4. One of the deepest expressions of the longing to matter is the denial that we are indeed composed of matter. How could we, as mere matter, subject to the same laws of nature that govern other physical systems and destined to disappear, succeed in mattering as much as we aspire to matter?
5. Ironically, our longing to matter is itself an outcome of the laws of nature.
6. The most fundamental of all physical laws, the law of entropy, is implicated in our longing to matter, while the laws of biology, also implicated in our longing to matter, evolved as life's (local) resistance to the law of entropy.
7. To be alive is to be in resistance to entropy.
8. The mattering instinct forces us into the sphere of values without equipping us to see our way through.
9. The inherent human dignity we vaguely sense is traceable to the mattering instinct that we share.
10. Just as the language instinct results in the great variety of human languages, so the mattering instinct results in the great variety of incommensurable forms of human life.[1]

11. Beneath the incommensurables, four general mattering strategies are operating, sorting us out into four mattering types: *socializers*, *transcenders*, *competitors*, and *heroic strivers*. I represent these differences, and all the further differences to which they lead, on what I call the *mattering map*.

12. The four mattering strategies, interacting with our individually variable temperaments, talents, interests, passions, and influences, result in the individual *mattering projects* that propel us into our futures, giving us, in a sense, our reason to live.

13. The logic that seems implicit in the mattering instinct gives rise to the urge to universalize: *my* reason to live ought to be *your* reason to live. The seeds of intolerance sprout from this flawed logic.

14. The differences between us are such that there will always be socializers, transcenders, competitors, and heroic strivers, making it imperative that, if we are to live together with recognition of the dignity of human life in all its incommensurable forms, we find an objective standard that we all can accept to distinguish between better and worse ways of responding to the mattering instinct.

15. A person's overall effect on entropy provides such an objective standard. A life well-lived is a life that, while pursuing mattering in a way that best accords with a person's individuality, joins forces with life in its resistance to entropy.

A CRISIS OF MATTERING

"Longing on a large scale is what makes history," wrote the novelist Don DeLillo, and of no longing is this truer than the longing to matter. And that is why the theme of mattering, as timeless as all existential issues are, is also timely. Its time-liness relates to the paradoxical state of the world right now.

On the one hand, so much has been going measurably right. Life expectancy has more than doubled around the world. Extreme poverty has declined tenfold. Literacy in the world has soared, especially for girls. Global high school grad-uation rates have climbed dramatically in the twenty-first cen-tury; we are entering the first-ever period in human history when more than half of young people have a high school edu-cation. A majority of countries have become, for the first time in history, at least partially democratic. Women's participation in parliaments and the workforce around the world has risen significantly. Internet penetration continues to grow, expand-ing access to information and connecting people globally. In many parts of the world, there's not only increased time for leisure but an abundance of amusements with which to fill it.

Yet in this world of measurable progress, many people have felt increasingly aggrieved, frustrated, and in despair, and their discontent has produced political upsets and rights reversals that have taken pundits by surprise. Elites are per-ceived as garnering more than their share of everything, and the backlash of resentment has left in its wake a hankering for populism, sometimes darkening into fascism, with char-ismatic shysters promising trickle-down mattering, all while hungrily chasing their own power. *Tribalism* has become the word of the day, and tribalism has everything to do with the mattering instinct.

What we are experiencing is a crisis of mattering. Individ-uals can experience crises of mattering—we call them, tell-ingly, "existential crises"—and so, too, can societies.

Deepening the paradox, our current crisis of mattering

has been precipitated by some of the very progress that we've enjoyed. The global economy that lifted a billion people out of extreme poverty has also produced ever starker wealth inequality in a culture that increasingly assesses mattering in terms of wealth. The increasing inequity has worked to unravel the reciprocal loyalty that once held between corporations and workers. In today's workplace, workers are made to feel they are as fungible as snacks in a vending machine: identical, interchangeable, and easily restocked. The focused effort to encourage previously marginalized groups to realize their potential and enter the circle of accomplishment has made unencouraged others—specifically white, straight, nonwealthy males—feel that they and their potential don't matter, inciting resentment. Advances in AI are making everybody, even the so-called creatives, feel that redundancy is threatening us all, and that soon it will be AI systems that will rob us of our mattering. The growth of education that has disseminated the scientific worldview has decimated the sense of transcendent mattering previously provided by religion— the conviction that there is an omnipotent God, the creator of "the starry heavens above me and the moral order within me" (Kant) to whom we all matter.[2] Into the vast God-shaped hole in our hearts, contemporary culture has instead inserted such values as power, wealth, and fame, suggesting these are the best paths to salvation. But such an exclusionary salvation leaves many feeling that they don't, can't, and will never matter—to say nothing of how the desire to reach such goals intensifies the destabilizing competition among us, turning us into mattering adversaries instead of mattering allies. There just doesn't seem to be enough mattering to go around, and we scramble like children beneath a piñata.

Whatever crises of mattering were already in place were exacerbated when, in 2020, a deadly virus swept across the world. The proximity of death strengthens the urgency of our longing to demonstrate that we truly do matter. To think that it can all disappear so soon, your life that means all the world to you, and that the world will go on its merry way as if you had never existed at all: Such awareness jabs excruciatingly at the existential nerve. And this was a jab on a worldwide scale. We might have anticipated that dramatic effects would ensue, and so they have. The calamity could have drawn us closer to one another, seeing as how we were all in it together. But though displays of gratitude for heroic health care workers were moments of brightness that drew us together, the overall effect of the pandemic worked in the opposite direction, so that the divisions already in place among us only deepened and darkened. We even found new ways to oppose one another—the quarantine wars, the vaccine wars, the mask wars, the science wars. Even a subtle reminder of mortality is enough to intensify the clashing claims of mattering among us, and the reminders of mortality brought on by the pandemic were anything but subtle. Though the virus was ultimately tamed by science, the intensified crisis of mattering has lingered on, the psychic analogue of long COVID, and it calls for an urgent response.

AN URGENT INSTINCT–THAT WE MUST URGENTLY UNDERSTAND

Mattering is urgent. It holds the urgency of our wanting to get our lives right, to live the best version of ourselves that we possibly can. It holds the urgency of our obligations to do right by one another. It holds the urgency of our troubled times, when it seems that the kind of crisis of mattering that can derail people from their own lives is calamitously afflicting the whole of society. How can we begin to address these urgencies if we don't get a fix on the existential longing that defines us?

This book is a manifesto for placing mattering at the forefront of our comprehension of what it means to be human in the hope of finding ways to do justice to the hidden longing that shapes us into creatures to laud and creatures to fear but most of all creatures to understand.

But the book is more than a manifesto. The mattering instinct, I hope to show, animates the choices and struggles of people as they live out their lives. It generates the great diversity among us that amazes and dismays us. I will tell the stories of people, some famous, such as William James, the eminent philosopher and psychologist; some obscure, such as Lou Xiaoying, an impoverished Chinese mother. All the stories are of people whose lives are surprising, vivid, and moving because of the ways that they are shaped by the longing to matter. Many of these stories come from science, philosophy, psychology, and literature, which tells you something about where I personally am located on the mattering map and the element of autobiography that inevitably creeps in. Some of the stories I will tell are tragic while others are triumphant. Whether they are tragic or triumphant is the result both of how the longing to matter expresses itself in a person and how the world responds to that expression.

All living things can be wounded and wasted by what they meet with in the world. Our longing to matter puts us all the more at the mercy of the world—a reason in itself to see one another more mercifully.

CHAPTER 1

THE MOST PECULIAR AND MOST HUMAN THING ABOUT US

Humans have many traits that distinguish us from other animals. There's our furlessness that evolved when our ancestors moved from the shady forest into the savannahs and allows for dissipation of heat; our articulated digits that allow us to achieve a powerful grip and a dexterous way around tools; our upright posture that frees those dexterous hands while necessitating skeletal adjustments that contribute to our susceptibility to lower back pain; our outlier "encephalization quotient" that makes the ratio of our brain mass to our body mass about three times what would be expected compared with other primates; the sizable bulge of the brain's information-processing cerebral cortex, which had to get crinkled up in order to be crammed inside our skulls, giving it its distinctive walnut appearance while also contributing to the difficulties and dangers with which we give birth; our innate capacity for language that allows us to share information with each other and pass it along from one generation to the next so that we don't have to keep reinventing the wheel; our extended immaturity, beginning with the abject helplessness of our infancy, that has us learning to move our limbs and is prolonged into our twenties, when our frontal lobes, seat of inhibitory control and decision-making, finally fully emerge; our susceptibility to the blushing that involuntarily reveals certain of our emotions, such as embarrassment and shame, and which Darwin characterized as "the most peculiar and the most human of all expressions."[1]

But beyond all these unique features characterizing the complicated creatures that we humans are, the mattering instinct is the most peculiar and the most human thing about us. It is the most peculiar and the most human because it explains so much about our uniquely human behavior, meaning behavior that doesn't fit the kinds of goals adequate for understanding the behavior of other animals: avoiding pain and death; seeking the pleasures of food and sex—in short, behavior explicable by the Darwinian mechanism of getting genes replicated into future generations.[2]

In contrast, the mattering instinct marks an entirely different dimension that characterizes our lives, carrying us beyond the Darwinian imperatives to have us interrogating ourselves in a way captured by the cartoon on the next page.

The everyman pictured is, while just as driven by the creaturely Darwinian imperatives of *eat, survive, and reproduce* as other creatures, unconvinced that these provide an adequate answer to the question he's posing. It's in that posing that the mattering instinct is hatched. So long as the basic requirements for living a recognizably human life are in place—such requirements as sustenance, shelter, and safety[3]—the question occurs to us: What is it all about, this one life that is mine and that can't help meaning all the world

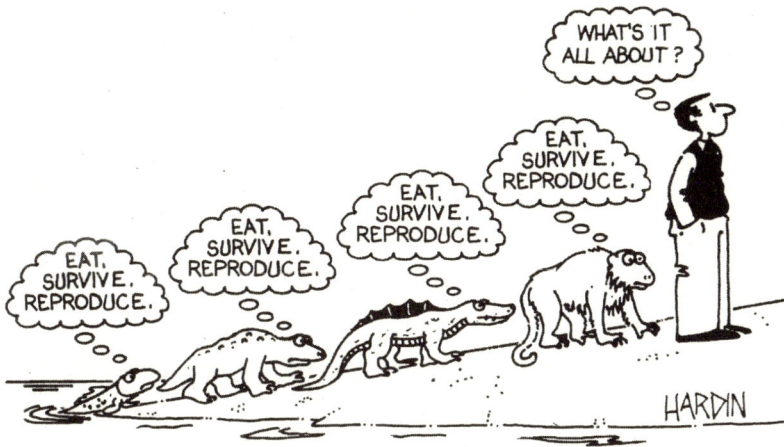

"What's It All About?" cartoon by Patrick Hardin

to me? Does the thing that I happen to be—this thing that, against all odds, has come into existence, the result of the capricious collisions of history, genes, and culture—matter so much as to be worth all the single-minded attention and bother I am forced to give to it for no reason other than its happening to be me?

Of course, I matter to myself—that's self-evident—but do I actually, truly, objectively matter? Does my objectively mattering just come along with my objectively existing, or is there rather something that I must *do*, something that I must *be*, to deserve all the attention that I can't help lavishing on myself? Should I pursue power or fame to vindicate my self-mattering, strive to have the fact of my existence register in as many lives as possible and in that way come to truly matter, or should I rather dedicate my life to the service of others? Should I strive to create something of beauty in the world, giving pleasure to many, or contribute to the ongoing search for knowledge that our self-characterization as *Homo sapiens* suggests we are supposed to be all about? Must I please a deity to whom I owe my existence and live out the purpose for which the deity might have created me, or live my life as if it were a work of art, cultivating such aesthetic qualities as style, originality, and coherence? Should I merge my identity with something greater than myself, something that will outlast me, perhaps a cause, such as justice for all, or, as in Buddhism, with reality itself so that my personal ego shrivels into the purity of nothingness? Or do I achieve mattering simply by doing my best by the people with whom the circumstances of my life have contingently bound me—my family and friends, my colleagues and neighbors?

In short, we long to live lives that we can regard as meaningful in our own eyes. This is the extra imperative—the non-Darwinian imperative—that we demand of ourselves, and it motivates a vast array of meaning-seeking forms of human life.

The extra non-Darwinian demand is constitutive of what we are as a species. What we are, we humans, are creatures of matter who long to matter. It's a longing that makes us deeply different from all other species. And the array of meaning-seeking forms of life generated by our longing to matter makes us deeply different from one another. What renders us peculiar as a species renders us peculiar to one another, sometimes to the point of confoundment regarding how others are choosing to live their lives. Just as the language instinct results in the great variety of human languages that requires the art of translation, so too the mattering instinct results in the great variety of meaning-seeking forms of life that likewise requires interpretation.

YOU CAN NEVER BE SURE

William Stanley Merwin entered Princeton University in 1944 at the age of sixteen, waiting tables to help pay for what his scholarship didn't cover. In his junior year, he took a poetry workshop in Princeton's creative writing program, which was just getting started under the supervision of the literary critic and poet R. P. Blackmur.[4]

Blackmur greatly impressed William Merwin. But it was Blackmur's teaching assistant who inspired him "to be a poet and nothing but a poet."

He was a strange man, this teaching assistant, whose lips and fingers trembled with the passion of his views about poetry. Though he'd been born in Oklahoma, he had an accent that Merwin judged had been "affected in England." He told his student to get down on his knees to pray to the Muse and "said he meant it literally." As for publishing, he advised Merwin to "paper [his] wall with rejection slips." His decorating tip was no doubt informed by experience. Though well into his thirties, he was still only Blackmur's teaching assistant.

His name was John Berryman, and if you know something about poetry in the mid-twentieth century then you know the name. He was to become a key figure in the "confessional" school of poetry, a term he reacted to with "rage and contempt."[5] His 77 *Dream Songs* exploded the solemnity of high art like a concerto scored for farts. In the late 1960s, a time rife with experimentation, including in art, his reputation soared so high as to break free of the coterie of people who care about poetry, with popular media devoting feature stories to him, such as a story in *Life* magazine entitled, "Whisky and Ink, Whisky and Ink: A Hard-Living, Hard-Working Poet Named John Berryman Achieves Sudden and Deserved Renown."[6] His packed public readings, both in the US and abroad, were delivered with such raw emotional intensity as to make audience members feel like voyeurs. His celebrity didn't detract from his standing among the literati, who bestowed on him their glittering prizes—the Pulitzer, the National Book Award, the Bollingen Prize for Poetry.

William Stanley Merwin, who became known out in the world as W. S. Merwin, also went on to poetic glory, though of a quieter kind, collecting, among other things, two Pulitzer Prizes. In his poem entitled "Berryman," he gives us his memories of the poet as he'd known him back in the day.[7] The poem provides the descriptions of John Berryman that I've been referencing, right down to the trembling lips and affected accent.

Berryman was long gone by the time that "Berryman" was published, dead at fifty-seven. He had been teaching at the University of Minnesota, fired before that from the University of Iowa after a fight with his landlord led to his being arrested, jailed overnight, and fined for disorderly conduct and public intoxication. It had been, to say the least, a turbulent life, a mix of devotions and demons. On January 7, 1972, the day before winter classes were scheduled to begin, he jumped from the Washington Avenue Bridge into the icy Mississippi River. He had resolved to die two days before but had returned home in defeat and written a poem about the failure. This time he approached the task having drunk heavily all day. Climbing over the high railing of the bridge, he briefly turned back to the passing motorists and waved in his last act of ambiguity.

"I will tell you what he told me," begins Merwin's "Berry-man." And it ends with these two stanzas:

I had hardly begun to read
I asked how can you ever be sure
that what you write is really
any good at all and he said you can't

you can't you can never be sure
you die without knowing
whether anything you wrote was any good
if you have to be sure don't write

The lives of the poets are known to be difficult, and these last two stanzas tell us why. To premise your mattering on your poetry, flaying yourself raw so that you can touch the world skinless the better to take it in and transmute it into art . . . and then never to know whether anything you wrote was any good? To live out every day in the presence of such doubts is to live with unease, your whole life at the mercy of your art.

But then poets are a breed apart, praying to the Muse to grant them the genius to weave words into wonder. The rest of us are thankfully different. Only we're not. It's not the specific way that we respond to the mattering instinct that breeds the unease. It's the mattering instinct itself. Even if we pursue our lives far from the rarified air breathed by poets, the unease of the poet is the unease of us all.

Angela Rubino is a wife and mother of two, who having transplanted herself from New York now lives in Rome, Georgia. She's worked in restaurants and flipped houses for a living, buying them and then selling them at a profit. But these facts weren't why a major newspaper devoted a story to her in 2022, seeing in her a harbinger of the changing political winds sweeping across the American landscape.[8]

Rubino had never before had much use for politics. But all of that changed in 2020 when political activism took over her life. Her activism took the shape of many activities, including, at least on one occasion, dumpster diving, when she thought she'd heard, while standing outside the county election board, the whirr of a paper shredder within. Under the cover of darkness, she returned that night. Hoisting herself up on the metal rim of the dumpster, she spotted two clear plastic bags crammed with paper shavings, and the rush of vindication sped through her. She emerged from the dumpster shaking off bits of trash and feeling like a patriot. She hauled the contents back to her home, intending to put them together like a jigsaw puzzle, to assemble a picture of the Big Lie that was, she was convinced, the stolen presidential election of 2020.

What could matter more than saving the country from the lying and cheating that was corroding it from within? To this end she'd taken on her local school board, challenging their curriculum for pornographically grooming children for sexual predators. She'd organized meetings of her neighbors to put up signs all over the county, attacking candidates who were RINOs, Republican in name only. She'd rallied her neighbors to oust the former county election board so that its members had now been replaced with only those who acknowledged the Big Lie. With her online moniker of @Burnitdown, her life had been taken over by a cause larger than herself, and in it she had finally found her purpose.

She had wondered about that purpose for a long time, tracing it back to a moment when she was eight years old, sitting in the back seat of her mother's car on the way to religion class.

"The thought just came into my head. I was thinking, 'What are we doing this for? What are we doing any of this for if we're just going to die? You die, and it's over. So, what's the point?' I felt afraid. Afraid to the point of not wanting to think about that anymore."

She had never stopped thinking about it, though, and she traced its effect on her to the reason she had been so drawn to the Make America Great Again movement. Donald Trump was the first politician to give voice to her private thoughts about what America was becoming, which made her feel "recognized and even important." She had never voted before, never felt herself mattering as a citizen until Donald Trump came onto the scene.

There were so many people who made people like her feel that people like her didn't matter—not only didn't matter politically but in any way at all. When she and her fellow activists got together to put up lawn signs, their talk was about the billionaires—Bill Gates and his world vaccination program; Elon Musk and his brain chip company, Neuralink: *"Can you please stop trying to chip me?"* (This, of course, was before Elon Musk allied with Donald Trump.) They talked about the Hollywood movie stars, indulging themselves in any way they see fit, even drinking the blood of other people to stay forever gorgeous. *"And they say we're weird?"*

It was dizzying for Angela, this new way of looking at everything in which she was caught up, cutting herself off from the sources of information that she used to trust, sus-picious of almost everything, believing almost no one other than those who shared her suspicion.

"Sometimes I'm like, what if I'm wrong?" Rubino mused. "It crosses my mind. Then I ask God: If I'm doing something wrong, please give me the strength to figure it out. Because I really want to understand what the point is. This can't be what life is, that you get up and go to work and come home. That as humans, we're nothing."

There it is, served up straight, the longing that is the most human thing about us and also the most poignant. John Ber-ryman had cautioned the young William Merwin that when it came to writing poetry, you can never be sure if anything you wrote is any good. You die without knowing. If you have to be sure, don't write. And so it is with our longing to matter. We can never be sure. We die without knowing. If we have to be sure, we can't live.

When I first began to write about mattering, I had used the phrase "the will to matter," intentionally echoing the phi-losophers Arthur Schopenhauer and Friedrich Nietzsche, who had placed such stress on the will. For Schopenhauer, the ele-mental truth of us was described as a blindly directionless and insatiable Will: "The whole of Nature is what we know directly and intimately and find within ourselves as the Will." Nietzsche qualified Schopenhauer's blind Will by identifying it as the will to power: "This world is the will to power— and nothing besides! And you yourselves are also this will to power—and nothing besides!"

Only it's longing, rather than will, that better captures our situation.

Longings are the lengthened desires that won't let us go.

They hold within them the melancholy of unfulfillment or—what amounts to much the same thing—our inability to know whether they've been fulfilled. And that inability to know is exactly the case with the longing to matter. Although we can't conclusively know that we matter, we also can't help longing for that certainty, acting to appease the longing so that we can get on with our lives—whether it's praying to the Muse for a glancing touch of genius, joining a political movement to overcome what we perceive as massive corruption, or any of a vast array of differing responses: our whole life at the mercy of our response.

I represent that vast array of differing responses with what I call the mattering map, a concept I first introduced in a book published in 1983.[9] The map is composed of a multitude of regions, each region offering a different answer to the question of how to pursue a life that matters. Our location on the mattering map influences the mattering projects that we undertake, which, in channeling our longing to matter, propel us into our future, giving us a reason to live. While the mattering instinct expresses our distinctiveness as a species, our mattering projects express our distinctiveness from one another.

The variety of mattering projects is immense, testifying to the vast creativity our species has devoted to the mattering instinct. Our mattering projects can be selfish or altruistic, individualistic or communitarian, competitive or cooperative, religious or secular, creative or destructive. But whether it's tending one's garden or one's cause, one's relationships or one's reputation, one's immortal soul or one's net worth, these mattering projects become the loci of some of our deepest emotions. Our evaluations of how well our lives are going are dependent on our evaluations of how well our mattering project is going.

The late philosopher Bernard Williams, who had used the phrase "ground projects" for what I am calling mattering projects, wrote: "For a project to play this ground role, it does not have to be true that if it were frustrated, or in any of various ways he lost it, he would have to commit suicide, nor does he have to think that. Other things, or the mere hope of other things, may keep him going. But he may feel in those circumstances that he might as well have died."[10] Our mattering projects, as opposed to the other projects we might take up, possess an existential dimension. For example, though many of us may take seriously our pleasure in music, few would say, as the late opera singer Montserrat Caballé once said, "When I am not singing, I have the feeling that I do not exist." That is rather a stark statement of the existential dimension that our mattering projects have for us.

When these mattering projects function as they should for us, then at least one of the two cornerstones of our flourishing, the longing to matter, is being met. (We'll look at the other cornerstone at the end of this chapter.) But the proper functioning of these projects in our lives doesn't mean that the doubt is entirely subdued within us. It never is, for reasons that derive from the very meaning of mattering.

THE MEANING OF MATTERING

We speak both of *what matters* and of *who matters*. In fact, we speak a great deal about both.

Consider *what matters*. In recent decades, the phrase *why X matters* has become a template for dozens of book titles, including *Why Beauty Matters*, *Why Emotions Matter*, *Why Family Matters*, *Why Genealogy Matters*, *Why Good Sex Matters*, *Why Jesus Matters*, *Why Knowledge Matters*, *Why Liberalism Matters*, *Why Money Matters*, and *Why Stories Matter.* The profusion of titles, many of them mutually exclusive—after all, if Jesus matters, then how, too, can money?—testifies to our preoccupation with what matters.

And it's not only the question of *what matters* but also of *who matters* that's urgent. Consider: In 2013, seventeen-year-old Trayvon Martin, a Black American, was visiting, together with his father, his father's fiancé at her townhouse in a gated community in Florida. While the grownups were out, Trayvon went to a nearby convenience store to get himself some snacks and, on his way back, was shot by a Neighborhood Watch volunteer, George Zimmerman, himself a member of a minority as a Hispanic American. Zimmerman found Trayvon suspicious looking—the boy's hoodie was prominently mentioned in news stories—and called the police, while he continued to trail the teenager, a course of action ultimately ending in the boy's death. Trayvon hadn't been armed. All that was found on him was a bag of Skittles and an iced tea.

After the acquittal of the shooter, the hashtag #BlackLivesMatter exploded onto social media. The three-word slogan soon went beyond mere hashtags and placards, following the deaths of two more unarmed Black Americans, Michael Brown and Eric Garner, to become a political movement. Those who opposed Black Lives Matter sometimes offered as rejoinders their own three-word slogans: "All Lives Matter," or "Bluc Lives Matter," this last referring to police officers. Of course, "Black Lives Matter" isn't inconsistent with either "All Lives Matter" or "Blue Lives Matter," since "Black Lives

Matter" isn't synonymous with "Only Black Lives Matter." The power and the poignancy of the original slogan lay in its minimalism. But what the battle of the slogans made clear is the potency of the verb *to matter*, in this instance applied not to the question of what matters but rather who matters.

So what exactly does the verb *to matter* mean? Here is a quick working definition: *To matter is to be deserving of attention*. It's the same whether we are speaking of what matters or who matters. The thing or the person that matters makes a claim on us; at the very least, a claim is made on our attention.

The claim of being deserving of attention may be based on consequences that would ensue from paying attention or not paying attention—as when we ask, say, does voting really matter? We're asking whether voting makes a difference, and so whether it's worth our while to pay the attention called for in voting. It's still the question of being deserving of attention, but what decides the issue is the consequences. In other circumstances, claims of mattering—of being deserving of attention—are independent of considerations of consequences, as when we assert that Black lives matter or that all lives matter. Here it's intrinsic mattering, having nothing to do with consequences. And what intrinsic mattering comes down to is being deserving of attention. To claim that Black lives matter, as all lives matter, is to make claims regarding the deservingness of attention.

This leaves us with two more terms to explicate: *attention* and *deservingness*.

Attention is a mental phenomenon studied by contemporary psychologists, cognitive scientists, and neuroscientists—in other words, it is a subject for the empirical sciences.

The best definition I know of the phenomenon was given

THE MOST PECULIAR AND MOST HUMAN THING ABOUT US

by the philosopher and psychologist William James. Attention, he wrote, is "the taking possession by the mind, in clear and vivid form, of one out of what may seem several simultaneously possible objects or trains of thoughts. Focalization, concentration of consciousness, are of its essence. It implies withdrawal from some things in order to deal effectively with others and is a condition which has a real opposite in the confused, dazed, scatterbrained state which in French is called *distraction*, and *Zerstreutheit* in German."[11]

James implies that attention is something we do. "It is the taking possession by the mind." The world's languages agree. In English we *pay* attention, while in other languages we *give, lend, gift, dedicate, sacrifice, prepare, turn, attach, apply, infuse,* and *arouse* our attention. The linguistic formations all imply that there is activity and agency in attention. His definition also makes clear how attention, as an activity, is to be distinguished from the broader notion of consciousness. After all, that confused, dazed, scatterbrained state is a state of consciousness, though the "real opposite" of paying attention.

His definition also entails that attention is limited and selective: *withdrawal from some things.* Every act of attention is an act of exclusion. In paying attention to something, we are forced to ignore a multitude of other things. And he ties this limitedness and selectivity with attention's usefulness: *in order to deal effectively.* Contemporary psychology agrees. Attention's limitedness and selectivity is crucial to its usefulness and linked to the reason why organisms evolved attention in the first place: to pay attention to changeable things in the organism's immediate environment that can help or hinder it, nourish or annihilate it. That unpleasant smell, for example, may very well signal toxicity. Note the presence of the word *changeable*. The function of attention is tied to what is variable, not just to what is relevant to fitness. Oxygen, our heartbeat, gravity, and many other things are vital to our survival, and our unconscious mental processes must take them into account. But they tend to be constant, so there is no need to allocate our limited window of attention to them, unless circumstances alarmingly change.

The agency entailed in the act of paying attention means that we have some control over what we do and don't pay attention to. You may be unable to remain oblivious to the bad music blasting in your gym or the rank smell seeping into your kitchen—stimuli that are intense or that pop out of your surroundings. But you can decide to pay no attention to, say, gossip or popular culture, social media or your weight. You can decide that they simply don't matter, which is to say that they're not deserving of your attention. And this brings us to the second component of the English verb *to matter*—namely deservingness.

Deservingness introduces an entirely different level of consideration into our preoccupations with mattering. It's a level that goes beyond the psychological, beyond the empirical altogether. Deservingness draws us into the nonempirical sphere of values and justifications, of *ought*s and *ought-not*s. This is the sphere that philosophers call normative, because it invokes norms of justification. The mattering instinct means that we are normative creatures down to our core. We think and act and shape our lives within the sphere of justifications. Instead of calling ourselves *Homo sapiens*, we might better have christened ourselves *Homo iustificans*.

It's the presence of deservingness in the concept of mattering that raises us up into an entirely different order of both complexity and perplexedness. The mattering instinct has us straining beyond the empirical for the normative knowledge that eludes us. We are carried over into the sphere of values and justifications without being equipped to see our way through. Here is the epistemic elusiveness that injects the unsubdued doubt—and hence unease—into the heart of what it is to pursue a human life.

THE MOTHER OF ALL MATTERING QUESTIONS

We speak both of what matters and of who matters. And behind our preoccupations with both is the most urgent of all our mattering questions, which is voiced in the first person: Do *I* matter? This is the mother of our mattering questions. Ultimately, we want to know *what* matters because we desperately want our own lives to be driven by what matters. We want to know *who* matters because we desperately want to be numbered among the ones who matter.

Self-mattering—feeling ourselves overwhelmingly deserving of our own attention—is baked into our identity. The usefulness of attention, to which William James alluded, is its usefulness to ourselves. So it's no wonder that the greater part of our attention is given over to ourselves, whether overtly or tacitly. Throughout the enormous complexity of how the mind works, our self-mattering is presumed. And yet, astonishing creatures that we are, we are able, by way of the capacity for self-reflection with which our brains come equipped, to step outside of our self-mattering, which is to step outside ourselves, to pose the mother of all mattering questions. We'll look more closely at how this comes about in chapter three, Becoming Human.

It's the deservingness component that separates the mattering for which we long from such empirical psychological states as having confidence or self-esteem. You can go online right now, or schedule a visit to a psychologist, and take a test that measures your confidence or self-esteem. There will be a series of statements to which you respond with the degree of your agreement, such as: *I feel that I am a person of worth, at least on an equal plane with others. I feel that I have a number of good qualities. All in all, I am inclined to feel that I'm a failure.* The test may even provide a numerical score, similar to an IQ test. The Rosenberg Self-Esteem Scale, for example, which is one of the most widely used measures of self-esteem and from which I've taken the above statements, provides a numerical value from 1 to 30, with any score under 15 indicating low self-esteem. It was none other than William James who first formulated the concept of self-esteem, offering an equation as its definition.[12]

But these assessments of how good you feel about yourself, often in relation to others, aren't tests of whether you truly, objectively, *existentially* matter. To figure out that question, the mother of all mattering questions, you can't take an empirical test. Your self-esteem score, whether high or low, may be grounded in self-delusion, and the mother question is a demand for the answer that lies on the other side of self-delusion. Do I truly and objectively matter? I know that I can't help feeling that I do, but do I really?

When it comes to our own mattering, we are staunch realists. We don't want feelings. We want the facts.

A BEGUILING POLYSEMY

Linked with the English verb *to matter*, there is, of course, the noun. Matter, as noun, means the stuff of the universe. Or to put it a bit more precisely, matter is what composes the things that take up space and that also have mass and volume. Their mass and volume are composed of matter.

We learn the properties of this stuff through the science of physics, which has revealed to us the complicated structure of matter, the elaborate choreography of its constituent particles as described by quantum mechanics, its convertibility into energy as described by special relativity, and its capacity to warp the geometry of space-time as described by general relativity.

Whatever its details, matter is quintessentially objective, meaning that it exists independent of perception. If you doubt that the far side of the moon, which can't be seen from the earth because of its synchronous rotation with the earth, existed until it was photographed by the Soviet Luna 3 space probe in 1959—or maybe not even until the Apollo 8 astronauts first viewed it in person in 1968—then you doubt the existence of matter.

The verb *to matter* was derived from the noun, and the noun was derived from the Latin word for mother, *mater.* When we speak of our *alma mater*, for example, we are suggesting that our educational institutions function as our nurturing, or nursing, mothers.

How did mothers get mixed up into the stuff of physics? It goes back to Aristotle, who had hypothesized, against his teacher Plato, that there was a basic undifferentiated stuff—a pure receptivity without any qualifying attributes—that goes into the being of such things as take up space.[13] Since there was no word in ancient Greek for such pure receptivity, he appropriated the Greek word for wood—*hyle*—to do the trick, only abstracting from it any differentiating features that make it wood as opposed to, say, marble or clay. *Hyle*, in Aristotle's metaphysics, is passive receptivity awaiting form.

It was this passive receptivity that the Latin scholars who translated Aristotle were trying to capture by the word *materia*, which they substituted for Aristotle's *hyle* by way of metaphor. Just as mothers are mostly passive in generating humans, or so Aristotle and his followers thought, receptacles of incubation awaiting the primary activating form provided by seminal males; so, too, is matter mostly passive in generating things, awaiting the reception of activating forms.

You might find it surprising that females were presumed to have so little effect on conception, given how many children look like their mothers. But since females were considered, for Aristotle and his followers, as failed males, no very great role was assigned them in determining the form of the child. The resemblance of children to their mothers was attributed to some minimal contributions of the material cause, while maintaining the overall passivity of females in the act of conception.

Matter, of course, turns out to be far more interesting than Aristotle had thought—not passive at all but holding vast quantities of potential energy, as described by the most famous equation of physics: $E = mc^2$. The science of physics has revealed ever more about the astonishing attributes intrinsic to matter, confuting many of our untutored intuitions and requiring daunting mathematics to express. And still so much about the nature of matter eludes us—including how, at least in some configurations of matter, such as your working brain, matter manages to wake up to the world and pay attention to it. This is the problem that has come to be known as "the hard problem of consciousness." I think it would better be called the hard problem of matter.[14]

In any case, though Aristotle got the nature of matter as wrong as he got the nature of mothers, his thinking provided a useful concept for referring to the constituent stuff of things with mass and volume. And it's from the noun that we derive the verb.

Why should undifferentiated stuff be related to what merits the commandeering of our attention? What's the conceptual metaphor that links the noun and verb? Perhaps it lies in matter's being so fundamental, the very stuff of things, which in turn suggests the very core of things, its essence. An obsolete meaning of the noun meant exactly that, as when, in 1611, Ben Jonson wrote in his theatrical masque *Oberon, The Faery Prince*: "He is the matter of virtue." Perhaps this is the train of thought that got us, in English, from the noun to the verb.

It's a twisting semantic history that ends in the word's polysemy—one word crammed with more than one sense. It's a beguiling polysemy that allows us to elegantly express the core of what we are: matter longing to matter. A presumption that females matter less than males gave us the Latin *materia*, which gave us the English noun *matter*, which then yielded us the verb by which we can challenge presumptions as to whose lives are and are not fully deserving of the attention that is accorded some.

THE TWO CORNERSTONES OF OUR HUMANNESS

The longing to demonstrate that we do indeed matter—the mattering instinct—is one of the cornerstones of our humanness and a key to our flourishing. The other cornerstone is our connectedness to others. I want to end this chapter by speaking about connectedness, both because it's often confused with the longing to matter and because, even though the two corner-stones are distinct, they interact profoundly with each other.

But first a word about the meaning of *flourishing*. In its broadest sense, to flourish means to develop successfully. We can speak, for example, of a business or a neighborhood as flourishing. In living things, to speak of flourishing includes organic healthiness. And in us, flourishing includes not only organic healthiness but also emotional satisfaction. As we'll see in chapter two, The Transformation from Within, flour-ishing always demands resistance to what is regarded as the supreme law of physics, the law of entropy. Biology is nature's response to the law of entropy, a central point that was argued by the physicist Erwin Schrödinger.[15]

Now to the difference between the need for connected-ness and the longing to matter. Connectedness intrinsically involves our relationships with others, while the longing to matter does not. More specifically, connectedness is the feel-ing that there are particular others who are prepared to pay us special attention whether we deserve it or not. When it comes to connectedness, justification is beside the point, another dif-ference between it and the mattering instinct. Just as we speak of love as being unconditional, so, too, in our need for con-nectedness, the special attention to us from specific others must be unconditional.

While our mattering instinct is unique to us, our need for connectedness is not. It derives from our being members of a gregarious species, evolved from gregarious species. To require special attention from other creatures of one's kind is what it means to be a member of a gregarious species. Of course, our human need for connectedness is more complicated than it is in other gregarious species, as just about everything in us is more complicated.

We are not only gregarious but altricial—meaning born helpless and requiring long periods of care from others. (The root comes from the Latin *alere*—meaning to nurture, to nurse—making for the other half of *alma mater*.) We are born into a helplessness unmatched in the animal kingdom, and if, in our prolonged immaturity, no caretakers regard us as deserving of their special attention, whether we deserve it or not, we die. Our need for connectedness, in its most fundamental sense, begins here.

But other species, too, are altricial. What distinguishes our need for connectedness is the inordinate length of our immaturity, which is due to how unprepared for a human life we are when we emerge from the womb and into the world. Our brains take an exceedingly long time to get themselves fully equipped to meet the complicated challenges of human existence, with the last piece of our brains not fully wired up until our mid-twenties. That would be the frontal cortex, which is the most recently evolved part of the human brain. It is, in the words of the primatologist Robert Sapolsky, "where the sensible mature stuff happens: long-term planning, executive function, impulse control, and emotional regulation. It's what makes you do the right thing when it's the harder thing to do."[16]

While other primates can, within minutes of their birth, at least cling to their mother's fur and in this way hitch a ride, leaving the mother's arms free to travel the treetops, the newborn human will lie helpless where it is put. At around four months old it will figure out how to control its arms well enough to reach for something, and at around six months old it will, often to enthusiastic applause, manage to roll over.

The extraordinary helplessness is due to our being born with only about 30 percent of our eventual brains developed. Fetuses would need to be gestated nine to twelve months longer for their brains to reach the comparative neurobiological and cognitive level at which chimpanzees are born. Why then aren't they? For those of us who have gone through pregnancy, the question is apt to produce a dramatic eye roll. Nine months is plenty long.

But beyond the eye roll, there is biology. The reason for the less-than-impressive state in which we emerge from the womb has to do with both the size and the complexity of the human brain—which is, in its full development, the most complicated object yet discovered in the universe. It's hard enough to get the heads of our offspring through the birth canal, given the outlier encephalization quotient that has our brain mass disproportionately large compared to our body mass. And then there are the energy demands of the fetus, once again due to its proportionately bigger and energy-hungry brain. Beginning in the second trimester, the human fetus demands an exponentially growing number of calories from the mother's body. At between thirty-eight and forty weeks, the energy demands of the fetus become more than double the mother's normal metabolic rate at rest. Birth takes place right before the critical stage is reached, when the fetus's energy demands would compromise the mother's health.

With only 30 percent of their eventual brains, neonatal humans have a lot of catching up to do. During the first year of life, the circumference of the baby's head will more than double to keep pace with its extremely rapid brain growth.

But though the neonatal brain may be 70 percent lacking, it is already equipped to pay attention. And what it pays attention to are other humans. An hour-old baby will stare at faces longer than at any other pattern. They are even prepped to betray their innate biases. Within a few hours of birth, they are showing a preference for faces that adults judge pretty.[17] Isn't that precocious of them, if also superficial? In fewer than four days after birth, they are able to distinguish the face of their primary caretaker. By four months old, even though the visual system is still underdeveloped, their brains, as studied through neuroimaging, are processing faces at almost adult levels.[18] Within fourteen months, they are checking out their caretakers' reactions to unfamiliar things to learn how to react.[19] Should they be frightened of that shiny thingy or explore what it can do and what it tastes like? Feel friendly toward that stranger whose hair isn't on his head but hanging beneath his chin, or retreat cowering behind their caretaker?

Our brains not only are prepped to pay attention to others, they are prepped to pay attention to who is paying attention to us. We have a "gaze detection" system that is exquisitely sensitive to whether another person is looking directly at us. Studies that record the activity of single brain cells have discovered that there are designated cells that fire only when someone is staring directly at you; if their gaze is averted the slightest bit, different neurons will fire.[20] The sensitivity of gaze detection explains the almost spooky ability to tell when somebody is staring at you from the periphery of your visual field, raising your hackles. Aiding this capacity is the fact that the human eye has the greatest amount of visible white among primate eyes. This contrast between the white sclera and the darker iris and pupil makes it easier to determine precisely where someone's gaze is directed.

So we pay attention to others and we pay attention to

whether others are paying attention to us. Our need for connectedness presumes these mental activities but goes beyond them. It requires that there be particular individuals whose special attention to us we feel we can automatically expect. As it was in the extreme helplessness of our prolonged immaturity, so it continues throughout our life. We pay special attention to whether certain people are paying special attention to us. They are the people whom we consider to be *in our lives*—typically our family, friends, and romantic partners, maybe our colleagues and community members. We do not have to love them. We do not even have to like them. Sometimes we can bloody resent them. But we can't help paying attention to whether and how they are paying attention to us. That is connectedness, and without it we can't flourish.

Of course, we expect a certain degree of attention from random folks that indicates that, at the least, they recognize that we are, like them, a person. That is what the most basic rules of civility are about: don't interrupt others while they're speaking, don't shove people out of your way to get to where you're heading, as if they're nothing more than inanimate objects. But from the people we count as in our lives we expect a great deal more.

It would be nice to be able to define the need for connectedness in terms of a mutuality of expected attention—that there are others in our lives from whom we can expect their special attention to us and to whom, in turn, we are prepared to pay special attention. It would be nice, since it would be descriptive of a less one-sided attitude toward the people we regard as in our lives. But if I described it in this nicer way then I wouldn't be describing the need for connectedness as it actually characterizes *all* of us, whether we have advanced to mutuality of connectedness or not. What we need, *all* of us, is to feel that there are particular others who will pay us special attention, whether we deserve it or not. That was what we needed in our helpless beginnings, and that is what we continue to need, whatever else we are prepared to extend to the others we regard as in our lives.

Our childhood family—where such a family is interpreted in the broadest sense to mean the setting in which a child is raised—is responsible for providing us our first feelings of connectedness. If things have gone reasonably well for us, we felt special attention coming to us just by having been born into our families or adopted into them. We didn't have to be anything other than what we were to get our caretakers to pay us the special attention we desperately required. There is no such thing as a perfect family, though there are plenty of families that possess the mythology that they are a perfect family. A more useful concept is a good-enough family. A good-enough family is one in which every family member equally feels that they belong, with each person feeling that they matter to the others as much as anybody in the family does.

And how sensitive we all are, from an early age, to any inequalities in the amount of attention meted out within a family. A child senses the differential in attention that a sibling gets from a shared caregiver with the acute accounting of a miser counting her returned change down to the penny, ever alert to the unfairness of being cheated. The imbalance of attention within a family, if it's not in your favor, can be a secret hurt that shapes your life, as an old injury shapes a lasting limp.

A mother of three sons once told me that her middle child, who was then five, informed her that she didn't love him as much as she loved his brothers. His evidence: When she was washing the dishes at the kitchen sink, if her oldest or youngest son asked her a question, she would turn off the water the better to hear them. But she left the water running when her middle son spoke. Though the mother had been entirely unconscious of her behavior at the sink that had transmitted so much information to her middle son, once he said it, she knew that it was true. She confessed to me that she found her middle son less interesting than his brothers. "He's kind of a little pedant, always going to great lengths to split hairs and explain the obvious." I should mention that the little pedant grew up to be a be a professor of mathematical logic.

As we emerge from the cocoon of our families, our need for connectedness is broadened to take in others outside our families. Foremost are our peers, our friends and classmates. We can't regard their attention to us as a given, as we hopefully could within the bosom of the family. The notion of popularity emerges quite early in childhood, growing ever more urgent in adolescence. Are we popular? What do we have to do to become more popular? The very word reeks of the adolescent turmoil accompanying our growing concern about how much attention we can expect to get in the extra-familial social world. Our teachers, coaches, mentors, and other authority figures might also become others whose special attention we strive to receive. Sexual and romantic desires kick in, as we experience the crushes that single out certain people to whom we are paying a specially charged kind of attention and from whom we desire reciprocal specially charged attention.

Our need for connectedness matures as we do—if, in fact, we do manage to mature. But whether we mature or not, our flourishing will remain dependent on the need that comes from our being gregarious creatures who inhabit a world of social relationships.

But gregarious creatures, inhabiting a world of social relationships, is not all that we are, and connectedness is not all that we require for our flourishing. There is also the demand that forces us into the space of justifications, focused, by way of the mother question of all mattering questions, on ourselves, the person with whom we are forced to keep company every waking moment of our lives. To satisfy this self-directed demand, which is the mattering instinct, is just as essential to our flourishing as are the needs we have as gregarious creatures.

Both of these needs, for connectedness and for mattering, are fundamental to our flourishing. In the absence of connectedness, we experience the anguish of loneliness. And in the absence of a sense of intrinsic mattering, we experience the kind of anguish that, in its most extreme form, becomes chronic depressive disorder or dysthymia. The term *dysthymia* derives from the ancient Greek word *thumos*, which was used by philosophers like Plato to mean the spirited part of our psyche that drives us forward into our future. And that is exactly what we lose in dysthymia. Our spirit flags, and we plunge into a blackness through which it becomes impossible to see our way forward into our future.

In one of his most famous statements, Sigmund Freud declared, "Love and work are the cornerstones of our humanness." Freud was right about the duality at our core, only I would amend his statement. For Freud's "love," I would substitute connectedness, since our need to feel that we are being paid special attention by those we regard as in our lives can assume forms quite distinct from love. And for Freud's "work"

I would substitute the sense of mattering—which in Freud's case, derived from his work.

Chapters five and six will explore the four strategies for responding to the mattering instinct that sort us out into socializers, heroic strivers, competitors, and transcenders. Among heroic strivers, the striving may be intellectual, artistic, physical, or ethical. Freud was, unsurprisingly, a heroic striver of the intellectual kind. His groundbreaking psychological work was the mattering project that made his life feel worth pursuing. "What would one do when ideas failed, or words refused to come? It is impossible not to shudder at the thought," he wrote to Oskar Pfister, a Swiss Lutheran pastor and lay psychoanalyst with whom Freud kept up a long correspondence.[21] Freud was like most of us in universalizing his mattering strategy, assuming that what it took for him to feel that he mattered, his work, is what it would take for any of us to feel that we matter. The urge to universalize our own response to the mattering instinct comes almost as naturally to us as the mattering instinct itself. We'll look at the urge to universalize more closely in chapters six and eight.

We are far more aware of our need for connectedness than of our longing to matter, which tends to keep itself hidden from view. In fact, keeping itself hidden from view is integral to the way that the longing to matter functions within us, burrowing itself down deep into our mattering projects, so that we don't have to confront the unease provoked by the mother of all mattering questions. It's only when our mattering projects are failing us—or we are failing them—that the existential doubt comes bursting forth. So far as our own flourishing is concerned, hidden is exactly where we want our longing to matter to be, along with the existential doubts it arouses. But as we'll see in a later chapter, this hiddenness encourages the faulty logic we exercise in universalizing our own response to the mattering instinct.

The hiddenness of the mattering instinct, as compared to the overtness of the need for connectedness, provides the explanation for something that has surprised me over the years in my discussions with people on the theme of their mattering. Often when I first broach the subject, people automatically complete the verb *to matter* with the prepositional phrase *to others*, almost as if the phrase is entailed in the verb. It isn't. Even the one psychology book that I've found that is called *The Psychology of Mattering* presumes that the verb *to matter* entails *to others*. The book turned out to be about the need for connectedness and not the longing to matter.

The two core needs share some of the same vocabulary, being focused on attention, which aids the confusion. But while connectedness intrinsically involves others, the longing to matter does not—not intrinsically, although some people respond to it by way of connectedness. These are the people I call socializers. And while the longing to matter intrinsically involves norms of justification, the need for connectedness does not. The fact that the notion of mattering involves deservingness—and so norms of justification—raises this aspect of ourselves to a different order of cognitive complexity and explains why it's our species alone that harbors the longing to matter.

No wonder then, that we are more overtly aware of our less complicated, non-justificatory need for connectedness, come to us by way of our being a gregarious species. No wonder, too, that connectedness is the cornerstone that has received the bulk of attention from psychologists. Connectedness, often referred to as belongingness, is a topic suitable for empirical study, and social psychologists have rightly made it a foundational concept in the field. Connectedness captures our lives as social beings, and we *are* social beings. But that's not all that we are, and not all of our longings are social longings.

Meanwhile the longing to matter has remained neglected. Overlapping as it does with questions both empirical and philosophical—the latter taking us into the extra-empirical realm of values and norms of justification—the longing to matter can't be adequately probed using only the empirical tools at psychology's disposal, its surveys and statistics. What we are after in our longing to matter isn't to feel that we matter but to be assured that we actually do—that the lives we are choosing to live are lives that actually matter. The reactions we get from others as to our mattering can often help but they often can't. There are those who enjoy loving relationships, respect and admiration, who yet battle with the desolation of feeling that they don't matter. We'll meet several of these people in the pages that follow.

The quotation from the philosopher and novelist Iris Murdoch that I've chosen for this book's epigraph observes that we seem unable to set forth what makes the human person precious and unique except by way of ideology and abstraction, by which she meant the questionable religious doctrines of the theologians and the dryly abstract moral theories of the philosophers. That is one of the challenges of this book, to express that uniqueness and preciousness while avoiding abstraction and ideology. We hardly have the vocabulary to discuss the cornerstone that yields us our existential dimension. We need an expanded vocabulary to do justice to that which is the most peculiar, most human, and most poignant thing about us.

CHAPTER 2

THE TRANSFORMATION
FROM WITHIN

One of my two daughters has always been an exuberant speaker, accompanying the rush of her sentences with wild hand gestures. When she was a little girl, we rarely got through a meal without some dish or cup getting knocked over. After one of these mishaps, involving grape juice on a white tablecloth, she exclaimed in genuine shock, "Look at what my body did!" Your body or you? I asked. "Not me!" she asserted emphatically. "It was my body!" Further questioning revealed that yes, barely out of toddlerhood, she was indeed a Cartesian dualist, believing herself and her body to be two distinct things. What she did "on purpose" was due to herself. She hadn't intentionally knocked over her cup. Ergo, it wasn't she but her body that had done it.

Cartesian dualism is named after the philosopher René Descartes (1596–1650) in recognition of such assertions as this: "And although possibly (or rather certainly, as I shall say in a moment) I possess a body with which I am very intimately conjoined, yet . . . it is certain that this I, that is to say, my soul by which I am what I am, is entirely and absolutely distinct from my body, and can exist without it."[1]

Descartes produced a subtle argument for his dualism, involving a philosophical thesis concerning essences—the properties of a thing that make it the very thing that it is—an argument that was resuscitated by one of the most brilliant of twentieth century philosophers, Saul Kripke.[2]

But subtle philosophical arguments have nothing to do with the intuitive appeal of the view. Cartesian dualism is our natural default. It seems to come upon us early in our development—as witness my daughter—in our valiant, if confused, attempt at making sense of ourselves and the world, of ourselves *in* the world.[3]

Not only was my little Cartesian daughter innocent of philosophy. She had also never heard tell of a place called heaven where people are said to go after they die. I mention heaven because a popular theory for why we are natural-born dualists, disinclined to believe that we are nothing but complicated material beings, is our fear of death. There is probably some truth in the theory, even if fear of death had nothing to do with why my death-ignorant child declared her independence from her body. Still, fear of death might help to explain why dualism lingers so persistently. If we're nothing but our material bodies, then what hope is there for surviving our death? Part of our resistance to the evidence for our own material composition might well derive from what the cultural anthropologist Ernest Becker had called "the denial of death" in his celebrated book of that name,[4] which not only posthumously won Becker a Pulitzer Prize but was, in its time, so well-known that it made an appearance in a scene in Woody Allen's 1977 film, *Annie Hall*.[5]

Becker argues that we alone are the animals who know that we are animals, and we do everything in our power to deny it, since we know that to be an animal is to die. Self-deception—which puts us in the paradoxical situation of being both the deceiver and the deceived—is, for most of us, in Becker's view, a permanent condition. If that sounds like a difficult state of mind to maintain, teetering dangerously close to the neurotic, then you've grasped Becker's point. He diagnoses neuroticism as an almost universal condition, with denial of death the hidden motive behind our most distinctively human behavior: culture and religion; heroism and achievement; social stratification and identity; romantic fixation and ideological extremism. All of these distinctly human behaviors, Becker argues, are ploys of self-deception in the face of the inevitability of death.

Becker has a point, but he surely overstates it. Although our creaturely terror of death may contribute to our reluctance to acknowledge that we are creatures of "mere" matter, so too does the longing to matter that has us striving after lives we can regard as worth the striving. For how can mere clumps of matter achieve the mattering for which we long? That's the question that makes some balk at the material hypothesis. They find the notion of identifying the loftiness of our thoughts, the nobility of our aspirations, the grandeur of our creativity to electrochemical impulses carried along the neuronal circuitry crisscrossing the gelatinous matter of our brains tantamount to denying the loftiness, nobility, and grandeur. Those physical processes might be causally correlated with what we experience in our *être intime*, they protest, but the *être intime* must itself be of a different essence, more numinous and exalted. Call it spirit, soul, mind, consciousness—whichever word best resonates with the value-laden mystery of what we are. But do not identify the god-haunted being of us with the laboratory stuff of physics, chemistry, and biology.

Becker underestimated our species. As difficult as it is, we can accommodate ourselves to the fact of our death—but not to the thought that our lives count for nothing, that we might as well not have bothered to show up for our existence, for all the difference it makes. We are not inveterate neurotics but rather matter longing to matter, and for those who feel the material hypothesis lessens our mattering, dualism is the preferred option.

Given the link between the longing to matter and dualism, it would be interesting to tether the longing itself to our being made of matter. That's the aim of this chapter and the next. Our deepest struggles—to persist, to thrive, to make a difference, to do right, to create beauty, to make sense of ourselves and our world—emerge from the physical forces that made us. These are the forces that coaxed intricate, sentient, and purposeful organisms out of the disorder and dissolution entailed in the direction of time itself, as described by the most fundamental law of physics.

The realm of impersonal physical forces and the realm of our meaning-seeking lives may seem incommensurable, but in our species they intermingle. In the being of each of us, they intermingle. It all begins with one extraordinarily singular law of physics, which, applying to all physical systems, applies to us. I don't think this reduces the wondrousness of what it is to be human—in fact, quite the contrary. But such judgments are subjective, so you be the judge.

THE SUPREME LAW OF PHYSICS

Six years after my first husband and I separated, I went back to the house we had shared for decades and where he was then living alone. I'd returned to be present for the appraiser, so that the division of our marital property might proceed.

It was a ramshackle old house, a despotically demanding house, which had consumed big chunks of my life in the struggle to keep it from collapsing. Still, the house had quirks that compensated for its disadvantages. A laundry chute to the basement had provided my daughters and their friends with hours of amusement, playing catch with stuffed animals that they dropped from the second story into the basement's laundry room or sending secretly coded messages up and down with a homemade pulley. A boarded-up "servant stairway" had been converted into a cabinet for oversized pots and pans, and sometimes, in the stillness of an early morning, I imagined I heard footsteps hurrying along the vanished passageway.

Over the years, I had come to think of the house as a tyrannical invalid and had assembled a team of specialists to aid in its survival. I should not have been surprised on visiting it after the passage of time to see its state of dissolution. The devastation in the small bathroom off the kitchen pantry was particularly grotesque: the ceiling heaving downward like a hammock holding a body, the wallpaper delaminating and mortified with water stains.

"Not exactly," said my soon-to-be ex-husband when I asked whether there had been a flood. "The toilet in the upstairs bathroom had a leak."

"Not exactly," he responded when I asked whether he

had summoned a plumber. "The leak spontaneously self-terminated."

I had to laugh at his response, delivered deadpan. The absurdity decked out in the precision of the physicist: It was very much his style of humor. He had known that I would laugh, as I had known that he had known. The recursion of our shared knowledge of one another rushed out of the past with its distinctive feeling of familiarity and warmth. We had known each other so long, having met when I was fifteen and he nineteen. I had once been so connected to his thoughts and desires that it was hard to tell where his had ended and mine began. No more though. Attention of that pitch requires emotions that had run their course. Hereafter our knowledge of each other would only decline.

This is what happens to houses and relationships when the energy necessary to keep them going is withdrawn. They run toward ruin.

And it's not only houses and marriages that work this way. Everything does. That's not just me being depressing. That's physics—in particular one law of physics so fundamental that it has been elevated to "the supreme position among the laws of Nature,"[6] the single scientific law that scientists confidently claim will never be overthrown by any future discoveries.[7] Physicists even tell us that it is the law that generates time itself—or at any rate, time's arrow, pointing us away from the unrecoverable past and toward the uncertain future.[8]

The law has more commonplace applications. It explains why a pot of soup removed from the stove will cool off until it is the same temperature as the room and then cease cooling. It explains why you shouldn't cry over spilled milk—or, at any rate, explains why the spilled milk will never become unspilled—and why you can't unscramble an egg. It explains why we weaken and wrinkle and grow forgetful with age, why there are innumerably more ways for things to go wrong than right, and why we have more names for negative emotions than for positive ones.

"Outside and within man is *l'autre*, the 'otherness' of the world," wrote the literary critic George Steiner. "Call it what you will; a hidden or malevolent God, blind fate, the solicitations of hell, or the brute fury of our animal blood. It waits for us in ambush at the crossroads. It mocks and destroys us."[9]

The scientific name for *l'autre* is the second law of thermodynamics. You wouldn't think that thermodynamics could be implicated in our existential dramas. It seems diminishing to subsume the human condition under a law that explains why a pot of steaming soup will, when removed from the source of heat, inevitably cool off and won't, no matter how long you watch it, spontaneously reheat. Even a malevolent God or the solicitations of hell seem preferable to accepting that soup going cold has anything to do with the thrashings of our soul. At least those hostile forces would have us in mind. So might insist a creature of matter in its longing to matter, preferring the malevolence of the universe to its utter indifference.

Thermodynamics literally means the dynamics of heat, and fittingly the field originated in the industrial age, when the complex relationships between heat and other forms of energy, temperature and work, were the first order of business. But the second law of thermodynamics spreads its explanatory net far beyond these topics in physics. It is acknowledged as fundamental in the fields of chemistry, evolutionary biology, information theory, and more. Though not yet widely acknowledged, it is equally fundamental in psychology, a point succinctly made in the title of a paper published in 2003, "The Second Law of Thermodynamics Is the First Law of Psychology."[10] The law itself can be succinctly expressed: In a closed system, entropy increases. From now on, I'll just call it the law of entropy.

I confess I'm enraptured by this law and have been ever since I was an undergraduate studying physics, suspecting that its hidden depths might shed some light on *our* hidden depths. If I seem to get carried away with details you find irrelevant, I announce at the onset that the brief excursion into the law of entropy is here because of its implications regarding the longing to matter. It's the law of entropy that necessitates the self-mattering of all living systems, from bacteria to us. All living systems must devote available energy to *locally* resisting the law of entropy. But, if you've read the introduction, with its fifteen key ideas, you know that I think much more can be gotten out of the law of entropy. We can use it to help us decide the normative questions, involving *ought* and *ought-not*, that our mattering instinct forces on us.

The word *entropy* was first coined in the nineteenth century by the physicist Rudolf Clausius. "I have intentionally formed the word entropy so as to be as similar as possible to the word energy: the two quantities to be named by these words are so closely related in physical significance that a certain similarity in their names seems appropriate." Like *energy*, *entropy* is derived from Greek roots. *Energy* is composed of *en*, "from within," and *ergon*, which means work. For his new concept, Clausius combined *en* with the Greek *trope*, which means transformation. Entropy literally means *transformation from within.* Less literally, it is the measure of the disorder of a system. It is the collapse of the system quantified.

Though the notion of entropy was first introduced to explain why heat always passes from a hotter body to a colder and never the other way round—such problems were central to the Industrial Age and its need to convert the burning of fuel into motion—the notion has the broadest applications. Wherever there is irreversibility, then there is the law of entropy. And since irreversibility generally reigns, so does the law of entropy.

Here is the difference between reversible and irreversible processes: If you film a billiard ball colliding with a second one on a table and then reverse the film so that it is playing backward, the reversed film looks perfectly believable. Unless you were informed, you wouldn't know the film was reversed. But if you film an irreversible process and then play it backward, you can tell that the film is playing backward, because what you are seeing could not have happened: The beaten egg separates so that its yolk emerges from the albumin, becoming a discrete blob in the midst of the glutinous whites, the whole glob then leaping up into the jagged open shell, which then seamlessly seals itself up into a perfectly smooth ovoid.

Most of the changes that we observe are irreversible, and so we tend to take irreversibility for granted. Our common sense about irreversibility is complacent and incurious, as if there is nothing here to explain, when in fact irreversibility once posed a problem so perplexing that it was officially labeled a paradox—the kind of contradiction-breeding puzzle that paralyzes the rational mind.

Consider a glass of water into which you put a small blob of black ink. At first the ink will form a discrete shape where it was dropped. But gradually the borders of the blob will break down and the ink will become dispersed throughout the glass, even without your helping the process along by stirring it. All by itself the water will change until it becomes homogenously tinted, and once it reaches that state, it will remain that way, all its future states undifferentiated from one another. That is the state called an equilibrium. You will never see the process reversing itself, the ink spontaneously separating itself back out. Think of all the work you would have to do, the infusions of energy you would have to introduce, to get the process to reverse itself and return to the initial condition, the water once again clear and the ink gathered into a discrete blob— for example, boiling away most of the water, leaving behind an inky residue and then letting the steam condense. That's a lot of work, and you know for a fact that it is not going to happen spontaneously. Were you to film the process of the blob of ink dispersing itself in the water and then run the film backward, viewers would know that what they were viewing had never actually happened.

And here is what is so baffling. The inky pool is a mixture of molecules of water and molecules of ink. Were you able to zoom in to the molecular level and view the molecules of ink dispersing themselves through the molecules of water, you would see a lot of molecules rushing about and banging into one another, the collisions deflecting their motions, the motions governed by the laws of mechanics, just like billiard balls scattering on a pool table. So far, so good. These random motions of the molecules of ink and water offer an explanation as to why the blob becomes unblobbed. But here is the puzzle: Eventually the ink molecules will become evenly dispersed throughout the water molecules, and we should ask why: Why should the random motions of the molecules end up in homogeneity? And once they do end up in homogeneity, then to our eyes, back up on the observable level rather than the molecular level, nothing will change in the glass, and again we should ask why. The molecules are continuing to behave exactly as before, moving and colliding according to the laws of mechanics. So why do we see no changes at all when we look with our eyes at the tinted water in the glass? Why do the random motions result in stasis, at least as far as observation is concerned? Why don't the ceaseless motions of the molecules ever result in, say, the ink molecules coming together into a discrete blob, as they were when the ink was first poured in?

The molecular motions that would result in that happening are perfectly possible. If again we zoom in to the level of the molecules and film the motions and then run the film backward, we would see nothing at all bizarre. Just as the filming of billiard balls colliding on a pool table can be run backward and we would see nothing to alert us to the fact, so too the filming of the motions of the colliding molecules can be run backward, and all would look normal.

We know the behavior of the molecules is reversible, and the change in the color of the water that is wrought by the molecules' motions is irreversible. But how can what we see be irreversible while what *composes* it is reversible?

This was the problem that struck scientists as so perplexing that it was elevated to the status of a paradox, the irreversibility paradox. There seemed only two choices: give up the claim that matter is composed of particles or give up the claim that entropy increases.

The person who solved the irreversibility paradox was a physicist named Ludwig Boltzmann, a citizen of the Austro-Hungarian empire, which was itself heading toward entropic collapse. In the process of solving the paradox, Boltzmann also clarified the notion of entropy, giving us our understanding that entropy is the measure of the disorder of a system, while also creating a new science: statistical mechanics.[11] As the name implies, Boltzmann made probabilistic reasoning central in his explanation. Since Boltzmann's time, we've gotten used to thinking that probability can play a pivotal role in scientific explanation. But the idea was iconoclastic when Boltzmann introduced it, seemingly running so counter to the aims of science, with its ironclad determinism, as to provoke robust opposition.

So, how did Boltzmann's explanation go? Back again to the glass of inky water, its color remaining an unchanging shade of gray even as its molecular activity continues on exactly as before. How many configurations of the molecules would realize the state of the glass when the ink was first dropped in? A definite number of ink molecules are dropped into the water, which means there is a definite number of possible configurations of molecules that realize the original shape of the blob. Now consider the number of configurations that would realize the state of equilibrium, the ink molecules dispersed throughout the water molecules. The number of possible ensembles that realize equilibrium will be enormously larger—by orders of magnitude—than the number of possible ensembles that realize the bordered blob. There are staggeringly more ways in which the ink can be evenly distributed throughout the water than there are ways it can be concentrated inside a discernible blob, meaning that disorder is far more probable than order. That was Boltzmann's game-changing insight, and it can be elegantly expressed in an equation that has come to be recognized as among the most fundamental in science:

$$S = k \log W$$

What the equation means is that the entropy (S) of any system is proportional to the number of indistinguishable configurations of its particles that it can assume without appearing to change to our eyes, which is the W. As W grows, so grows S. How fast S grows in proportion to W is calculated by the other factors symbolized in the equation. The k in the equation is a number known as the Boltzmann constant. It is a fundamental constant that relates temperature to energy that was first discovered by Boltzmann and that turns up in other important equations. The "log" in the equation stands for logarithm, a mathematical function you might remember from high school, the inverse of the exponential function that takes a number to its power, as in squaring, cubing, taking to the fourth power, and so on. So, for example, the log 100 (base 10) = 2, since $100 = 10^2$. The logarithm increases as W increases, but more slowly.

So long as we accept that matter is made up of particles, then it is the mathematical laws of probability that explain why entropy increases. This is why the law of entropy is accorded its "supreme position" by scientists, never to be overturned. As Sir Arthur Eddington put it, "If someone points out to you that your pet theory of the universe is in disagreement with

Maxwell's equations—then so much the worse for Maxwell's equations. If it is found to be contradicted by observation—well, these experimenters do bungle things sometimes. But if your theory is found to be against the second law of thermodynamics, I can give you no hope; there is nothing for it but to collapse in the deepest humiliation."

The reason for the unique inviolability of this one law of physics is that it rests on only two premises: the compositional nature of matter and the mathematical laws of probability. It is the latter that prove, with all the a priori finality of mathematics, that disorder is more probable than order.

It may not be immediately apparent how much likelier—by orders of magnitude—disorder is than order. I have a friend whose vindictive ex-husband gave their young child a puzzle of the Sistine Chapel for Christmas, knowing that his overworked ex-wife would have to devote many hours to "helping" the child with the puzzle, which consisted of more than a thousand pieces. Of course, there is only one right way—that is, ordered way—to arrange all the pieces. How many wrong, that is, disordered ways, are there to arrange them? Imagine that the pieces are all the same size and that, properly assembled, they fill a square thirty-two inches by thirty-two inches. Suppose there are 1,024 pieces. Ignore, for simplicity's sake, the straight-edged pieces along the perimeter, and instead imagine that the pieces are all attachable on four sides. That would mean that there are 5.42×10^{2639} wrong ways to put the pieces together. To give you some idea of how enormous this number is, consider that the number of particles in the visible universe is 10^{70}.

That was a vindictive ex.

BIOLOGY'S RESPONSE TO THE LAW
OF ENTROPY

What are the implications of the law of entropy for our own lives? The good news is you can let yourself off the hook a bit: The states constituting your well-being and happiness are highly ordered and therefore improbable. If you are not having a great day, that may just be life (and statistics). The bad news is that since disordered states are far more probable, you have to *work* for your well-being and happiness.

The overwhelming probability of disorder over order is the difference that holds the answer to why all living systems must devote so much energy to resisting the entropic transformation from within. All life, all flourishing, depends on capturing energy (from sunlight or food) and applying it in local anti-entropic resistance. And the more complicated the system, then the more ways for it to be disordered, and hence the more resistance required. Again, our brains are the most complicated objects yet discovered in the universe and, not coincidentally, require a lot of energy.

Here is a thought experiment to bring home the truth of how much more likely disorder is than order and the implications for our flourishing. First, list all the things that presently could happen to you that would significantly enhance your flourishing. Some of them might be highly unlikely, such as winning the lottery (even more unlikely if you've never bought a lottery ticket), others not quite so improbable. Now list all the things that presently could happen to you that would significantly diminish your flourishing. Compare the number of possibilities on your first list with the number of possibilities on your second list. If you have done it right, the result should be disheartening. The preponderance of possibilities in our disfavor explains why there are so many more negative emotions than positive ones, so many more bad choices that lay open to us than good ones, so many more ways to achieve unhappiness than happiness—all because there are so many more ways to achieve disorder than order. It also explains why it's so much easier to destroy than to create. To destroy is to work in the direction of entropy, while to create is to resist entropy. Almost all the things worth doing in this world—learning, loving, creating—require our resistance to entropy.

Schopenhauer, philosophy's reigning pessimist, wrote, "Every possession and every happiness is but lent by chance for an uncertain time, and may therefore be demanded back the next hour." Boltzmann demonstrated how right Schopenhauer was. Not only our health and happiness but our very survival demands that we are constantly required to pit ourselves against the laws of probability and resist the entropic transformation from within.

And resist we do. All living things do. The law of entropy states that *in closed systems* entropy increases. But we aren't closed systems. No living organism is. Entropy, as its very etymology implies, is an inward process; it describes what happens to a system that doesn't have recourse to external sources of energy. Being a closed system isn't compatible with being alive. Existence demands persistence, and persistence demands resistance. And that's exactly what living organisms do: resist. To maintain life demands what's called "negative entropy," or "negentropy," which are processes that lead to a local decrease in entropy *within* a system, though that isn't to say that the law of entropy is violated.

Living things are actively self-organizing and self-maintaining, taking in free energy from food, sunlight, or dissolved minerals that is put to work in metabolism, which generates high-entropy wastes expelled into the surroundings, thus increasing the overall entropy. (Life makes a mess, some lives more than others.) Eventually, the low entropy of the living organism can no longer be maintained. Senescence is built into an organism, with different species having evolved different natural lifespans. Our finally succumbing to the law of entropy is, like all other inherited aspects, a product of natural selection.[12] Natural selection focuses more of its attention on mutations that favor reproductive success at an early age, since survival is always chancy. The longer something lives, the greater the chance that something out there will do it in—competitors, predators, pathogens, droughts, falls, famines, floods, fires. It's a matter of the odds, and natural selection "knows," so to speak, where to place its bets. (Any language that seems to anthropomorphize natural selection should be understood as figurative.) And there might well be trade-offs between traits that confer fitness in youth as opposed to those that confer benefits in old age. Though some organisms have an enviably long lifespan—the yew tree can live five thousand years, which means the oldest predate writing—senescence is an aspect of all cellular life. Senescence is a consequence of the trade-offs between vigor and longevity, with the non-zero probability of accidental death at any age favoring vigor at younger ages. Any vigor at an older age will have gone to waste if the organism is felled before that age, so natural selection will favor youthful vigor at the expense of older vigor. One of my earliest memories: spying on my grandmother, who lived with us. I watched her staring into the gilded mirror that hung over the buffet in our dining room and softly lamenting, in her thick Hungarian accent, "Ah, Helena Blau, where has your beauty fled?" Now I could tell her: It's entropy, Grandma. Grandma eluded the Nazis, but there's no eluding entropy.

With death, the organism reaches maximal entropy, its cold, decomposing corpse moving toward thermodynamic equilibrium with its surroundings. Ashes to ashes, dust to dust. Entropy always triumphs. But until it does, *vive la résistance*!

SELF-MATTERING: THE ORGANIZING PRINCIPLE BEHIND ALL THE INSTINCTS

And so we are brought back to the self-mattering that is a feature of all living things. Not only is self-preservation a prerequisite for an entity persisting rather than entropically falling apart, but natural selection ensures that self-mattering—at least of a primitive and proto kind that doesn't require the capacity for attention—is baked into the very thermodynamics of life, encoded in the genetic information responsible for the organism's adaptive behavior.

If an organism—any organism—were to have the capacity to articulate its deepest motivation, the motivation that's a prerequisite for all its other motivations that drive it on in its ceaseless tasks and activities—its scurrying, hiding, roaming, grazing, ravaging, raiding, mating—it would say that its own existence in this world, its persistence and its flourishing, *matters*. Its own life deserves the assiduous activity that every creature unthinkingly gives it. And if the genes could speak, since it's at their level that the machinery of natural selection is run, they would make for the best of self-esteem coaches. With all the conviction of a Rogerian therapist ministering unconditional positive regard, they would incessantly and urgently exhort the organism forward, whether it's the blade of grass struggling up through a crack in the sidewalk toward the sunlight, or a sea slug discharging its potent chemical mix against a predator: *You are special, oh so special. There is nothing in all the world that matters more than you, matters more than your own survival and flourishing!*

Biology's response to the supreme law of physics is what makes self-mattering deeper than any instinct, making it, rather, the organizing principle behind all the instincts. Just as no university has a designated Department of Knowledge, knowledge being the organizing principle behind all the academic departments, so too there is no designated instinct for self-mattering, self-mattering being the organizing principle behind all the instincts.

There is, of course, a dramatic difference between the proto self-mattering of the light-seeking blade of grass and the self-mattering of more complex organisms, such as you and me. At some point in the evolution of life on this planet, certain living systems evolved the capacity for attention. They became *observers*. Observers have more flexibility in resisting entropy. They can acquire information from their surroundings to take advantage of the sources of free energy needed to maintain the low entropy consistent with life (i.e., food) and avoid threats that would hasten their thermodynamic equilibrium with their surroundings (i.e., death).

In other words, attention is an adaptation that raises the proto self-mattering of living systems to something a little less proto and a little closer to what we find in us. A little closer, though still not there. The sea slug, even if it does have some rudimentary capacity for paying attention to its environment, which is unclear, is hardly thinking, "Out of my way, dammit, my life matters!" Whatever we mean by awareness of self, sea slugs lack it. But then other species do possess self-awareness, at least of a rudimentary kind—most convincingly chimpanzees, but also, arguably, orangutans, bonobos, dolphins, orcas, the bluestreak cleaner wrasse, elephants, rhesus macaques, and some birds, such as Indian crows and Eurasian magpies. At least these species seem to have some notion of their selves as a distinct thing among other things, with traits that either do or do not belong to it.[13]

But in us, self-awareness blooms into an entirely different order of complexity, enriched with nuances of thought, emotions, and attitudes. Our self-awareness encompasses our having a sense of our ongoing lives—of a past we recollect as our own, with such attendant emotions as nostalgia and regret, and of a future that we likewise anticipate as our own, with such attendant emotions as hope, dread, insecurity, worry, and a whole lot of fantasizing. Even though the notion of our lives is projected both backward and forward—we remember the past when we were and try to imagine the future when we will be—we live our lives forward and not backward. Our agency is future oriented, pointed in the direction of our self-interested survival and flourishing, just as the organizing principle of all the instincts—our self-mattering—would have it. As Søren Kierkegaard put it, "Life can only be understood backwards; but it must be lived forwards." We can even project our emotions into a future in which we will be absent, as for example the writer who confessed to me how he motivates himself to write by fantasizing the fame he will win after he dies. How can posthumous fame matter to you, I asked him, when you won't be around to reap any benefits from it? He shrugged. "What can I tell you? It matters to me. It keeps me going, gets me out of bed and to the keyboard." So used do we become to projecting ourselves forward that our self-interest can sometimes seem to extend even beyond our own existence—the shadow of the future in which we shall not exist yet casting itself backward over our present motivations and emotions.

SELVING: THE FEEL OF BEING ONESELF

Consisting of roughly 86 billion neurons, connected by roughly a hundred trillion synapses, the human brain is the most complicated object on this planet designed to resist entropy.

The brain of a human averages only three pounds in weight, but even at rest it consumes more than 20 percent of the body's energy. Just by actively thinking you're typically using up about 320 calories per day even if you never stir out of bed. If this book is pushing you to step up your thinking, even if only to disagree, then you are burning up extra calories, so you're welcome.

It's no wonder that our brains require so much energy, considering the vastness of organization that must be maintained to preserve their low entropy. The neurological system that we carry in our craniums is the most sophisticated mechanism any creature on this planet has evolved for trying to beat the entropic odds racked up against it. In other words, your brain—which the computer scientist Marvin Minsky ingloriously called a "meat calculator"—was built to preserve you. It makes tremendous demands on your existence while also increasing the odds that you will, with your excellent brain, be able to meet these demands. The welfare of itself—that is, of you—is the very function for which your brain evolved its stupendous complexity, with your self-mattering—that is, regarding yourself as deserving of your own attention— implicit throughout the entirety of the dynamic attentional-emotional-motivational system that is you. It's no wonder that the greatest proportion of your attention is given over to yourself—that's literally how we are wired.

Pursuing a human life is a demanding proposition, requiring countless observations, considerations, calculations, convictions, commitments, decisions, emotions, exertions, and above all attention. You have to pay ceaseless attention to the variable factors that you encounter that can potentially hinder or help you in your lifelong endeavor of surviving and flourishing. Your attention is not disinterested, in the sense of having no stake or vested interest. Your *interested* attention is almost always hovering, ghostlike, in the interface between you and your environment, because being in that interface facilitates the function for which attention evolved in organisms in the first place, which is to respond flexibly to changes in the immediate environment that can nourish or annihilate them.

There are exceptions to the constancy of self-attention. You might have sometimes experienced extraordinary intervals when your attention was drawn so fixedly toward something outside of you, perhaps as you concentrated on a task that so entirely absorbed your attention that you lost all sense of yourself—together, most tellingly, with the psychological sense of time's passage. That is how fundamental to us our self-attention is: Escape it temporarily, and you temporally escape temporality. These extraordinary episodes have come to be called *flow*, and they are so psychologically distinct precisely because they are so anomalous.

Of course, sometimes it really is you—and only you—that rivets your full attention—when you are introspecting, self-reflecting, self-analyzing, navel-gazing. Flow is at one end of the continuum, when attention to self is largely blotted out, while introspection is at the other end, with our attention to ourselves explicit: the very thing to which we are attending. And in between there is outwardly focused attention, whether to things, ideas, or other people, with our self-attention tacit. That space, with self-attention tacit rather than explicit, is where the bulk of our attention is spent. And it stands to reason that this is where our attention is generally cast—focused on things other than ourselves but with an implicit reference to ourselves, since it's this kind of attention that answers to the explanation for why organisms evolved the adaptation of attention.

You stand in the doorway, scoping out the scene of the party. You don't see anybody you know. They're all in jeans and sweatshirts. You're embarrassingly overdressed. Your eyes scan the room for someone you know, or someone you'd like to know, or, failing that, some food. You've skipped dinner, thinking you'd eat at the party. All you locate is a mess of nachos surrounding a bowl of neon yellow slop that looks squeezed from a tube. Wrong crowd for you, both sartorially and gastronomically. But you could still steal away. Nobody who knows you has spotted you. Uh oh, somebody is waving at you. Too late. No wait, she's waving at the guy standing to your left. But now that guy has turned toward you, and you recognize him as the one who invited you to this convivial disaster. Now it's really too late.

In none of these perceptions are you distinctly attending to yourself. Rather, your attention to other things is suffused with self-referentiality, like a scent or a fine mist. The sense of you permeates the varying fluctuations of your attention, layering them with the warmth and familiarity of their being unmistakably your own—"that taste of myself, of I and me above and in all things," in the words of the poet Gerard Manley Hopkins, "which is more distinctive than the taste of ale or alum, more distinctive than the smell of walnut leaf or camphor. . . . Nothing else in nature comes near this unspeakable stress of pitch, distinctiveness, and selving, this selfbeing of my own: nothing explains it or resembles it, except so far as this, that other men to themselves have the same feeling."[14]

Linked to our "selving" is the full exquisite mechanism of human emotions. Our entire emotional repertoire, so rich and nuanced, has evolved to give us feedback regarding how things are going for us so that we might adjust our responses accordingly. Affection, aggrievement, anger, annoyance, anxiety, apathy, arousal, awe, bewilderment, boredom, confidence, confusion, contempt, contentment, courage, curiosity, desire, despair, disappointment, disgust, distrust, dread, embarrassment, enthusiasm, envy, excitement, fear, frustration, gratification, gratitude, grief, guilt, happiness, hatred, hope, horror, hostility, humiliation, hurt, indifference, indignation, interest, intimidation, jealousy, loneliness, love, lust, outrage, pain, pity, pleasure, pride, rage, regret, rejection, relief, remorse, resentment, sadness, shame, shyness, surprise, suspicion, trust, wonder, worry, and other emotions that we haven't gotten around to naming:[15] The complexity and variations of our emotional repertoire correspond to the complexity and variations of the situations to which we feel that we must give our full attention because they have implications for our own well-being. The emotions themselves, the *feel* of them—are designed to get our full attention. Just try to ignore the surges of love, anger, surprise, fear. And those emotions—both the painful and the pleasurable ones—have cognitive content. They are giving you constant readouts on the way that the world is impacting your lifelong ambition of surviving and flourishing. They are also energizing you to respond to the changing circumstances around you, if a response is called for: the anger that moves you to rear up and resist, the loathing that causes you to withdraw. Self-mattering is implicit throughout the whole expanse of the attentional, emotional, and motivational structure that is us.

You reach into an oven to remove a pan and . . . #@$%*&! You don't have to explicitly think out, step by step: *That is pain. The pain is mine. I hate the pain—it hurts! The pain deserves my attention. I ought to do something to stop the pain, like drop the #@$%*&! pan.* Rather all these elements of self-mattering— attention, emotion, and motivation—are merged together in the unity of experience that the processes of your brain smoothly produce. Human consciousness is anything but simple!

Human attention is itself an anti-entropic process of vast complexity, executed at multiple coordinated levels. The kaleidoscopic profusion of distributed activity in the brain—the colors, contours, and motions in 180 degrees of visual field; the sounds from twenty to twenty thousand cycles per second; the sensations from the skin, joints, and viscera; memories from the past and plans for the future; and sheer random, unbidden activity, mind-wanderings and fantasizings—are filtered and organized, with the maps and networks representing the focus of thought becoming amplified, synchronized, and suffused throughout with the selving that ensures the thought of you is almost never entirely absent from your mind, a linchpin for your inner coherence. In fact, some contemporary theories of schizophrenia posit that it's precisely this "selving," which they call, somewhat less poetically, *ipseity*—from the Latin *ispe* for self—that is lacking from those suffering from schizophrenia.[16]

In the complexities of our working brain, selving is intimately fused with the entire interconnected system of attention, emotions, and motivations. Is it any wonder then that David Hume could not locate a single perception of the self, "simple and continued"?[17] To turn your eye inward and search for the simple and continued perception of self is like constantly halting a film to search, in frame after stilled frame, for the motion you see when the film is running.

We can try not to feel ourselves deserving of our own special attention to ourselves, but such an aim isn't compatible with pursuing our lives. Any mattering project you might possibly undertake, including trying to transcend your own ego, is saturated with your self-mattering. Even the yogi, meditating on his mountaintop, is motivated by self-mattering. After all, the yogi isn't going to be satisfied with his life if some other yogi, maybe on the next mountaintop over, manages to transcend his ego. It's the transcendence of his *own* ego that is the yogi's mattering project.

Being motivated by self-mattering isn't tantamount to selfishness. Selfishness means caring only about getting results that benefit yourself, while self-mattering is having our brain function as nature has built it to function—as the outcome of biology's response to the law of entropy. Within the normal course of your life, engaged as you are in all its myriad details, there is no distance to be gained between you and your self-mattering, no question as to whether you will regard your own flourishing as deserving of your special attention. Your self-mattering is one with your engagement in your life. It's one with your being you.

CONATUS

It was the philosopher Baruch Spinoza who intuited how our identity is not static but rather dynamic, fused with the very process of persisting. His intuition is compressed in a single word that he introduced: *conatus*, derived from the Latin *conare*, meaning to strive.

Spinoza defined *conatus* as the striving of a thing to persist in its own being and to flourish, and he asserted that a thing's conatus is what makes each thing the very thing that it is.[18]

Spinoza lived his brief forty-four years in the seventeenth century, at the very dawn of modern science, when it was still feeling its way toward the optimal balance between empirical observation and a priori mathematics that characterizes the physical sciences. Spinoza himself, as thoroughgoing a rationalist as the history of philosophy ever produced, who made every claim for reason that has ever been made, veered toward the radically nonempirical. And yet so many of his intuitions have proved so prescient that Albert Einstein repeatedly called out Spinoza's scientific vision as being, of all worldviews, the closest to his own.

Centuries before the formulation of the law of entropy, Spinoza intuited that persistence demands resistance. Identity is an ongoing dynamic process, a *striving*, in which self-mattering is implicit. For Spinoza, the fact that you matter to yourself is a tautological fact about your personal identity, tantamount to asserting that $x = x$, where you are the x. He was wrong about our self-mattering being a tautological fact about us, ultimately coming down to pure logic and nothing else. As an extreme rationalist, Spinoza was intent on demonstrating that all facts ultimately come down to pure logic and nothing else. Spinoza notwithstanding, the self-mattering that is baked into our identity is baked into it by way of the laws of nature—the law of entropy that determines the transformation from within of all physical systems and the laws of biology that dictate the resistance to entropy of living systems. These are empirical laws, not deducible through pure logic. Nevertheless, though our self-mattering is not tautologically one with our identity, it is so fused with our identity that it can almost seem like an instance of $x = x$.[19]

After all, who exactly are you? What is it that picks you out from all the other persons that have ever been, or are, or will be? The answer is that you are the person who, in explaining why _____ (fill in your name) matters to you, doesn't have to cite any fact other than your identity. For all other people who matter overwhelmingly to you—that infinitely precious child, parent, sibling, lover, or friend for whom you might even be motivated to sacrifice your life—to explain why they are so deserving of your attention requires your citing the extra fact of your relationship with them: They are my beloved child, parent, sibling, lover, or friend, you explain. But if somebody should ask you why _____ (fill in your name) is so deserving of your attention, it is sufficient to answer, "Because I *am* _____." Enough said.

Enough said, only not. As baked into our identity as self-mattering is, we yet demand a *reason* for it, a reason that *justifies* it to ourselves; otherwise the great conative project of being ourselves can lose its forward thrust, becoming a striving that we aren't convinced is worth the effort.

How this demand for a reason justifying our self-mattering arises in us is the story of the next chapter. Just as our self-mattering is implicit in our being alive, so our demanding of ourselves a *reason* for our self-mattering is implicit in our being human. That extra demand is, of course, the mattering instinct.

Is it any wonder that living a human life is so unremittingly demanding? It demands not only the struggle against entropy but also the struggle to convince ourselves that we are *deserving* of the struggle.

THE SCIENCE OF MATTERING VS. THE SCIENTIST WHO MATTERS

It is poignant that the man who gave us the crucial insight in understanding how our lives demand our constant struggle against entropy was himself so tragically ill-equipped for it.

Much about the life of Ludwig Boltzmann is perplexing. He himself perplexed himself. But about one thing he left us with no uncertainty. He knew exactly what most mattered to him in satisfying his longing to live a life that matters. "It must be splendid to command millions of people in great national ventures," he wrote, "to lead a hundred thousand to victory in battle. But it seems to me greater still to discover fundamental truths in a very modest room with very modest means—truths that will still be foundations of human knowledge when the memory of these battles is painstakingly preserved only in the archives of the historian." That's the project to which he dedicated his life, discovering fundamental truths that would be foundational in future knowledge, and he succeeded as few people had. And yet despite his brilliant success in realizing what he imagined as the most splendid of all lives, Boltzmann is one of science's tragic figures.

Outwardly, Boltzmann hardly fits the tragic image. Short and corpulent, a man who loved his Viennese roast pork and potatoes downed with steins of beer—he was horrified when, while lecturing at the University of California, Berkeley, he learned that Berkeley was a dry city—he had a high-pitched voice and his nearsightedness eventually became so acute that he would pile two or three pairs of spectacles onto his nose to read the sheet music when he played the piano. Though a brilliant and enthusiastic lecturer, he could also veer suddenly into inappropriately personal directions. One former student, Lise Meitner, a physicist who helped discover nuclear fission—and ought to have won the Nobel Prize[20]—wrote that Boltzmann had been inspirational as her professor, but added that he was amusingly uninhibited when he lectured and would, midlecture, launch into "how much difficulty and opposition he had encountered because he had been convinced of the real existence of atoms."[21]

Meitner's reminiscence is lighthearted, but there was nothing lighthearted to Boltzmann about the professional resistance he met concerning the "real existence of atoms." This might surprise you. Don't all scientists believe that atoms exist? Not necessarily, and for philosophical reasons that had great currency in Boltzmann's day, when a radical form of empiricism, sometimes called phenomenalism or positivism, dominated. Radical empiricism can crudely be expressed by the slogan "to be is to be observable," or even more radically, "to be is to be measurable." Atoms aren't observable and therefore, according to radical empiricism, don't exist. Reference to them in theories should be interpreted as only imaginative aids in grasping theoretical abstractions. They are imaginative metaphors, not to be interpreted ontologically—that is, as having any implications concerning what actually exists.

Radical empiricism held much sway in the scientific community of Boltzmann's day and was later invoked to rule out the existence of genes, germs, tectonic plates, and, in behaviorist psychology, mental states and even consciousness. One of Boltzmann's contemporaries was the influential physicist and philosopher Ernst Mach. As a physicist, Mach primarily studied the physics of shock waves. You may recognize his name from the Mach number that measures speed relative to the speed of sound. To break the sound barrier something must travel at a speed exceeding Mach 1. As a philosopher, Mach is associated with radical empiricism, which rendered him a vehement critic of Boltzmann's work. Once, when attending a lecture by Boltzmann, Mach was unable to contain his impatience and interrupted the talk to shout out, *"Atome? Haben Sie einen gesehen?"*—that is, "Atoms? Have you seen one?" This was devastating for Boltzmann. He later reported that Mach's words continuously "ran around in my head."[22]

There are scientists still who remain indoctrinated with radical empiricism, regarding "to be is to be observable" as tantamount to the scientific outlook. But this was not Boltzmann's understanding of science. From his point of view, if an explanation of observable phenomena, such as all those covered by the law of entropy, requires you to infer the real existence of unobservable particles of matter, then you are *scientifically* justified to infer the real existence of those particles. A satisfactory scientific explanation can expand our ontology. Boltzmann's explanation of the law of entropy demanded the real existence of the particles of matter—molecules and atoms—unobservable though they may be, and in his view his successful explanation demonstrated the wrongheadedness of radical empiricism rather than the other way round. Since when should bad philosophy be allowed to dictate to successful science? This was Boltzmann's plaintive query. Bad philosophy, in the form of radical empiricism, was impeding scientific progress and in the process beating him down. "Shouldn't the irresistible urge to philosophize be compared to the vomiting caused by migraines, in that something is struggling to get out even though there's nothing inside?" he asked in exasperation in a letter to his friend Franz Brentano, a philosopher.[23]

And it wasn't only radical empiricism that Boltzmann was battling. He was also attacked for injecting the mathematics of probability, first developed by Blaise Pascal to analyze games of chance, into the explanation of a fundamental law of physics. Scientists have by now accommodated themselves to statistical explanations, but it took some getting used to.[24] Reducing a law of nature to statistical reasoning meant a law of nature could in principle be violated, even if the violations would be statistically improbable. The ink molecules dissolved in the glass of water could, improbably, blunder their way back into a discrete blob. Boltzmann's explanation of the law of entropy doesn't rule out occasional fluctuations leading to decreasing local entropy, even though the overwhelming probabilities will prevail, which is sufficient to explain why entropy increases.

The lack of absoluteness for which Boltzmann's work allows didn't sit well with many of his contemporaries. There was, for example, Lord Kelvin (Sir William Thomson), another scientist immortalized by a scale of measurement. He's the *K* in the Kelvin scale of temperature above absolute zero. Lord Kelvin was an early supporter of the new science of thermodynamics as it pertained to heat but objected to the turn that thermodynamics had taken with Boltzmann and his probabilistic reasoning. The great German physicist Max Planck—who, ironically, would go on to be one of the founders of probabilistic quantum mechanics—also initially balked at Boltzmann's probabilistic treatment of entropy. Planck would eventually come round—as most scientists would—to the legitimacy of probabilistic scientific reasoning, even at the most fundamental levels of physics, but in the meantime, these rejections from those in a position to evaluate Boltzmann's work in explaining the law of entropy deeply wounded Boltzmann.

Boltzmann complained bitterly that his work was not getting a fair hearing and that his accomplishment in solving the irreversibility paradox was being ignored. When in 1896, the German mathematician Ernst Zermelo, himself a student of Planck, published a critique of Boltzmann's solution, Boltzmann began his response with a bit of sarcasm: "Herr Zermelo's paper indeed shows that the relevant works of mine have not been understood; even so I am bound to be pleased by this paper as the first indication that these works have been paid any attention at all in Germany."[25]

Boltzmann had devoted his life to a single project—explaining the law of entropy and thereby solving the paradox of irreversibility—and he can't be faulted for taking his project seriously. It was tantamount to taking his life seriously. The attacks and dismissals made Boltzmann obstinate, obsessive, and finally ill. Even a buoyant nature can be brought down by criticism and derision, especially when the target is a person's mattering project.

When it comes to the four mattering strategies that we'll examine more closely in coming chapters, Ludwig Boltzmann was every inch a heroic striver. Boltzmann explicitly put his mattering project in heroic terms, comparing his project to commanding millions in great national ventures. "But it seems to me greater still to discover fundamental truths in a very modest room with very modest means—truths that will still be foundations of human knowledge when the memory of these battles is painstakingly preserved only in the archives of the historian." And that's exactly what Boltzmann had done. What's more, he *knew* that he had done it, which makes him, in some sense, more fortunate than many other heroic strivers. Recall John Berryman's words to the young William Merwin: "You can never be sure. You die without knowing whether anything you've written is any good." That's the lot of the poet, but not of the scientist. Science has a methodology, involving predictions, that allows the physical world itself to weigh in on whether one's theory is any good. Boltzmann's theory, with its elegant equation, would prove to be powerfully explanatory for a rich diversity of complex phenomena, from the stellar and galactic dynamics of astrophysics to the evolution of all living systems. Boltzmann, a heroic striver, had succeeded heroically. Why, then, did he become so desperately unsatisfied with his life? Why was the recognition of his peers of such overwhelming importance to him that, in its absence, his future increasingly came to seem to him not worth pursuing?

Boltzmann himself makes it clear why, as a scientist, recognition of what he had accomplished was so overwhelmingly important to him. For the truths one has discovered to become "foundations of human knowledge" others must recognize them as important truths. Boltzmann succeeded in this as well, of course. He succeeded magnificently, with his equation for entropy among the most important in the history of science. But he didn't live to see this, and he despaired that the philosophy of his day would continue to block his science from becoming recognized.

Certainly, other scientists have died before knowing how fundamental their discoveries would prove to be. Gregor Mendel comes to mind, the monk whose experiments with pea plants led to his posthumously being recognized as the father of genetics. Mendel's results were misinterpreted as demonstrating, albeit with mathematical rigor, what was already assumed—namely that hybrid plants and animals revert to their original forms. The fact that his work pointed to discrete carriers of traits, later to be named genes, was entirely missed, as were the evolutionary implications entailed in his demonstration of the recombination of traits. Mendel had made some effort to get his work recognized. He was not simply an isolated monk. He'd become a monk mainly to get an education, having been born poor. He presented his results in two lectures to the Natural History Society in Brünn, and published a paper, "Experiments on Plant Hybrids," in the society's journal. But compared to Boltzmann's efforts to get his work recognized, Mendel's efforts were minimal. "My time will come," he is reported to have said. And indeed it did, when his results were discovered in a library thirty years after his death. Boltzmann's posthumous fame arrived more quickly. Four months separated his death and the first phase of his vindication.

Perhaps one of the reasons that Boltzmann took his peers' dismissal so much harder than had Mendel—in addition to differences in temperament, which are always significant—is that, in Boltzmann's case, bad philosophy was holding sway over good science, and that bad philosophy had become accepted by scientists as part of science itself—a maddening situation to a scientist like Boltzmann. And unlike Mendel, Boltzmann had devoted so much effort to getting his work understood by his peers, and so had less faith that his time would come.

As the nineteenth century waned, so, too, did Boltzmann's well-being. Friends and family noticed that his enthusiasm for life was dwindling, an inner darkness overtaking him. He decided to move away from Vienna and accept an academic post in Leipzig. The move required much wrangling with the bureaucratic bloat of the Austro-Hungarian gatekeepers. And when he finally managed to move to Leipzig, it did nothing to lift his gloom. A colleague of his reported to a friend that "anyone who got to know the ill and depressed Boltzmann in his Leipzig period" would hardly believe that this was the same energetic man of former times. Soon he was wrangling to move back to Vienna, desperately seeking external circumstances that would reconcile himself to his life.

Among the more obscure of psychiatric disorders is one called *lethophobia*—the fear of forgetting. Boltzmann was overcome by the fear that he would, midlecture, suddenly lose his memory, which, because of his failure to get his work recognized, contained precious truths that only he possessed.

His doctor diagnosed neurasthenia—unsurprisingly, since it was the catchall diagnosis of the nineteenth century. The new disease had been formulated in terms of energy—the "nervous energy," it was hypothesized, on which we run. The concept of energy, raised to scientific prominence, was offered as an explanation for the "disease of modernity," dissipating our energy. This is when the term "enervated" originated. When the diagnosis of neurasthenia was first introduced, in America, it was said to most especially afflict competitive businessmen and intellectually overstimulated women. As the nineteenth century progressed, the disease was seen to be far more widespread, the pathological expression of modernity itself. Boltzmann, with his cluster of symptoms both physical and mental, was seen by his doctors to present a classic case.

In 1905, a young patent official in Bern, Switzerland, published a paper that left little doubt about the reality of the constituents of matter, even if directly unobservable. But Boltzmann's mental state had so deteriorated that, as far as we know, he took no notice of it. The patent officer was Albert Einstein, and the results reported in his 1905 paper would be cited when, in 1922, he won the Nobel Prize in physics. Einstein's paper definitively explained the phenomenon known as Brownian motion, named after a Scottish botanist of a century before, who had observed grains of pollen under a microscope and seen them jiggling about, as if they were alive. When you watch dust motes flitting about randomly in a sunbeam, you are witnessing Brownian motion. Einstein demonstrated that what explains the motions of these bits of matter is their being bombarded by the unobservable particles of their medium. His reasoning yielded equations for calculating the size and number of particles from the effects of their impact. Three years later, the French physicist Jean Perrin performed a series of experiments that proved the accuracy of Einstein's equations for predicting Brownian motion under varying conditions.

Einstein's paper, fortified by Perrin's measurements, provided the empirical evidence required for asserting that the particles of matter really exist. At least one of the two disputed premises on which Boltzmann's work was founded had been vindicated, though Boltzmann gave no indication that he had read Einstein's paper. By this point in his life, not only was he no longer doing creative scientific work, but he took little interest in the work of others.[26]

"How I envy you your constant cheerfulness and satisfaction," Boltzmann wrote his friend Brentano. "You are in truth a genuine philosopher. I have reached 62 years of age, and I have gained no peace of mind."[27]

Boltzmann's doctor, seeing the accelerating decline of his patient, advised him to give up his work, or at least to take a vacation. Boltzmann took a vacation.

In a hotel room in Duino, Italy, while his wife and children waited for him to join them on the beach, Ludwig Boltzmann took a short cord dangling from a casement window and hanged himself. He was scheduled to return the next day to Vienna to resume his course of university lectures. He left behind no suicide note. Horrifically, his corpse was discovered by his teenage daughter, Elsa, who had been sent by her mother to see what had delayed her father.

He is buried in the Zentralfriedhof, Vienna's largest cemetery, his grave inscribed with the equation he had spent his life defending: $S = k \log W$. He died before the scientific community would come to recognize the immensity of explanation compressed within it. And still the implications of Boltzmann's equation are forthcoming, including its implications for clarifying some of the mysteries of our lives, and most certainly of Boltzmann's life. The man who understood entropy as nobody before him had, converting his quest to explain its logic into the mattering project of his life, is one of science's most tragic figures.

It would be hasty to attribute Boltzmann's suicide to the lack of recognition his work had received. Some scholars have argued that Boltzmann might have suffered from bipolar disorder. Even Boltzmann acknowledged his mood swings. On his sixtieth birthday he fell to reminiscing, observing that he had been born on the night between Shrove Tuesday and Ash Wednesday, and suggesting, likely in jest, that perhaps this fact explained his lifelong swings between joy and misery. Nevertheless, there can be little doubt that the frustrations and disappointments he experienced in regard to his life's work took a great toll on him.

The physicist David Goodstein began his book *States of Matter* by noting a curious coincidence: "Ludwig Boltzmann, who spent much of his life studying statistical mechanics, died in 1906 by his own hand. Paul Ehrenfest, carrying on the work, died similarly in 1933. Now it is our turn to study statistical mechanics. Perhaps it will be wise to approach the subject cautiously."[28]

A mere four months after Boltzmann's death, Max Planck, whom Boltzmann had resented as someone hostile to his probabilistic physics, published his equation for black-body radiation, kicking off the quantum revolution that has embedded probability into the very foundations of physics. The Boltzmann constant turns up in Planck's equation, and it was Planck who dubbed it "the Boltzmann constant." Perhaps Boltzmann might have taken some life satisfaction in this homage from Planck and in the indication that one of the great obstacles to the acceptance of his own work—the hostility toward probability in physical explanations—was about to crumble.

But fantasizing about how it might have gone differently for Boltzmann isn't thinking thermodynamically. Disorder is far more probable than order, as Boltzmann explained for us. Once the disintegration from within has sufficiently progressed, it takes that much more energy to reverse it, a law that holds for our psyches as for all else.

All tragedies are thermodynamic.

Grave of Ludwig Boltzmann, physicist, in Zentralfriedhof
(Central Cemetery), Vienna, Austria

CHAPTER 3

BECOMING HUMAN

Being human seems quasiparadoxical, lodged as we are between two seemingly inconsistent truths.

Our self-mattering and our longing to matter seem irreconcilable. How, given the laws of nature that made us, is there room in our psyche for the longing to take form? Self-mattering is wired into our brains. We feel ourselves, insistently and persistently, deserving of our own attention—so very much attention!—not as an outcome of the decisions of our will but rather the outcome of our being ourselves. How then can we come to feel compelled to dedicate so much of our available energy to striving to prove to ourselves that we are deserving of our own attention—when to feel that we are deserving of our own attention is to be ourselves?

The physical laws that shaped us would seem to preclude the most peculiar and most human thing about us, the very aspect that transforms us into the fascinatingly complicated creatures that we are, endowing us with our existential dimension and challenging us to figure out the right standard for judging whether we are living as we ought to be if we're to satisfy our longing to matter. Nature would have seemed to leave no room for such creatures as we are, and yet here we are: matter longing to matter.

I've mentioned that the resolution of the paradox rests in our capacity for self-reflection, but at first glance it's hard to see how. Self-mattering is as apparent in the emerged self of self-reflection as in the submerged self of our moment-to-moment, day-to-day pursuit of our lives. In self-reflection, we consider ourselves stretched out over time, remembering ourselves as we once had been, as far back into childhood as our memory can take us, and likewise projecting ourselves forward in time, anticipating our future selves. And tripping along beside the emerged self of self-reflection, as its dogged companion, is our ever-faithful self-mattering.

Our past self matters to us because it's ours, permeated with such painful emotions as regret and remorse and also with nostalgia, itself a kind of longing for what is done and gone. Even sweet memories are sorrowed with the loss we feel in time's passage.

We regard our future self, too, as mattering—in some sense, mattering even more than our past self does, because there is nothing we can do to change the facts of our past self, whereas we feel that we can change at least some of the facts of our future self by our anticipation of it and the plans and precautions we undertake for the sake of it. We care passionately about our future self because it is ours. What it will experience is what *we* will experience.

Our past self may be more filled in for us, our memories denser with details than our anticipations of our future self can be, since those remembered details come from what actually happened to us, whereas our future self has yet to be, which makes our anticipations of it vaguer and more shadowy. But the vagueness doesn't make our future self matter any less to us, as indicated by the intense emotions that we feel for it— all those hopes and fears that we focus on it.

Both in our submerged self as we go about the business of living, and in our emerged self that stretches out in time in our self-reflection, the conative drive of our self-mattering is inextricably bound up with our being ourselves. How then can there be space enough, even within the distancing of self-reflection, for the longing to matter to take form? That's the question to which this chapter is devoted.

This will be the most philosophical chapter in this book, but only because we are, in our longing to matter, philosophical creatures. You don't need to have been a student of philosophy. The ponderings and reflections that everyone falls into, at least once in a while, are preparation enough.

AN EXISTENTIAL DRAMA IN ONE ACT

I was hurrying down a crowded stretch of Manhattan's Madison Avenue during the noontime crush, rushing to an appointment for which I was late, when I caught a glimpse of an anxious-looking blonde woman reflected in a store window. There was something about her that gripped me. It took a few moments, and then I realized what it was. She was me.

A strange moment, to say the least: to have glimpsed myself as just one of the throng that was out there, a person in the sea of people through which I was desperately trying

85

to make my way to avoid being any later than I already was. And then to realize that no, that one wasn't out there. That one wasn't a *that one* at all. It was me.

It was a trompe l'oeil at an ontological level, a trompe l'ontologie. It made it seem, momentarily, as if my personal identity could be a two-step process, as if God (so to speak) had first created the worldwide throng and then assigned each of us to our identities, as an extra fact about the world: Now this one is to be you. That two-stepness made it seem, for one vertiginous moment of metaphysical disorientation, that it was in the realm of possibility that I could have been assigned identity with another person out there in the throng. But that two-stepness was a momentary illusion brought on by whatever glitch I had just experienced in the part of the brain dedicated to recognizing our own mirrored reflection.[1] It's not that there was a separate her that then was assigned to be me. There is no her without her being me. That is who she is: me—and under normal circumstances, that is how we experience our being ourselves. There is no two-stepness about it. But here—because my identification of my reflection was split into two distinct steps, whereas it is usually, after about thirty-six months of age, experienced as instantaneous—it had seemed to me as if the fact of my being myself was split into two steps. As I said, a deeply strange experience.

But there is an experience that likewise registers high on the strangeness metric, although you have to think about it to fully appreciate its strangeness. Unlike my trompe l'ontologie, this experience is not born of a glitch in the brain but is common to us all. It lies at the furthest reaches of self-reflection.

Self-reflection is the capacity of the mind to take itself as an object of observation and investigation. We take other people as objects of observation and investigation—an adaptive capacity for such gregarious creatures as we are, highly dependent on our social relationships. In self-reflection we turn that capacity back on ourselves, observing ourselves almost as if we were another person, prepared to discover new things about ourselves, sometimes surprising. Since our capacity for self-reflection is dependent on our capacity to reflect on others, let's look at the latter capacity first.

We arrive into our extended helplessness ready to pay attention to others, learning to discern their individual traits so we can know what to expect from them in their behavior toward us. We can observe only their behavior, not the beliefs and desires that motivate that behavior, but we catch on remarkably early to the fact that others have beliefs and desires. Psychologists call this our "theory of mind," and by the toddler stage it's already functioning.[2] Four-year-olds demonstrate the capacity to grasp that others have beliefs and desires distinct from their own, a sophisticated and adaptive capacity. Theory of mind is highly useful to such creatures as we are, not only because of our prolonged helplessness but also because of the social worlds that we continue to inhabit as gregarious creatures, our continuous need for connectedness that is lived out in the web of our relationships among people whose inner lives are not exact replicas of our own, to say the least.

In self-reflection, we turn our adaptive theory of mind back on ourselves. We didn't need Sigmund Freud to know that our own selves, like the selves of others, are not transparently open to our view and present us with multiple mysteries. "I study myself more than any other subject. That is my metaphysics, that is my physics," wrote the great sage of self-study, the sixteenth-century's Michel de Montaigne.

And this turning of our theory of mind back on ourselves is likewise useful to us as social creatures. Self-reflection allows us to debug our suboptimal ways of thinking and behaving—for example, those eureka moments that people experience in psychotherapy. ("My romantic relationships keep failing because I only choose rejecting partners and that's because rejection is what I think I deserve!") And self-reflection also allows us to anticipate how others will see us, again a useful adaptation for us social creatures. As Robert Burns had charmingly put it:

> O wad some Pow'r the giftie gie us
> To see oursels as ithers see us!
> It wad frae mony a blunder free us,
> An' foolish notion.[3]

But in fact some Pow'r did gie us that giftie, that Pow'r being natural selection.

And once our capacity for objectively reflecting on ourselves is in place, with the distancing from the self that is inherent in our turning our theory of mind back on ourselves, then one of the most salient features of ourselves can't help making itself recognized, namely how very much we matter to ourselves.

We are each in a uniquely privileged position to view the self-mattering that is pounded into our identity. The view afforded by seeing "oursels as ithers see us"—at once inside ourselves and yet outside ourselves in the extreme distancing to which self-reflection can deliver us—makes clear not only the magnitude and unrelentingness of our self-mattering, but also its arbitrariness.

Here is Sartre's famous *nausea*, directed not only at the arbitrariness of things in the external world—the lumpy roots of the chestnut tree sinking into the ground[4]—but rather the arbitrariness of our own self-mattering laid bare in the coldly objective gaze we cast on it in self-reflection. The brute contingency of the conative force of self-mattering, pushing us into our future, rests on nothing more substantive than one's happening to be who one happens to be. The arbitrariness is as disruptive to our sense of ourselves as anything short of a glitch in the brain could be. Stay with it long enough—which is admittedly not to everyone's taste—and you can begin to feel yourself untethering from your very self.

And that is because of how deep down in our being our self-mattering is—deep down, but still, because we possess it by virtue of the physical laws by which we function, and not, despite Spinoza, by virtue of logic—separable from us, and because separable from us, questionable by us, and because questionable by us, we question it, determined to do something about it, to justify our self-mattering enough so that we can feel that we've earned it, or at least are on our way to earning it, by way of the mattering projects of whose significance Franz Kafka took the true measurement: "The fact that our task is exactly commensurate with our life gives it the appearance of being infinite."

What transpires in the self-reflective questioning of our self-mattering is a drama worthy of staging by Samuel Beckett.[5] In the intimacy of our own minds, we each mount *An Existential Drama in One Act*, the one act being the act of self-reflection at its farthest reaches, where one's own self-mattering can strike you with, as the philosopher Thomas Nagel puts it, "detached amazement": "Each of us lives his own life—lives with himself twenty-four hours a day. What else is he supposed to do—live someone else's life? Yet humans have the special capacity to step back and survey themselves, and the lives to which they are committed, with that detached amazement which comes from watching an ant struggle up a heap of sand."[6] It's in that special capacity that the longing to matter quickens into a motive powerful enough to shape our lives.

I'd indicated earlier that I'm taking some liberty in describing the longing to matter as an instinct. What I'm arguing is that the mattering instinct is not, in itself, an adaptation, that is, a distinct psychological faculty with an evolutionary function. It is instead engendered by two other features of the mind interacting with each other. It is thus closer to what evolutionary scientists call a *spandrel* (from the architectural term for the tapering space between two arches, namely a feature of an organism that was not directly selected for its adaptive value but arose as a by-product of other features). In the case of the mattering instinct, the first feature is the self-mattering that is necessary for our pursuing our lives and is pounded into our very identity. The second is the cognitive capacity to reflect and analyze on all things, including the self. Longing to matter—that is, the mattering instinct—is what happens when our cognitive processes try to rationalize our self-mattering.

AN ALTERNATIVE THEORY

To appreciate that the mattering instinct represents a distinctive theory, it helps to consider alternatives. One alternative is that a concern with our own mattering is a manifestation of a specific adaptation, namely monitoring how we matter *to others*. The existential concerns I have emphasized, which involve the inner interrogation of the self, would be, on this alternative interpretation, a gauge for keeping track of what others think of you; that is its adaptive function. As one social psychologist put it to me, "Inner processes serve interpersonal functions."[7] He pointed out that his way of explaining the existential dimension—in effect, explaining it *away*—fits a straightforward evolutionary account, since what others think of us has direct effects on our survival and reproduction, whereas how we make sense of our self-justifying existential dilemma does not.

Are these two different theories of our longing to matter—one which sees it as separate from our concern with mattering to others, the other which doesn't—distinct enough that we could decide whether one or the other is likely to be true? I think it is possible in theory to design psychological experiments that could decide between them, though difficult in practice. Until I or someone else does, here are some phenomena that I think are better explained by the theory that our longing to matter is separate from our longing to matter to others. There are examples of people pursuing mattering projects in the face of general rejection, as we saw in considering Ludwig Boltzmann. There are the values we embrace, and that motivate us to do things that we know will alienate others—even the others who mean the most to us. There are people's religious and spiritual impulses that speak to our existential dimension apart from our social relationships. There is the despair of self-loathing that can afflict even the most highly regarded among us, when, for example, they consider themselves frauds and imposters. And if the inner process of interrogating our self-mattering is really only a way of assessing how much we matter to others, why don't we experience it as such? Why does it feel like a longing to prove our own intrinsic mattering, our deservingness and worth, rather than a longing to be admired, respected, even loved?

These specifically existential obsessions will be further explored in the vignettes and reflections of the following chapters. I believe that they reveal deep and autonomous concerns that arise from our self-reflective interrogation of ourselves, separate from our concerns for how others regard us.

You needn't have a distinct memory of engaging in such existential self-searching. Many of us submerge our existential dimension so successfully within our mattering projects that we fail to see any trace remaining in our daily lives—as if those mattering projects that keep us engaged in our lives weren't in themselves something more than a trace of the longing to matter.

We are the species caught between the biologically determined directive of paying ourselves the ceaseless attention needed to resist entropy and the doubt that we truly merit it. Engagement in our lives requires our being passively receptive to the biologically determined directive, but the brains we have evolved are capable of stepping outside our lives to cast a coldly appraising eye on that directive and raising the doubt that we *Homo iustificans* live to obliterate.

A PHYLUM OF OUR OWN

Our evolutionary lineage has us belonging to a species of African apes. Species: sapiens; Genus: Homo; Family: Hominidae; Order: Primates; Class: Mammalia; Phylum: Chordata.

Biologists are eager to stress the validity of the classifi-
cation, pointing out the many ways in which we are like the
other animals from whom we most recently diverged on our
way to evolving into humans. "We are apes in every way, from
our long arms to our tailless bodies, to our habits, and temperaments," writes the primatologist Frans de Waal.

There is something refreshing in the insistence on our
ape-ness. It strips away the romanticizing anthro-mythology,
whether religious or secular, that we have adopted to exaggerate our differences from the other animals. Biologists agree
that we share 98 to 99 percent of our DNA with chimpanzees,
who are more closely related to us than they are to gorillas, a
stunningly demythologizing fact. There are, in other words,
sound scientific reasons for classifying us as a species of African ape. But then, in the course of our evolution, we became
the African ape with the longing to prove to ourselves that the
self-mattering without which we cannot live is actually justified, striving to earn on our own merits at least a smattering
of mattering that we can claim with integrity. (It was Rich-
ard Thaler, a Nobel laureate in economics, who suggested to
me in conversation that quantity of mattering: a smattering.
Leave it to an economist.)

All other creatures capable of attention have their attention just as fixed as we do on the conditions that promote or
impede their own survival and flourishing. But they, unlike
us, don't feel called upon to justify their fixation. They simply
don't do justification. Not even the much-praised bonobo, the
laid-back hippie primate who would rather make love than
war and to whom we are so often unfavorably compared, with
primatologists chiding us, "Why can't you be more like your
sweet-tempered cousin, the bonobo, instead of your hell-

raising cousin, the chimpanzee?"—not even the bonobo has the wherewithal to look squarely at where its attention is over-whelmingly fixed—namely on the self—and to summon the question as to whether it merits such a fixation. By posing that question we became something so radically new, with motiva-tions so unlike those of other apes, as to merit a new phylum.

To propose a phylum of our own isn't biologically naive, or yet another example of romantic anthro-mythology. In practice, taxonomy isn't determined only by evolutionary relatedness but also, to some extent, by phenotypic distinc-tiveness. If gerrymandering weren't allowed in the Linnaean classifications, we'd be classified as a type of fish![8] I'm suggest-ing that an outstanding phenotypic distinctiveness, overrid-ing evolutionary descent, might warrant a new phylum for us: *Homo iustificans.*

Once we've been propelled, by the extreme reaches of our self-reflection, into confronting the mother of all mattering questions, it's never entirely gone—pushing us to undertake the mattering projects that require such a great deal of energy but that are well worth their energy expense if we are to get on with the business of getting on. Still, beneath all the multi-tude of details to which we must attend in pursuing our lives, the mother question hovers close, and it will burst forth and overtake us at certain junctures in our life, hissing its litany of self-doubts and self-denunciations. Any intimation that our mattering project, however we are pursuing it, is failing us—or more to the point, we are failing it—and something vital in us begins to cave, as it did so tragically for Ludwig Boltzmann, despite his heroic accomplishments, and as it did for John Ber-ryman too, despite his accomplishments and acclaim. The vital resistance before the formidable entropic odds from which our brains were built to defend us takes a great deal of energy, and that energy can drain precipitously away when the defenses we have built around our sense of mattering are breached.

For this is a most remarkable fact about our species: Once the question of our own mattering has been encountered, it forever after has the clout to take us over. We will risk our lives, we will even terminate them, if we come to believe that such a sacrifice is required for us to matter—yet another indication that it isn't the denial of death but rather the affirmation of our mattering that explains so much about our distinctively human behavior. Just so long as the thresholds for living a recognizably human life are being met, then the longing to matter motivates us.

The longing to matter doesn't have to motivate you to do something big with your life, although for some people it does. It doesn't need to send you seeking the kind of recognition that will have your name be remembered long after you are gone, although that is what some seek. And it doesn't have to include the belief that you matter to the cosmos at large, in the form of a transcendent presence that you may or may not call God and who, in being mindful of your existence, ensures that you matter, although again that belief is necessary for some among us. Although all these aspirations may be generated by the mattering instinct, they don't have to be for it nevertheless to be working within you, seeing you safely, more or less, into your future.

Wherever human life is pursued, so long as the thresholds for such fundamental needs as nourishment and health, safety and security, connections with others and opportunities to think and imagine for ourselves are being met, then there is a life being shaped by the longing to matter, the same for all of us, even if it motivates us to such a vast array of different mattering projects.

There is something estimable about the pursuit of mattering, this extra burden that we take on ourselves in seeking to justify our biologically mandated self-mattering. I don't mean to deny that it can motivate us to petty and even deplorable behavior that we will regret, or in any case ought to. We'll look at the ways that the mattering instinct can lead us astray in chapter seven, Getting Mattering Wrong. And yet even in those whose mattering projects we may deem morally toxic, this too is as true of them as of anyone else: that though the laws of physics and biology conspired to shape them into a creature who can't help regarding themselves as overwhelmingly deserving of their own attention, they nevertheless have it within them, in resistance to such overwhelming natural forces, to summon up the mother of all mattering questions and feel compelled to shape their lives as an answer to it. And in that there is something in them, as in everyone, that is estimable.

If the mattering of a thing is measured in how deserving of attention we rate the thing to be, then each of us, simply in being ourselves, would seem to rate ourselves as the thing that objectively matters the most in all the world. But short of serious mental problems, we all acknowledge this to be an untrue assessment, and we set about trying to close the gap between how much we feel that we matter and how much we actually matter. Like the legacy student whose place at a university is a given but who nevertheless works hard to earn admittance on their own merit, so we work to earn at least some of the disproportionate sense of our own mattering that is one with our being ourselves.

So yes, there can be mattering projects that are destructive, aims that are heartless, savage, and unforgivable unleashed by the mattering instinct. But in each of us the longing that makes us human speaks to something estimable in demanding that we justify ourselves to ourselves. That estimable something is what we vaguely have in mind when we speak of the dignity inherent in being human. To claim this human dignity isn't to deny dignity to the other animals with whom we share the planet—and not very well, I might add. Animals don't possess their dignity in virtue of being similar to us but rather in virtue of their own distinctive natures. "[Animals] too live amid a staggering, and today an increasing, number of dangers and obstacles, many of them of our making. They too have an inherent dignity that inspires respect and wonder," writes the philosopher Martha Nussbaum, and she is right.[9] But to claim our unique human dignity is to honor what is so remarkable in being matter longing to matter—the staunchly realist position we take toward our own mattering that has us striving to earn the smattering of mattering that will reconcile us with our self-mattering selves. Plato wrote that even in our reaching for beauty, there is beauty. So, too, in our reaching for mattering, there is mattering.

The laws that apply to all other organisms as much as they apply to us carry us this far: They carry us to our theory of mind, which can then be turned on ourselves, and in the turning we are transformed into something so different, with such an added and burdensome requirement for our flourishing, that we merit a new phylum. Our flourishing will now require our convincing ourselves that we have a reason to flourish, and we are prepared to devote a great deal of our energy to what it takes to convince us. This is the inflection point where the narrative of our lives goes beyond a Darwinian narrative, becoming uniquely our own. If free will exists anywhere, then here is where it is to be found: in this sphere of *oughts* to which the mattering instinct carries us, transforming us into the normative creatures we are, who think and act and shape our lives within the sphere of justifications.

We are in strictly human territory now.

A DIFFERENT TELLING

I want to end this chapter with an altogether different way of speaking about our becoming human. It bypasses all discussion of entropy and natural selection in favor of a story.

It's a story about a garden called Eden. The Greek translation of the Hebrew Bible called it *parádeisos*—paradise—borrowing the word from the Persian *paridáyjah*, meaning an enclosed pleasure garden that was restricted to royalty. It was here, within this protected place, that, according to the ancient story, the first man and woman came to be.

Everything within the garden was there for the taking—orchards that tended themselves, producing figs and pomegranates, olives, almonds, and dates; vines hung heavy with clusters of grapes; melons whose flesh was golden, ruby, or celadon; shrubs thick with clustering berries of vermillion, indigo, and black. Animals flitted or lumbered around the two of them, some so large as to shake the ground. But none of these animals threatened the two, for in that garden it was only the flesh of the fruits and vegetables that was eaten by the man and woman, as well as the animals.[10] Birdsong filtered down from the lush foliage above them, along with the sun that dappled the grasses soft beneath their naked bodies.

There must have been much for the two to talk about,

everything being so new to them, including themselves. They were delightfully companionable, marveling as to how it seemed that they had been made for each other, since of course they had been. In their innocent nakedness they would have found their way to pleasure, just as the animals around them did. Nothing had been forbidden to them except for the fruits of the two trees that grew in the very center of the garden.

These trees were interesting, to the woman especially. One tree's fruit yielded knowledge, they were told, the other's eternal life. It was the tree of knowledge that most drew her. Having no idea of death, she would not have known what was so special about eternal life.

A talking snake is a part of the story. It lures the woman into eating from the tree of knowledge. As a child this part of the story baffled me. Not the talking snake part. I was perfectly willing to countenance a snake that can speak. No, the baffling part was God's forbidding knowledge—an obvious good—to the woman and man. I imagined that the woman found it baffling too, which was what drew her constantly to the tree of knowledge, while the man amused himself in other ways, maybe figuring out ways to travel the forest canopy as nimbly as the monkeys or learning to hold his breath as he plunged his head under the cold running streams. When the woman tried to discuss the tree of knowledge with him, he told her that it wasn't theirs to think about.

Perhaps the snake had overheard the woman trying to discuss the forbidden tree with her mate. So that when the snake found her once again standing under the tree and gazing up, he didn't so much tempt her as just speak aloud what she had already been wondering, which was what could possibly be wrong about knowledge?

When I got a bit older, I thought I understood. It was knowledge of good and evil that the fruit supposedly yielded. Now that made sense to me. The Abrahamic religions are all about the meta-ethical claim that we humans can't reason our way toward morality and so must depend on the word of God. But then I thought a bit more, and the story of the tree of knowledge again ceased making sense, since even after the woman and the man ate from the forbidden fruit, they were morally clueless—otherwise what is the latter part of the Bible all about, with its extensive litany of *oughts* and *ought-nots*? The meta-ethical claim would be uprooted if that tree really had granted knowledge of good and evil.

Still, eating the forbidden fruit did make a difference. One bite and the woman was experiencing the emotion of shame. Shame, not guilt. Guilt would have been the result of thinking she had done something wrong in disobeying the Rule-Giver. But shame is the emotion we feel when we consider ourselves as others see us and know that they would be seeing something about us that we would rather they didn't. Guilt impels us to perform reparations, but shame impels us to hide. And in the story of Eden that was exactly what the woman and her mate did, after she shared the fruit with him. They hid.

It was their nakedness that was shaming them, the nakedness of an animal. That was the shameful truth that they wanted to hide away: their commonality with the other animals. They had been promised they were special, but they saw in their nakedness that they were not—at least not yet, there in that protected garden. They were merely animals that could speak—and the snake could do that too.

The tree of knowledge then is not so much about knowledge of good and evil as it is about the capacity of knowing ourselves—in modern terms, turning our theory of mind on ourselves. And although moral knowledge is arguably impossible without the capacity to turn our reflection on ourselves, the two are not equivalent. By biting into the forbidden fruit, the first man and woman were seeing their animal nature—a good start for the search for moral knowledge but hardly amounting to the possession of a moral compass.

How was the woman punished? With the difficulties of childbirth. Unlike other animals, the woman's big-brained offspring would introduce into the birth process not only great physical pain but also the risk of death for them both, mother and child. A more than fitting punishment for a creature who had chosen the capacity to know herself over eternal life.

This story, the first *human* story of the Bible, belongs to the woman. It's entirely her drama. The Bible pays no attention to the motivation of her mate in choosing to take his first bite. She offers him the fruit, and he bites. Wouldn't he have spoken his reservations, given her a lecture on the folly of disobeying the Rule-Giver, telling her that just because she had gotten herself into trouble that was no reason for him to follow suit? Perhaps he bit into the fruit because he couldn't tolerate the woman knowing more than he? In any case, he too had disobeyed and had to share the woman's expulsion from paradise.

The Bible presents the exit from paradise as a fall, but not in my retelling. Paradise was living in a purely Darwinian existence just like all the other animals. Paradise was feeling no need to seek the values that could justify ourselves to ourselves, just as the other animals feel no need. Once we knew what we knew about ourselves, it was time to move on. We weren't banished from the garden but left of our own choice, although full of uncertainty. That is the excruciating aspect of the exit from paradise—not the justificatory work that we feel called upon to do but the uncertainty over whether the work ever accomplishes its aim. The knowledge of ourselves born of the fruit transformed us into values-seeking creatures who lacked the knowledge of values, despite the fruit that the garden had grossly mislabeled. And we never know whether all our normative struggles to go beyond the Darwinian instincts of the animals have added up to a hill of beans—or rather, to skip several chapters ahead in Genesis, to an ill-chosen portion of potage. By the sweat of our brow, we toil at trying to convince ourselves that we deserve the self-mattering that makes us who we are.

Actually, the original Hebrew literally translates as the sweat of our nose—בְּזֵעַת אַפֶּיךָ—which sounds far less dignified. The Bible's language proceeds to rub our noses in our lack of dignity—stressing not only the indignity of the end that awaits us but of the very stuff that makes us: "You will return to the ground, for out of it you were taken, for dust you are and to dust you will return."

Despite the Bible's harsh description of our material being, we left paradise endowed with something estimable. We are dust with dignity. We are dust that does justification, seeking and holding to values, even if they are false values. And so we remain, dust with dignity, no matter how morally misguided and even perverse the acts to which we might be led in our longing to matter.

Genesis soon gives us a story about the perversity as well. Cain and Abel were the first children born after the departure from Eden. Striving to matter to God, one brother kills the other. The first of our many murders has been committed in our pursuit of mattering—or more particularly, in our striving to matter by competitively mattering more to God. Many murders will be committed in that same striving, in not only the pages of the Bible but the pages of history and continuing into our day.

In the story of Cain and Abel, God admonishes the murderer—"The blood of your brother cries out to me from the soil!" (4:10). Cain's response, which is to complain that his punishment is too great to bear, shows once again that his parents ingesting the forbidden fruit didn't yield much in the way of inherited moral knowledge. The first murderer appears to have no idea of what was so terrible in his act. It's his own vulnerability, unprotected from God, that concerns him. God only promises that those who harm him will themselves be harmed, without enlightening him further as to why murder is wrong.

It's not until Genesis gets round to the story of the flood that a moral explanation of sorts is given. Murder is wrong "for in God's image he made humankind" (9:6). On the basis of this phrase many have claimed, and still claim, that our mattering derives from God alone. In the absence of God, all is permitted, including murder.

But not on my allegoric reading of Genesis. On my reading, it was only upon our leaving the protected garden to take up the burden that makes us human that we acquired the intrinsic dignity that renders murder the singular abomination it is.

Our exit from the mythical garden was more than a giant step for humankind. It was a giant step into humankind.

The ancient story leaves us with the image of the many "winged-sphinxes" that guard the way back to Eden, a fiery sword flashing in their hands. But the sphinxes are unnecessary. We all know that there is no going back to what we left behind in becoming human.

CHAPTER 4

LIFE, LIBERTY, AND THE PURSUIT OF EUDAIMONIA

In identifying the two cornerstones of our humanness as love and work, what exactly was Freud claiming? Was it a claim about happiness: that as long as things are going reasonably well in regard to our loving and working, then we will be reasonably happy? And am I similarly making a claim about happiness, only modifying the two cornerstones to connectedness and a sense of mattering? These claims about our cornerstones: Are they about happiness or about something else?

They are about something else. Ludwig Wittgenstein is reputed to have remarked, "I don't know why we are here, but I'm pretty sure it is not to be happy." Freud himself seemed to agree, once saying that the goal of psychoanalysis was to turn "hysterical misery into ordinary unhappiness."

We are distracted by happiness, the shiny bright object of our emotional lives. Of course we want happiness. Happiness feels great. From tranquil contentment to rapturous joy to every shade in between, happiness is the positive emotion par excellence. That everybody wants happiness seems about as obvious as any generalization about us can be. One could argue that we aren't frivolous in wanting to be happy. After all, the American Declaration of Independence lists the pursuit of happiness alongside life and liberty as among our inalienable rights.

Happiness is an emotion, and like all the emotions, it is a reaction we evolved to give us feedback about our immediate circumstances, so that we might pay attention to them and how they are affecting our lifelong striving to survive and thrive. In terms of neurobiology, happiness is a surge of neurotransmitters like serotonin and endorphins, and the feeling of that surge is good.

What characteristically provokes our happiness, in all its varieties, is having a desire satisfied. The desires might vary in terms of how important to you they are, and so the degree of happiness when they are satisfied. You find an item that had been lost; you make a quip that cracks up the room; you snag a hard-to-get concert ticket; you solve a knotty problem that had been driving you nuts; you discover that the person you presently feel is the love of your life feels the same way about you; the result of your medical test comes back negative; your teenager transmits a subtle sign that, beneath the loathing and contempt, the sweet breath of the child still persists: Any one of these occurrences, and vastly more, will occasion some variety of the emotion of happiness. And, of course, we are not the only creatures who experience happiness, as anyone who has ever lived with a tail-wagging dog knows.

The emotions, being so closely tied to circumstances in which we find ourselves so that we might adjust our actions accordingly, are episodic. They are not designed to be self-sustaining, which makes the pursuit of happiness as a lifetime goal frustratingly futile. That surge in neurotransmitters is not designed to last.

What then did Thomas Jefferson mean by endowing the pursuit of happiness with so much gravitas? He was known as a meticulous and deliberate writer, and his choice of the phrase was a considered one. He had arrived at it by modifying John Locke's specification of our inalienable rights, in his *Two Treatises of Government*, as life, liberty, and property.

It is almost certain that what Jefferson had in mind was not the episodic emotion of happiness, but rather what the ancient Greeks had called *eudaimonia*. The term is composed of *eu*, which means good, and *daimon*, which means spirit, and the etymology suggests that, unlike the more fleeting emotions of happiness, eudaimonia is connected with more enduring features of ourselves.

The term is most saliently tied to Aristotle and his *Nicomachean Ethics*, sometimes described as the first attempt at establishing a science of happiness. But a first attempt at a science of eudaimonia is closer to what the philosopher was up to. In fact, Aristotle was at pains to distinguish what he meant by eudaimonia from happiness. He emphasized that our pursuit of eudaimonia typically involves struggles and suffering—in other words, unhappiness. "Eudaimonia, then is not found in amusement; for it would be absurd if the end were amusement, and our lifelong efforts and suffering aimed at amusing ourselves."

Aristotle is associating eudaimonia with our lifelong efforts, quite different from the happiness that responds to our ever-flowing stream of wishes and wants that itself changes with our circumstances. And he is pointing out that these lifelong efforts on behalf of eudaimonia often involve struggle and suffering. There are frustrations, discouragements, disappointments, and perhaps even long bouts of boredom—emotions that are anything but happy. Eudaimonia can exist alongside such unhappiness, because our sense that we are living our lives well can coexist with such unhappiness. And that is what eudaimonia is about: the sense that we are living our lives well, the sense that, all in all, we are flourishing.

Eudaimonia, unlike happiness, is a positive state that only humans feel. Like the mattering instinct itself, eudaimonia requires the self-reflective act of taking a step away from the successive moment-to-moment experiencing of our lives as we are submerged in them and assuming the wider-angle perspective of self-reflection, from which we can assess how well our lives, stretched out over time, are going. The assessment that they are going well is eudaimonia, accompanied by a feeling of reflective satisfaction. And the claim that connectedness and mattering are the two cornerstones of our humanness is the claim that they are what are required in experiencing eudaimonia.

A life that has not succeeded in establishing connectedness with others whom you regard as in your life and from whom you can expect special attention is not a life that feels like it's going well. And a life in which you feel like you don't matter in the way that most matters to you is not a life that feels like it's going well.

It's only relatively recently that psychologists have caught up with Aristotle in their drawing a distinction between episodic happiness and what they call life satisfaction, or sometimes subjective well-being, both of which approximate what Aristotle meant by eudaimonia. "Altogether, I don't think that people maximize happiness in that sense. . . . This doesn't seem to be what people want to do. They actually want to maximize their satisfaction with themselves and their lives. And that leads to completely different directions than the maximization of happiness," remarked the cognitive psychologist Daniel Kahneman, a Nobel laureate in economics.[1] Life satisfaction, subjective well-being, the sense of flourishing: These all are terms that indicate the reflective, wide-angle feeling of satisfaction with how one's life is going over the long term. They are all approximations of the Greek term *eudaimonia*, all of them indicating something other than happiness.

What psychological researchers want is quantitative data, and that poses a problem in gathering data about life satisfaction versus episodic happiness.

For episodic happiness, quantitative data is relatively easy. You ask subjects to keep an emotions journal, jotting down how many times in the day they feel happy and under what circumstances. Testing for life satisfaction, a self-reflective emotion, is trickier, requiring a person's integrative evaluation of their lives over the long term. Our sense of life satisfaction not only involves our self-reflective capacity for thinking of ourselves stretched out over time, but, at an even higher level of abstraction, implicitly involves counterfactual thinking: How does my actual life compare to other possible versions of it?

One test devised to measure life satisfaction is called the Cantril Ladder, which gets at the counterfactual aspect. A participant is asked to imagine a ladder consisting of alternative possible lives that they might presently be living, starting with the worst possible life they can imagine for themselves, level 1, and proceeding upward to the best possible life they can imagine for themselves, level 10. Then they are asked to say at which level of the ladder their present life is.

And what psychologists have found is that a person can be experiencing a paucity of happiness, as measured by an emotions journal, and yet rate their life satisfaction as high. Happiness feels great, and misery feels miserable, but sometimes we feel that misery is worth it if demanded by one of the two cornerstones of our humanness. Our negative experiences need not adversely affect our life satisfaction.

So far, this book has concentrated on how we became creatures motivated by the mattering instinct. Now it turns to the ways that the mattering instinct affects our psychology. But in this chapter, focusing on life satisfaction, I want to consider both cornerstones of our humanness. I begin by discussing connectedness, the cornerstone with which we are more familiar.

THE PARENTHOOD PARADOX

The sense of connectedness a parent feels with their child, the sense that their life is interwoven with theirs, is intense. There is no mystery in this. The mechanism of natural selection consists of some genes getting replicated into future generations more than others. Those who make the survival and flourishing of their offspring a top priority, who automatically *feel* that it is a top priority, are more likely to have offspring who survive. We evolved to care immensely about our offspring. Their prolonged helplessness is answered by our prolonged emotional involvement with their lives. The involvement well outlasts the child's helplessness—tends to last, in fact, as long as the parent does. The connectedness a parent feels to the child they raise isn't perceptually cued by the genetic facts, but rather by the child's adorableness and helplessness, the feeling of responsibility for their welfare, and the tenderness that nurturing encourages. We care about an adopted child as much as the child who shares our DNA. Nothing else in our relationships quite compares with the degree of connectedness forged in the parent-child relationship, excepting romantic love. And in the case of romantic love, the sense of our life being interwoven with another's life is by no means guaranteed to last as long as we do. Natural selection's interest, so to speak—which always comes down to the brass tacks of genes being replicated into future generations—is more cynically short-term when it comes to romantic love.

The intensity of the connectedness that parenting induces sometimes results in a parent's entirely changing the sense of their life. Their child's well-being, about which almost all parents are strongly inclined to care, becomes the parent's mattering project—which is to say, their means of responding to the mattering instinct and affirming their own mattering. But whether or not the raising of a child is put to work in satisfying a parent's mattering instinct, parents tend to overwhelmingly feel that their children matter. And that is indeed fortunate for the children, but is it so fortunate for the parents?

A few years ago, there was a rash of popular articles and books devoted to the so-called parenthood paradox. Some researchers claimed that, although prospective parents imagine that children will increase their happiness, the reverse is true. Parents tend to experience less happiness than the childless—and the younger and more dependent the children, the steeper the decline in happiness. The parents pay a prohibitive "happiness penalty." And yet here we are with the desire to nurture as strongly entrenched as ever. Women are having children later in life but having them at a higher rate than a decade ago, with the sophisticated technologies of modern science abetting their efforts.[2] Hence, the parenthood paradox. Are people just being foolish in deciding to have children, not foreseeing that they will pay with their happiness?

First, we can ask whether the premise of the parenthood paradox is true: Do parents really pay a happiness penalty? Those of you who have been through it—and especially those currently in the thick of it—know that parenthood ushers in a host of intense emotions, and many of them are negative, including worry, fear, self-doubt, frustration, exhaustion, anxiety, stress, anger, and mind-screaming boredom.

Of course, there are also positive emotions, above all overwhelming love and tenderness. And yet these positive emotions intensify the fears and worries and self-doubts. Are you doing right by these vulnerable beings who are so helplessly dependent on you? Every step of the way, as they progress from infancy, to childhood, to (God help us) adolescence, to adulthood: Their issues and problems are your issues and problems. The intense connectedness comes at a price. Your life will never more be entirely your own. Mixed in with all that love is not only resentment but also guilt over the resentment, and resentment over the guilt over the resentment.

It's good to acknowledge the negative aspects of parenting, shattering the sentimentalized picture that belies the ambivalence.[3] Still, some researchers may have exaggerated the proportion of negative to positive emotions, downplaying the complexity of factors that influence the episodic happiness of parents. Daniel Gilbert, author of the book *Stumbling Toward Happiness*, declares that, even though people refer to kids as "bundles of joy, they're not a source of happiness." In his book and public lectures, he produces a bar graph showing that childless adults are happier than parents. Another graph shows self-ratings from "about 1,000 American mothers" of happiness during daily experiences like talking with friends, eating, grocery shopping, doing housework, and spending time with children. On average, the only activity that these mothers didn't rate higher than spending time with children was doing household chores. "How happy are women when they are with their children? It's like scrubbing the toilet," declares Gilbert to hearty audience laughter. "It's not even as good as shopping for the things you need to scrub the toilet."[4] Even heartier laughter.

But the situation is more nuanced, even when it comes to the episodic emotion of happiness, let alone life satisfaction. For one thing, it is not inconsequential that those "about 1,000 mothers" were American. Two surveys, from European and Anglophone countries, found that the United States had "the largest happiness penalty for parenthood among the 22 developed countries, even after controlling for a host of individual-level variables that affect parental happiness."[5] The negative effects on parental happiness were explained by the presence or absence of social policies that allowed parents to combine their ability to financially support their families with other obligations. And this was equally true for fathers and mothers. "Since the U.S. is the only major industrialized nation left without guaranteed parenting leave, paid sick and vacation days, and one of few rich countries that fails to subsidize childcare, it isn't surprising that U.S. parents have the biggest happiness gap compared to nonparents. The U.S. simply asks too much of parents at a time when the economic costs of supporting children are enormous and the time to raise them effectively has been whittled away by employers that favor long hours and no breaks."[6]

Even among underserved American mothers, factors in addition to social support influence episodic happiness. For example, some researchers have looked at what they call child-centric parents, measured by the degree to which the parent is invested in their child's well-being. These parents report an increase not only in life satisfaction but also in day-to-day happiness: They enjoy spending time with their children. The authors of a study that compared child-centric parents to others concluded: "From this perspective, the more invested parents are in their children's well-being—that is, the more 'child-centric' parents are—the more happiness and meaning they will derive from parenting."[7]

"Parents who are more invested in their children's well-being" sounds dangerously close to moralizing. After all, what kind of parents are not heavily invested in their children's well-being? Even the title of the article reporting the results is moralistic. "Parents Reap What They Sow: Child-Centrism and Parental Well-Being." What is being blurred in this notion of child-centrism is the difference between those parents who make the raising of their children their mattering project and those who don't, even though they might be just as invested in their children's well-being. Just as it is important to distinguish between happiness and life satisfaction, so it is important to distinguish between connectedness and the mattering instinct. It would be unfortunate if child-centric mothers—and let's be honest, it's overwhelmingly mothers who would be most sensitive to the subliminal moral message—read such findings and drew the conclusion that, to be the best mothers they can possibly be, they have to trade in their mattering projects for the one that merges their mattering with the raising of their children. This comes close to the idea that the very purpose of women is to raise children.

And bear in mind that these studies concerning child-centric parents were testing the effects of such parenting on the parents' own well-being. They didn't look at the effects of child-centric parenting on the child, which are not always good. Child-centric parenting can morph into overparenting that leaves a child with a diminished sense of self-reliance, or with unreasonable expectations as to how the world will cater to their needs, or with forever feeling the burden of exaggerated parental attention on their achievements. The last decade has seen names for these different forms of overparenting, including helicopter parents (always hovering), snowplow parents (clearing away all obstacles), and tiger parents (pushing their children to high levels of achievement). Yet to be experimentally explored are the correlations between these forms of overparenting and those child-centric parents who identify their own mattering with the raising of their children.

In assessing how parenting affects episodic happiness, not to speak of life satisfaction, I have not mentioned money, but it must be mentioned. Researchers have found that an adequate amount of both money and maturity—the two tend to be linked—is a big factor in how much happiness parents report. "Children are positively correlated with happiness for wealthy people aged over 30."[8] But even single mothers of limited means—who are the parents who experience the steepest happiness penalty—more often than not rate their lives as a better life compared to the counterfactual life they imagine without children. Most parents say that their lives have more meaning than they would have had if they had foregone parenthood, and an astonishing 88 percent of American parents agree with the statement "having children is one of the most important things I have done."[9] Again, the importance of distinguishing between episodic happiness and eudaimonic life satisfaction is born out.

Measures like the Cantril Ladder can deliver important quantitative data. But conversations can catch subtleties that slip through the quantitative nets. I can't leave this discussion of the parenthood paradox without quoting from a conversation I had with one single mother.

She's a scientist who works on environmental issues, and her daughter, whom I'll call Molly, was then six. What Molly's mother had to say not only made the distinction between happiness and life satisfaction clear. It also hinted at the complicated ways that connectedness and mattering can be intertwined in evaluating how well our lives are going. Molly's mother was forthright in expressing the decline in her happiness that being Molly's mother has meant.

I don't have any time for anything other than work and taking care of her. I don't even have time to swipe left or right on any of those dating apps, much less go out on a date. But the deepest change has been in how I think about my work and the emotions it stirs up in me. Obviously, I've always been concerned with what we're doing to our planet. But now my fears about the future are more nerve-racking. The future means so much more to me because that's where Molly will be living her life. So, you asked me whether I'm happier now than before I had a child? No, definitely not. Negative feelings gnaw at my happiness. Like recently, Molly has learned how to read, and she's so proud of herself, which of course makes me feel happy and proud, but then there's this. The fact that this is a milestone on the way to her future makes me immediately start thinking about the existential dangers looming in her future. But in some sense, I'm grateful for that. It's the way I ought to have been feeling all along, about all the children of the world whose futures we're threatening by ignoring what we're doing to the planet. But somehow it took my having Molly in my life to get me to feel the appropriate sense of urgency. I had to love a child that much. And it makes the work that I do professionally mean all the more to me. Not only personally but professionally, my life feels more meaningful, and I wouldn't trade it for any other life.

Quite obviously, the claim that parenthood, despite its trials and tribulations, can boost life satisfaction is not tantamount to the claim that it is *required* for boosting life satisfaction, much less that it is required for feeling that you have a stake in the future, as one prominent American politician suggested, going so far as to argue that the childless are necessarily indifferent to the future and so their votes ought to count less than those who have children, although he attributed this indifference mostly to childless women. Molly's mother was making her point based on her own scientific work, which counted for her, together with her connectedness with Molly, as the two cornerstones of her flourishing, regardless of the effects on her happiness.

MATTERING AND LIFE SATISFACTION

Parenthood, ensured by natural selection to be a powerfully sustained form of connectedness, presents perhaps the most widely shared experience in which happiness and life satisfaction can diverge, though romantic relationships, which also involve intense connectedness, can also part the two. Most of us know what it means to suffer for love of the romantic sort, a great theme in narrative art, from Goethe's novel *The Sorrows of Young Werther* to such cult movie classics as *Brokeback Mountain* and *Eternal Sunshine of the Spotless Mind*. The last of these three masterpieces, *Eternal Sunshine of the Spotless Mind*, is the most perfect of the many great movies made from a Charlie Kaufman script. It tells the story of two lovers, Joel Barish (Jim Carrey) and Clementine Kruczynski (Kate Winslet), whose love affair involves such fulgurating pain that they undergo treatments to have all memories of it erased from their brains. But the movie, while brilliantly dramatizing what it might feel like to undergo the progressive blotting out of targeted memories, also suggests that the intensity of romantic pain can be worth it.

But how about the other cornerstone of our flourishing: the sense of mattering? Here too happiness and life satisfaction can diverge. There are ways of pursuing mattering that all but ensure the struggle and suffering to which Aristotle alluded in distinguishing eudaimonia from happiness. In fact, mattering is closer to the kinds of examples Aristotle probably had in mind.

Aristotle was—no surprise—a heroic striver; that is, someone whose mattering instinct demands that they achieve excellence in at least one area. In fact, Aristotle gave us a passage that could be adopted as the marching orders of all heroic strivers: "We must not follow those who advise us, being men, to think of human things, and, being mortal, of mortal things, but must, so far as we can, make ourselves immortal by straining every nerve to live in accordance with the best thing in us."

To live in accordance with the best thing in us: These are words that capture how the mattering instinct expresses itself in the life of a heroic striver, whether the best thing in them is conceived of as artistic, athletic, intellectual, ethical, or some combination. (For Aristotle, it was the combination of the intellectual and the ethical.) To strain every nerve: The burden that all of us share in trying to earn what biology dictates—namely our feeling that we are deserving of all the attention we give ourselves—is made that much more burdensome for heroic strivers, with frustrations, disappointments, self-doubts, and self-criticisms par for the course.

The striving of heroic strivers has got to be heroic— heroic for *them*—which means that the more talent they have, the more excellent their achievement must be for them to regard their lives as going well. It is never easy to be a heroic striver, no matter your level of talent. Low-hanging fruit, even if it would be a high reach for others, will not suffice to gain heroic strivers the requisite sense of mattering that reconciles them to their lives.

It isn't only heroic strivers that experience the struggle and suffering that life satisfaction can demand, and the next chapter will examine the lives of transcenders, socializers, and competitors. But in the rest of this chapter, it will be heroic strivers I'll consider to demonstrate how life satisfaction can tolerate much unhappiness.

A person need not possess outsize talent to have the temperament of a heroic striver. They only need to be striving to achieve standards of excellence that are high-reaching for them. To have, for example, your mattering project focused on your marathon running doesn't mean that you see yourself breaking world records. One recent runner in New York's marathon race had a shirt that read on the back: *I am a slow runner. Please let there be someone behind me.*

But when heroic strivers do happen to be endowed with unusual talent, then the results can be astonishing. Heroic strivers can become, with not only the requisite talent but also the requisite circumstances that allow the talent to be expressed, the people who push our species to a new level of achievement, so that we can all partake, if only at a remove, in their triumph. They are the people about whom biographies are often written, and we love those biographies.

There's a Yiddish word, *kvell*, that has no English equivalent. It's a verb that means to take pride in another's achievement. It's typically used to describe the pride a person takes in their own children or grandchildren, but I think a more impersonal kvelling is what we do when it comes to heroic strivers heroically achieving. Not bad for a bunch of stand-up apes, you might find yourself thinking as you kvell at an Isaac Newton for discovering the mathematical equations that express the gravitational pull governing motions on earth and in heaven; kvell at an Albert Einstein for replacing Newton's conception of gravity with the mathematics of distortions in the curvature of space-time created by matter; kvell at a Michael Jordan as, soaring toward the basketball hoop, he defies the laws of gravity.

The lives of these heroically achieving heroic strivers give us pleasure, often considerably more than those lives gave the people who lived them.

In the beginning of this chapter, I quoted the rueful comment attributed to the philosopher Ludwig Wittgenstein. "I don't know why we are here, but I'm pretty sure it is not to be happy." And happy he was not, though one might have thought he had sufficient reason to be. Born into one of the wealthiest and most cultivated families in Austria and given every advantage, Wittgenstein pursued a life in philosophy that was so successful as to define what it was to do philosophy for many of the philosophers of his generation and beyond. He managed to inspire two different schools of philosophy—logical positivism and ordinary language philosophy—through the two distinct phases of his philosophical life.

Wittgenstein was a heroic striver extraordinaire. Money meant nothing to him. He gave the bulk of his inheritance to his brothers and sisters, explaining, "They have so much money already that some more won't do them any harm."[10] Fame, too, was of no concern, though he was a celebrity of sorts, at least among a cohort of analytic philosophers. The esteem in which he was held by American and Anglo philosophers bordered on veneration. The philosophers I knew who had been in his inner circle, all getting on in years when I was a young philosopher, went so far as to mimic his tics— the long, anguished pauses punctuated by Germanic guttural noises; a characteristic movement of his head, which, though normally tilted, would be thrown back as he directed his gaze into the distance. How it amused me to watch my philosophical elders from across the pond unconsciously performing their rituals of reverence.

Wittgenstein first appeared on the philosophical scene not

in Austria, but in England. He had been studying aeronauti-
cal engineering at the University of Manchester and in the
course of his studies had become interested in problems in the
foundations of mathematics. He promptly took himself off to
Cambridge University to audit a class in mathematical logic
taught by the illustrious philosopher, logician, and coauthor
of the magisterial *Principia Mathematica*, Bertrand Russell. I'll
let Russell take up the tale from here. (You can listen to him
for yourself as he wryly tells the story of his first encounter
with Wittgenstein, which is even better than reading him.[11])

"He was queer," said Russell, using the word in its former sense of meaning *strange*, "and his notions seemed to me
odd, so that for the whole term I could not make up my mind
whether he was a man of genius or merely an eccentric. At
the end of his first term at Cambridge he came to me and
said, 'Will you please tell me whether I am a complete idiot or
not? If I am a complete idiot, I shall become an aeronaut, but
if not, I shall become a philosopher.' I told him to write me
something during the vacation on some philosophical subject
and I would then tell him whether he was a complete idiot or
not. At the beginning of the following term, he brought me
the fulfillment of this suggestion. After reading only one sentence I said to him, 'No! You must not become an aeronaut.'"

You can discern, in the uncompromising wording of
Wittgenstein's question to Russell—"am I a complete idiot or
not"—that Wittgenstein's notion of mattering was formidably
heroic. He was a formidable person in just about every respect
except his physical presence; he was short and slight. Though
philosophers like Bertrand Russell were entirely free of the
fear of God, being avowed atheists, many soon cultivated the
fear of Wittgenstein. Russell became so intimidated by him

that he eventually decided that he did not have what it took to do mathematical logic, suffered a near-suicidal depression as a result, and eventually bucked himself up by writing popular books on philosophy that eventually garnered him a Nobel Prize in Literature. I have little doubt that he would have preferred the respect of Wittgenstein.

But it is Wittgenstein's lack of happiness I want to discuss, not Russell's. Those who knew him paint a picture of intense struggle and suffering. His classes, held in his rooms in Whewell's Court, Trinity College, became legendary, the spartan room crowded with attendees, both students and other faculty. Wittgenstein sat in the center of the room on a plain wooden chair. There, as one attendee put it, "he carried on a visible struggle with his thoughts." He often expressed disgust with his own confusions, issuing such statements as "I'm a fool!" "You have a dreadful teacher!" "I'm just too stupid today." He spoke without notes, struggling to disentangle problems, which he believed to be the substance of philosophical work. Philosophy, he had opined, "is a battle against the bewitchment of our intelligence by means of our language." The disgust he felt with himself, as he judged himself losing the battle to language, was on pitiless display. Sometimes he announced that he wouldn't be able to continue the lecture, but he always did, finishing at 7 p.m. and then rushing off, exhausted and often revolted, frequently taking himself straight to the cinema to escape from the battery of self-reproaches.

"As he struggled to work through a problem one frequently felt that one was in the presence of real suffering. Wittgenstein liked to draw an analogy between philosophical thinking and swimming: Just as one's body has a natural tendency toward the surface and one has to make an exertion to get to the bottom—so it is with thinking. In talking about human greatness, he once remarked that he thought that the measure of a man's greatness would be in terms of what his work *cost* him. There is no doubt that Wittgenstein's philosophical labors cost him a great deal."[12]

This characterization of Wittgenstein comes from the philosopher Norman Malcolm. Malcolm was an American graduate student at Harvard who came to Cambridge University to study with the philosopher G. E. Moore. But once at Cambridge, he quickly fell under the aura of Wittgenstein and remained a devotee for the rest of his life. The evidence from correspondences is that Wittgenstein did not think much of Malcolm's abilities as a philosopher, but then he didn't think much of anybody's abilities as a philosopher, often including his own. However, he did consider Malcolm a friend. Wittgenstein's friends were important to him, and the force of his charisma was such that people were willing to put up with a great deal to have Wittgenstein regard them as a friend. The stringent standards he applied to himself were applied to others, his volcanic temper easy to awaken. Malcolm described his friend's moods: "Of the things that came to his attention in the normal passage of events, hardly any gave him pleasure and many produced in him an emotion that was not far from grief."[13]

The themes of struggle and suffering are repeated by others who knew Wittgenstein as well as it was possible to know him. David Pinsent, a young mathematician who had first met Wittgenstein in Bertrand Russell's rooms at Trinity College and enjoyed a friendship with him until Pinsent's death as a test pilot during World War I, recorded in his journal the severe unhappiness that Wittgenstein often experienced. Pinsent wrote that Wittgenstein expressed his horror "that he was *de trop* in this world," a phrase that literally means too much, too many, and meant by him to convey his own redundancy—an elegant way of confessing to the sense that one has failed to demonstrate one's mattering.

In 1947, Wittgenstein resigned from his position at Cambridge, and in the summer of 1949, he went to visit Norman Malcolm in Ithaca, New York, where Malcolm was teaching at Cornell University. This was surprising, since on a prior short visit to the US, he had decided he disliked the country: "The people are awful." Nevertheless, he traveled once again to the US and stayed with the Malcolms for three months. He had suffered ill health while still in England and had been diagnosed with anemia. While in Ithaca his health deteriorated. When he returned to London, the cause of his malaise was discovered. He had advanced and inoperable prostate cancer, which had spread to his bone marrow and was causing the anemia. He started undergoing treatments, but by February of 1951 his decline was such that it was decided to discontinue further medical intervention.

His English doctor was named Edward Bevan, and because Wittgenstein had confessed to a horror, not of dying, but of dying in a hospital, Edward and his wife, Joan, invited Wittgenstein to live with them as the disease advanced. Joan Bevan was at first intimidated by her houseguest, but since he avoided all serious topics of discussion with her, she was not made to feel, as she put it, her "inferiority."[14]

Once Wittgenstein's treatment was suspended, he seemed to take heart, telling Joan Bevan, "I am going to work now as I have never worked before." He threw himself into writing a large portion of the book posthumously published under the title *On Certainty*.

He just made it to his sixty-second birthday. "Many happy returns!" Joan Bevan wished him. "There will be no returns," Wittgenstein responded with his uncompromising insistence on accuracy. On the following morning, he composed his last philosophical thought: "Someone who is dreaming who says, 'I am dreaming,' even if he speaks audibly in doing so, is no more right than if he said in his dream 'it is raining,' while it was in fact raining. Even if his dream were actually connected with the noise of the rain."

This is very characteristic of Wittgenstein's style of philosophizing, at least in the second phase of his philosophical life, out of which came his posthumously published *Philosophical Investigations*, in which carefully designed examples, analogies, and metaphors are meant to do the bulk of the work rather than explicitly laid out arguments. The style is by its nature ambiguous, which provides endless opportunities for interpretation. Language-games are an important concept in this second phase of Wittgenstein's philosophical work, and Wittgenstein's work from this phase itself presents an absorbing language-game.

That night Wittgenstein's condition deteriorated, and when Dr. Bevan told him that he was not likely to survive more than a couple of days he uttered one word: "Good!"

Joan Bevan was with him through his last night, sitting by his bedside. Right before he lost consciousness, he murmured to her, "Tell them I've had a wonderful life."

These last words baffled Norman Malcolm. "When I think of his profound pessimism, the intensity of his mental and moral suffering, the relentless way in which he drove his intellect, his need for love together with the harshness that repelled love, I am inclined to believe that his life was fiercely unhappy. Yet at the end he himself exclaimed that it had been 'wonderful'! To me this seems a mysterious and strangely moving utterance."

But, of course, Wittgenstein, in his last utterance, was harkening back to the distinction Aristotle had drawn millennia before in his first attempt at a science of eudaimonia. You can have a life that is more struggle and suffering than happiness and yet is, in terms of satisfaction, a wonderful life: the very life one would have chosen. Those closest to Wittgenstein saw only the day-to-day unhappiness and never saw what Wittgenstein himself acknowledged about himself. For example, in one of his private manuscripts, in 1931, he wrote, *Die Freude an meinem Gedanken ist die Freude an meinem eigenen seltsamen Leben*: "The joy of my thoughts is the joy of my own strange life."[15]

For all of us, the joy that derives from our life satisfaction is the joy of our own strange lives. They are strange not (in all likelihood) as Wittgenstein's life was strange. But since life satisfaction demands our successfully responding to the longing that originates in each of us from the estrangement from ourselves that we all, however obscurely, have experienced, we also can lay claim to strangeness. The mattering instinct is our way of finding our way back to ourselves from that estrangement, and we are willing to put up with struggle and suffering to get ourselves there. To be matter longing to matter is indeed a strange business.

A JAMESIAN TALE

Loneliness is the result of connectedness eluding us. And what is the result of the sense of mattering eluding us? The result is psychologically disastrous, the kind of rupture that is described as an existential crisis. It's a sense of ungrounding from one's life that threatens the conative drive that pushes us against entropy and into our future. At its most extreme, a person can fall into that death-within-life that is called persistent depressive disorder. One can barely tolerate being in the presence of the self. This is the psychological analogue of an autoimmune disease: It's the self rejecting the self.

The human brain, which evolved to respond with utmost flexibility to the changing circumstances that could do it in, can be done in by its own longing to matter. The debilitating anguish of loneliness is not unknown in other species, but only we can suffer by believing ourselves *de trop*. To be human is to have found a new way to be destroyed.

The disaster from within can seem to come on a person precipitously, like a malevolent stranger leaping out from an alleyway. But almost always the condition has been preceded by long preparation, the ground for the ungrounding silently laid.

William James, with all the eloquence at his command, gave us a ravishing account of what it is like to be vanquished from within by the mattering instinct. In *The Varieties of Religious Experience*, a book replete with firsthand accounts of unusual experiences gathered from James's wide reading as well as personal correspondences, there is this:

> Whilst in this state of philosophic pessimism and general depression of spirits about my prospects, I went one evening into a dressing-room in a twilight, to procure some article that was there; when suddenly there fell upon me without any warning, just as if it came out of darkness, a

horrible fear of existence. Simultaneously there arose in my mind the image of an epileptic patient whom I had seen in the asylum, a black-haired youth with greenish skin, entirely idiotic, who used to sit all day on one of the benches, or rather shelves against the wall, with his knees drawn up against his chin, and the coarse gray undershirt, which was his only garment, drawn over them inclosing his entire figure. He sat there like a sort of sculptured Egyptian cat or Peruvian mummy, moving nothing but his black eyes and looking absolutely non-human. This image and my fear entered into a species of combination with each other. That shape am I, I felt, potentially. Nothing that I possess can defend me against that fate, if the hour for it should strike for me as it struck for him. There was such a horror of him, and such a perception of my own merely momentary discrepancy from him, that it was as if something hitherto solid within my breast gave way entirely, and I became a mass of quivering fear. After this the universe was changed for me altogether. I awoke morning after morning with a horrible dread at the pit of my stomach, and with a sense of the insecurity of life that I never knew before, and that I have never felt since. It was like a revelation; and although the immediate feelings passed away, the experience has made me sympathetic with the morbid feelings of others ever since. It gradually faded, but for months I was unable to go into the dark alone.[16]

James describes this case as exemplifying "the worst kind of melancholy" that can befall a "sick soul," which was his phrase for those who are temperamentally inclined toward depression. He attributes his account to an anonymous correspondent whom he identifies only as a French doctor. But it was William James who was the sufferer in question, as he confided to both his oldest son, Henry, and to the French translator of *The Varieties of Religious Experience*. It isn't hard to imagine why James, then defeated by the mattering instinct, would find this pitiful specimen of humanity terrifying.

The crisis occurred probably in the winter of 1869, when James was twenty-seven or twenty-eight and living in Cambridge, Massachusetts, with his family. The dejection over what he refers to as his "prospects" had been stretched out over years, during which he applied himself to first one endeavor and then another. Coming from a well-connected family, every opportunity had been offered him to try out first one of his talents and then another. But so far nothing had stuck. No project called to him as the one on which to stake his mattering.

When he was eighteen, he had studied with William Morris Hunt, a leading portrait and landscape painter of the day. William's father, Henry James Sr., expressed disapproval, though not because he wanted his son to be more practical and businesslike. He had inherited a considerable fortune from his own father, also named William James, who had immigrated from Ireland and became an entrepreneur and Albany's first millionaire. Henry James Sr. devoted his life not only to systematically reducing his sizable inheritance but also to theological studies, which were of a mystical bent. His books, which he felt were never properly regarded, developed the theme of "the immanence of God in the unity of mankind," and include *Christianity: The Logic of Creation* (1857), *Substance and Shadow: or Morality and Religion in Their Rela-*

tion to Life (1869), and *The Secret of Swedenborg, Being an Elu-cidation of Divine Natural Humanity* (1869). "Tell them I'm a Lover of Books, a Student. Better yet, tell them I'm a Seeker of the Truth," he instructed his sons to respond when they were asked by their schoolmates what it was their father did for a living.

Obviously, practicality was not on the father's mind in discouraging his firstborn's artistic pursuit. It was rather a scientific career that Henry James Sr. had in mind for his son, and perhaps, as some have speculated, for a self-interested reason. Disappointed that his theological writings had been largely ignored, Henry James Sr. hoped that if his brilliant son were to become a reputable scientist and endorse his father's religious views, he would finally gain the longed-for recognition. He craved the imprimatur of an established man of science and perhaps cherished hope that such a man would emerge from his brood of five—four boys and a girl. His secondborn, Henry James Jr., became, of course, the celebrated novelist. But it was his firstborn, William, whose intellectual inclinations were most like his own, on whom he fastened his hopes for his own validation.[17]

The youngest child was the only daughter, Alice, and between Henry and Alice there were two boys, Robertson (Bob), and Garth Wilkinson (Wilkie), who both served in the Civil War, marching off together, Wilkie seventeen and Bob not quite sixteen, the minimum age for the army. The father had discouraged the enlistment of the two oldest sons, who were of age. He had apparently decided that two big careers were enough for five children, and William and Henry were the chosen ones. Wilkie and Bob volunteered to serve as officers in the newly formed, and controversial, Black regiments, the 54th and 55th Massachusetts, raised by the abolitionist governor John A. Andrew. Their adult lives were tragic. Wilkie died broke at thirty-eight of kidney failure, perhaps brought on by the injuries he sustained during the storming of Fort Wagner, the Union debacle that was the subject of the 1989 film *Glory*. Robertson battled alcoholism throughout his life and died alone in 1910, the same year as his brother William, who was by then a renowned member of both the Harvard community and the wider community of international scholars.

Theirs was a family in which the distribution of attention—and thus the distribution of the sense of being deserving of attention—had not, by any means, been equitable. Short of abuse and neglect, this is one of the most harmful effects that our families can have on us, given how fundamental the mattering instinct is. To a child, the family constitutes the whole world, and if that child is made to feel that they matter less within that world, then they will be fortunate if they can ever regain the lost ground in the world at large. The despair of a child: How little even now it is understood.

Of course, having a psychologically dominating parent's attention focused on you in the hopes that you will vindicate their own mattering can be as detrimental as being ignored, and the father's great expectations for his eldest son weighed heavily on the young William. Still, though Henry James Sr. hoped for something other than art for William, he decided to let his multigifted boy give it a try, and so the whole family decamped to Newport, Rhode Island, where the prominent artist William Morris Hunt resided. But after a year William decided art was not his life's calling, declaring, "Nothing is more contemptible than a mediocre artist." The family moved back to Cambridge, Massachusetts, where William enrolled, through his father's connections, in the Lawrence Scientific School at Harvard. "The Harvard to which James came in 1861 was a relatively mediocre educational institution," to quote none other than *The Harvard Crimson*,[18] and it was enough to have family connections, which William's father had in abundance, to win admission.

James remained at the Lawrence School for three years, studying chemistry and anatomy, without ever getting an undergraduate degree, and then switched over to the Harvard Medical School, where standards were similarly slipshod. His studies there also failed to inspire him, but eventually, doing the bare minimum, he managed to pass the final exam, his father's good friend Oliver Wendell Holmes Sr. being conveniently assigned as his examiner. William had acquired a doctor's degree but no intention of ever practicing, having only again wasted his own time and disappointed the expectations of his father.

As 1869 drew to a close, he wrote to one of his friends, apologizing for not having written to him in a while. "I have been a prey to such a disgust for life during these past three months as to make letter writing almost an impossibility. My own condition I am sorry to say goes on pretty steadily deteriorating in all respects."[19] He spent long periods being able to do nothing but lie prone in bed—he referred to his "great dorsal collapse"—contemplating suicide.

Meanwhile his brother Henry, younger by fifteen months, was beginning to make a name for himself in the literary world, in the United States and abroad.

The drawn-out crisis of James's youth, painful to read, was balanced by a later life of prodigious productivity and success. He had the great good fortune of seeing his ideas reach a wide international audience, where they were valued for the same reasons that he saw value in them. And for this, he pronounced himself grateful. "He did not seek the fame that found him. Yet he prized the honors that had come to him so abundantly, although mainly because of the assurance which they brought him that he had done and was doing the best work he was qualified to do," wrote one of his colleagues.[20]

Harvard University, where he made such a poor showing as a student, continues to take pride in him in concrete ways—quite literally. A fifteen-story building, designed by the renowned architect Minoru Yamasaki, constructed of precast concrete panels, is christened William James Hall. Built in the early 1960s, it houses the Department of Psychology. In the seminar room on its top floor, departmental meetings and job talks are still conducted under his large and soulful portrait—I can't say under his watchful eyes, since his gaze is averted. The artist has caught him in the pose of self-reflection—the focused inward probing that he had refined into a scientific instrument of precision.

The christening of the building is justified. It was William James who created Harvard's Department of Psychology, which prior to its inception had been enfolded within the Department of Philosophy. In fact, it can justly be said that William James brought the study of psychology not only to Harvard but to the United States. He is widely recognized as the founder of American psychology, especially after the 1890 publication of *The Principles of Psychology*, which is nominally a textbook, but is something wonderfully more, as evidenced by the fact that it has not been rendered irrelevant by the accelerated advancements in the behavioral sciences. Though James had never been able to probe the different parts of a working brain with functional magnetic resonance imaging; though he knew nothing of the neurotransmitter serotonin and how medications that block its reabsorption have been relied on to combat the kind of death-within-life to which he was no stranger; still *The Principles of Psychology* remains the masterpiece that his academic contemporaries immediately recognized it to be, crowning the twelve years of arduous research and writing that had made James, as well as his editor, despair of ever seeing the final product. He later rewrote some of the chapters for a condensed version, *Psychology: Briefer Course*, which became the most important psychology textbook in the country. His own students playfully dubbed the longer version "James" and the shorter one "Jimmy."

Above all, in everything that William James published, whether intended for students of psychology or of philosophy, or for the wider nonacademic audience, the warmth and vibrancy of his personality floods the pages, so that you feel his living presence still. He is one of those writers who invites an intimate relationship. This is true still, more than a century after his death. His style is so bracing, so direct and lively, jolting the reader's attention with its originality. Here, for example, is his description of drunkenness: "Sobriety diminishes, discriminates, and says no; drunkenness expands, unites, and says yes. It is in fact the great exciter of the *Yes* function in man, it brings its votary from the chill periphery of things to the radiant core. It makes him for the moment one with truth."[21] The Yes function: an aid to overcoming philosophical skepticism, while also known to motivate some regrettable decisions at 2 a.m. Still, James's willingness to embrace both metaphysics and life, often in one extravagant move, picks him out as distinctive in the somber gallery of philosophers.

James's enthusiasm extended to sports and adventures. He played tennis, skated, cycled, rode horses, hiked, and climbed mountains. In 1898, when he was fifty-six, he was diagnosed as having overtaxed his heart when getting lost on a hike in the Adirondacks. (A very nineteenth-century diagnosis! Fit people today are rarely diagnosed with overtaxing their heart from strenuous exercise.) His health deteriorated, and he resigned from Harvard in 1907, writing two of his most important works in philosophy in the three years that preceded his death.

In 1909, he met Sigmund Freud at a conference at Clark University in Worcester, Massachusetts. It was Freud's first and only visit to the United States, and he had expressed eagerness to meet James. They walked together to the train station, and on the way, James was overtaken by an attack of angina pectoris. He calmly removed his packet of nitroglycerin tablets from his pocket and told the younger man to walk on without him while he recovered. Freud remarked that he hoped he could stare down his own mortality with as much equanimity.

James died a year later, at the age of sixty-eight. His wife, on reading the autopsy report, wrote in her journal, "Acute enlargement of the heart. He had worn himself out."

William James, despite the early years of debilitating depression, became a man of vibrant energy, of bracing force and irrepressible buoyancy, unaffectedly in love with life, open to the abundance of experience, both his own and others', of whom he was such a keen student. Or at least that is the impression he gave, as conveyed by the tributes that flowed forth following his death. How did the transformation come about, from a person who could barely rouse himself sufficiently to respond to a friend's letter to this figure of life-embracing vitality forcefully imposing himself on two academic fields with an influence that is still palpable today?

William James's own analysis of such transformations focuses on the will. In *The Principles of Psychology*, under the heading "The Obstructed Will," he describes the kind of paralysis of the will that characterizes "the moral tragedy of human life." For such an afflicted person "the pungent sense of reality" fails to take hold and rouse them from "the grumbling and rumbling in the background—discerning, commenting, protesting, longing, half resolving." The result is that the individual lives with a "consciousness of inward hollowness, which is one of the saddest feelings one can bear with him through this vale of tears."[22]

As the fundamental problem, according to James, is one of the will, so too must its solution derive from the will. In an effort almost analogous to the fabled Baron Münchausen's pulling himself, as well as the horse on which he sits astride, out of a swamp by his own hair, a person who suffers from an obstructed will must will themselves back into willing, and thereby will themselves back into productivity, into the future-oriented activity that will submerge the self-doubts and resurrect the will to live. It is in the effortful resistance of the will, asserting itself against the deadening hollowness within, that salvation lies. "The *âme bien née* [well-born soul], the child of the sunshine, at whose birth the fairies made their gifts, does not need much of it in his life. The hero and the neurotic subject, on the other hand, do."[23]

This emphasis on the will reaches back to the sustained

crisis of James's youth. In a diary entry dated April 30, 1870, as a first indication of his recovering from his depressive breakdown, he had resolutely written, "My first act of free will will be to believe in free will."

Free will is, of course, a contentious issue. Is everything about us determined by prior causes, even the acts of the mind that we experience as decisions, or can decisions break into the chain of causality and produce an undetermined effect? It was the latter alternative that James was willing himself into believing, and with it, he was willing himself into believing in the power of his own willing self.

It was a passage from Charles-Bernard Renouvier, a contemporary French philosopher whom he had discovered several years before, who galvanized him into the decision to believe in the efficacy of decision-making. To will, wrote Renouvier, is to sustain a particular thought when there are other competing thoughts equally sustainable. The young and suffering James drew the conclusion that free will consists in the agency you assert over your attention.

There is a connection between James's later attention to attention and the thoughts that helped to lift him out of his crisis. To be free, for James, meant being able to decide what is deserving of attention, what matters, and in that agency to resurrect the sense of one's own life's mattering: "Hitherto, when I have felt like taking a free initiative, like daring to act originally, without carefully waiting for contemplation of the external world to determine all for me, suicide seemed the most manly form to put my daring into. Now I will go a step further with my will, not only act with it, but believe as well; believe in my individual reality and creative power. My belief, to be sure, can't be optimistic—

but I will posit life (the real, the good) in the self-governing resistance of the ego to the world." (Notice his use of the word *manly*. We will return to it.)

All his life, James would place great emphasis on the exertions of the will, not only in going forward with his life, but in his philosophical and psychological points of view. If you can will yourself into the belief in free will, so, too, he reasoned, can you will yourself into other beliefs. "Believe that life is worth living, and your belief will help create the fact," he argued in a lecture poignantly entitled "Is Life Worth Living?" James's thesis of voluntary conviction was not applied wholesale to every belief, of course—only those in which neither the evidence for nor against was probative. In such cases, if there were pragmatic benefits that would follow having the belief, then it is rational, he argued, to believe.

It was not only in regard to beliefs that James stressed the role of the will. We can also, according to him, will ourselves into emotions by deliberately assuming the characteristic postures and expressions correlated with them.

Say you are hiking in the woods and come upon a grizzly bear. The sight causes you to tremble. You might think that you tremble because you are afraid, but James inverts the causality. "My thesis, on the contrary, is that the bodily changes follow directly the PERCEPTION of the exciting fact and that our feeling of the same changes as they occur IS the emotion."[24] In other words, according to James, you do not tremble because you are afraid but rather are afraid because you perceive yourself to be trembling. Willfully cancel the trembling, and you annihilate the fear.

In so much of James's thinking you can hear the echoes sounding from the depths to which he had descended during his youth, the resistance to those depths that "the hero and the neurotic subject" is called upon to mount through sheer will. Though it is not easy to be a hero and a neurotic subject, still the very difficulties are what create the possibility for the most admirable of characters who forcefully mount their resistance: "And if a brief definition of ideal or moral action were required, none could be given which better fit the appearances than this: *It is action in the line of the greatest resistance.*"[25] The sick-souled have been granted the greatest of opportunities, since their persistence in existence requires action in the line of the greatest resistance.

"It was like a revelation; and although the immediate feelings passed away, the experience has made me sympathetic with the morbid feelings of others ever since." The sympathy that James puts into his concealed autobiography held true for him all through his life, with practical consequences. Beginning with the academic year 1893–94, James introduced Harvard's first course on abnormal psychology, having convinced Harvard's president, Charles William Eliot, of its legitimacy. It was probably the first course on abnormal psychology taught at any American college. His students remarked on James's unusual sympathy toward those whose life had come undone by their inner demons, his refusal to recognize a clear demarcation between the normal and abnormal. Once, when he had taken his students to visit two asylums, he remarked to them afterward, "President Eliot would not like to admit that no sharp line could be drawn between himself and the men we have just seen, but it is true."[26]

The evidence is that beneath the buoyancy and energy, there was always, in William James, a heavy psychic reality that necessitated the exertion of forceful resistance. The bear remained in his mind, even as he repressed the trembling. "There was, in spite of his playfulness, a deep sadness about James. You felt that he had just stepped out of his sadness in order to meet you and was to go back into it the moment you left him," wrote another colleague, John Jay Chapman, who knew James well.[27] And yet, too, there was a certain pride in the overcoming, a conviction that the overcoming itself brought out the best—the ideal, the moral—in him. Among his notes for a series of lectures he gave in 1896 at the Lowell Institute in Boston, "Abnormal Mental States," there is this scribbled comment: "Melancholy! Gives truer values."[28]

But what about the inclusion of the word *manly* that so often slips into James's theory of the will? Manliness was a characteristic obsessively discussed in James's day, and it came loaded—just as its correlate, *womanliness*, did—with *oughts* and *ought-nots*. Manliness was understood to be different from *masculinity*—a word that first began to be used sometime in the 1890s. All men possess, simply in virtue of being men, masculinity, but manliness was an attribute toward which men ought to aspire, just as women ought to aspire toward womanliness.

As an aspirational attribute, manliness was in flux during James's life. Various factors, including the closing of the American frontier, the rise of the urban class of clerks and shopkeepers, and the robber barons of the Gilded Age, con- spired to confuse its meaning, so that it wavered between the honorable, self-restrained refinement of the true gentleman and the chest-beating specimen of primitive virility, within which a certain childlike purity was preserved, represented by novels like *The Virginian*, published in 1902, or *Tarzan of the Apes*, published in 1912.

William James was not immune to his period's obsession with manliness, an obsession that has recently reemerged. In James's case, the obsession might well have been exacerbated by his having not fought in the war in which his two younger brothers had fought, thereby discharging the family's debt to their abolitionist ideals. William James's answer to the question of manliness came in his theory of the will, which could impose itself on beliefs, attitudes, and emotions, thereby reshaping all the inner contents of one's life. Manliness consisted, for James, in the control exerted over oneself; the more control needed, the greater the manliness. The seeds of his understanding of manliness lay in that resolution that had lifted him—Münchhausen-like—out of the paralysis of depression.

Is James then denying women the grounds for action "in the line of greatest resistance"? Is he denying women the possibility for achieving the "ideal of moral action"? And if he is—and the short answer is yes—is it because he believes that women lack the strength to mount such resistance? Or is it rather that he thinks they lack the motive to mount it, being more naturally "the *âme bien née*, the child of the sunshine, at whose birth the fairies made their gifts"? It is the latter. For William, women are simply—blessedly—less existentially challenged than men. Their souls, as he elsewhere put it, are more likely to be of the "sky-blue tint." "It is to be hoped that we all have some friend, perhaps more often feminine than masculine, and young than old, whose soul is of a sky-blue tint, whose affinities are rather with flowers and birds and all enchanting innocencies than with dark human passions, who can think no ill of man or God, and in whom religious gladness, being in possession from the outset, needs no deliverance from any antecedent burden."[29] He appreciated women's lack of the depth that can only blossom in darkness, a shallowness that handily made them more delightful and more available to offer their emotional support to existentially tried men such as himself.

It is hard to believe that such a penetrating observer of human nature, who generally didn't allow the conventions of his day to do his thinking for him, could sustain such an eviscerated view of one half of the species, blinding himself to the full existential complexity that comes to us not by way of our gender but by way of being human—and then further blinding himself to the idea that within that humanness, those whose sense of mattering is further curtailed and controlled by society may indeed have it harder. We now know, in fact, that women are more susceptible to depression than men,[30] and if depression is at all linked with limited control over one's life, with choices for responding to the mattering instinct as one sees fit arbitrarily limited, then we would expect that in times past women suffered depression at even higher rates than they do now. The irony is heavy when we're speaking of the man who originated Harvard's course on abnormal psychology. It is particularly mystifying how he could have maintained such a view of women given that his immediate family provided a living, breathing enactment of the full existential drama in female form: his sister, Alice.

Alice, too, had lain prone in her bed, often contemplating suicide—in fact, for the greater portion of her life. By the age of twelve she was already described as of "a nervous disposition," and at nineteen, when others of her circle were getting married off, she had her first attack of "nerves." The family was always vague in their letters about the nature of these attacks, but from her twenties onward her life story is largely told in terms of them. The doctors came up with an impressive array of labels—"neurasthenia," "melancholia," "suppressed gout," "palpitations," "nervous paralysis," "an excess of nervous sensibility," and of course the always serviceable "hysteria," derived from the Greek word for *womb*. But they could never diagnose a physical cause.

She herself might have had, at least in retrospect, a better idea than the doctors. Years later she was to describe in her journal her rage toward her father, who had such a formative influence over all his children, the original dispenser of their mattering. "As I used to sit immovable reading in the library with waves of violent inclination suddenly invading my muscles taking some one of their myriad forms such as throwing myself out of the window, or knocking off the head of the benignant pater as he sat with his silver locks, writing at his table, it used to seem to me that the only difference between me and the insane was that I had not only all the horrors and suffering of insanity but the duties of doctor, nurse, and straitjacket imposed upon me, too."

There was only a brief period of three years when Alice lived free of her undiagnosable illness—three years that happened to coincide with her teaching history for the Society to Encourage Studies at Home, a Boston-based correspondence school for women founded by Anna Eliot Ticknor.[31] She must have suddenly had some room to chase down her own kind of mattering for the first time. But after that brief respite, her "nerves" returned in force, and she became so overtaken with the desire for self-annihilation that she confessed it to her father, asking if to act on the desire would be a sin. He opined that it was not, and only requested that, if she decided to voluntarily die, she do it in a gentle way, such as refusing all sustenance. His tacit permission for her to kill herself gave her some minimal agency over her life, and that sliver determined her to keep living. But her life was such that when, at the age of forty-two, she was discovered to have advanced breast cancer, she greeted the diagnosis with relief, for now at last she had a diagnosable disease.

It was not until 1964, when the journal of her last four years of life was published, that Alice James was revealed to have been endowed with a substantial portion of the family genius for heightened consciousness. But she, unlike William and Henry, had not been able to cultivate her gifts into a sustained mattering project. If anything, her lifelong project was her invalidism, which at least got her the sympathetic attention of her family. Her unappeased mattering instinct may have clawed at her, making her want to end her own life, but the weighted connectedness she experienced within her family, which remained for so long into her adulthood the emotional center of her world, for better or for worse, was enough to circumvent suicide—barely.

In the setting of our families, our need for connectedness and mattering first emerge, tightly intertwined with each other. Our need to be regarded as special by those people who are overwhelmingly special to us, during the time when they composed the whole of the world as we knew it, becomes enmeshed with our sense of mattering as it extends itself forward into our lives. That original sense of mattering affects our assessments of how much mattering we can expect in the world beyond our families and how we can best achieve it. It's possible to outrun the influence of our families on these assessments—if outrunning is indeed what's needed for our flourishing—but it's never easy. It must be added into all the work that we must do to resist the entropic transformation from within.

The more you learn about the James family, the more you understand Henry James's decision to reside permanently in England. Henry gave Alice his share of the inheritance from the estate of their parents, so that, as a single woman, she could live on her own. After their deaths, she continued to live in the family domicile on Quincy Street, which stood on the site now occupied by Harvard's Faculty Club. I fume at every event I attend there over Harvard's failure to have preserved the home as a national treasure.

It was only when Alice was nearing her last decade that she forged what was to be her most important relationship outside of the family. This was with Katharine Peabody Loring, an energetic education reformer and activist. Alice joined her life with Katharine's in what was to become known as a Boston marriage. Her brother Henry writes of such a relationship in his novel *The Bostonians*. "I wish you could know Katharine Loring," Alice wrote in a letter to her friend Sara Darwin. "She is a most wonderful being. She has all the mere brute superiority which distinguishes man from woman combined with all the distinctly feminine virtues. There is nothing she cannot do from hewing wood and drawing water to driving run-away horses and educating all the women in North America." Eventually Katharine and Alice moved together to England, to be closer to Henry, and Katharine is responsible for Alice's diary coming down to us. She was the scribe, taking dictation when Alice grew too weak to write, and after Alice's death, she wrote out copies of the diary to give to Alice's surviving brothers.

Nevertheless, though her relationship with Katharine was deeply satisfying, the lack of some mattering project, comparable to those of her two brothers, which might have provided an application for her extraordinary intelligence, talent, wit, and will, meant her life was hardly one of flourishing. Assessing it as the end drew near, she wrote in her journal: "The fact is, I have been dead so long and it has been simply such a grim shoving of the hours behind me as I faced a ceaseless possible horror, since the hideous summer of '78, when I went down to the deep sea, its dark waters closed over me, and I knew neither hope nor peace."

One wonders, of course, what happened during the hideous summer of '78. One possible explanation: William James got married on July 10 of that year. Their father had first encountered Alice Howe Gibbens at the Boston Radical Club, attended by transcendentalists, philosophers, and writers. She was a serious and idealistic young woman, and Henry Sr. returned home to announce to William, then thirty-six, that he had met his son's future wife. The second Alice James seemed as free of neurosis as the James clan was thick with it, and she served as emotional ballast not only for William but for other members of the clan.[32] But the marriage of William to this other Alice seems to have had a disastrous effect on his sister. The relationship between the brother and sister had always been close, and William's strange flirtatiousness with his sister might have been, on his part, playful teasing, but it added more convolutions to the complicated love that Alice experienced within the family.[33]

It was not William the psychologist but rather Henry the novelist who perceived their sister with the keenest psychological insight. After reading her diary, Henry wrote to

William that it "puts before me what I was tremendously conscious of in her lifetime—that the extraordinary intensity of her will and personality really would have made the equal, the reciprocal life of a 'well' person—in the usual world—almost impossible to her—so that her disastrous, her tragic health was in a manner the only solution for her of the practical problems of life."

It's interesting that Henry posited, as the source of Alice's disastrous health, the extraordinary intensity of her will—the very aspect by which William was able to claim his "action in the line of greatest resistance." Henry saw in Alice what William would not allow himself to see. We have so many ways of not seeing the full reality of one another, even the reality of the people we most love—sometimes especially the people we most love, since we so ardently wish them to be as our own needs demand them to be. As William James had written in *The Principles of Psychology*, "The inner significance of other lives exceeds all our powers of sympathy and insight."

The two siblings, William and Alice, provide a case study that almost approaches a scientific experiment, with a test subject and a control. Brought up in the same hothouse household, the brother and sister sharing similarly depressive temperaments that demand such a heroic effort in resistance, one sibling's life became a triumph of activity and achievement, of full engagement in a community of thinkers among whom he was respected and loved, while the other lived a life that made her happily embrace the fatal disease that allowed her to retreat to bed and await the final withdrawal from life. One sibling not only was deemed deserving of the full attention of the "benignant pater" (whose head the other fantasized knocking off), but also was helped to the full range of that parent's influential connections, so that eventually, after much agonizing and wrestling with the downward pull of a depressive temperament, he still found his way toward a mattering project that gave him the impetus to push on into his future, the vigor of his push a countermeasure to the downward pull of temperament. The other was given the support of fluffed-up pillows and ineffectual doctors.

I remarked earlier in this chapter that heroic strivers can, when provided with both extraordinary talent and the circumstances that allow their talents to be expressed, produce the kinds of achievements that move us all forward. Those circumstances were provided to one sibling and not to the other—and how the difference made all the difference in the lives they led, the flourishing they enjoyed, the legacy they left behind.

William James (1842–1910), by Ellen Emmet Rand

Photograph of Alice James, taken by Katharine Loring

CHAPTER 5

THE CARTOGRAPHY OF
THE MATTERING MAP, PART ONE:
THE SOCIAL AND THE HEROIC

There was a new moon that June night hanging over the English town of Tring. The extra cover of darkness suited the purpose of the studious-looking young man who had taken the Midland train into Tring from London, pulling a large rolling suitcase behind him. He had also come prepared with a diamond-blade glass cutter, a wire cutter, a miniature LED flashlight, a bunch of ziplock plastic bags, and a pair of latex gloves that he'd pinched on his last doctor visit.

The narrow winding streets were largely deserted as he headed for a sprawling nineteenth-century redbrick building that had once been the private museum of Lord Lionel Walter Rothschild, the second Baron Rothschild. An avid gentleman naturalist, who used to ride around Tring in a carriage pulled by zebras, the baron had erected his museum, which contained the world's largest collection of taxidermied animals, on the manicured grounds of his country estate. His share of the family's banking fortune had reputedly been exhausted by his project of accumulating samples of every mammal, bird, reptile, and insect that had ever lived. Now, through the gift of the Rothschild family, the formerly private museum was a branch of London's Natural History Museum.

In preparation for tonight, the young man had visited the museum several months before, posing as a researcher on birds of paradise so that he could gain access to the extensive ornithological research collection, stored away in carefully labeled metal drawers and never publicly displayed. Nobody had objected to his snapping photos, and he had even signed the visitors' guestbook with his real name: Edwin Rist.

An American, Rist was then twenty-two years old and was a serious student of flute, attending London's prestigious Royal Academy of Music. But the passion that drew Rist to Tring on the night of June 23, 2009, wasn't for music but rather for art of a different kind—Victorian salmon fly-tying. This is an art only derivatively connected with the sport of fly-fishing, which typically uses artificial lures that can mimic the wiggling behavior of live bait to catch the attention of a passing fish. There is trout fly-fishing, where the artificial lures are usually made from bits of hair, rabbit fur, and the feathers of chickens and turkeys. And then there is salmon fly-tying—in particular what is called classic or Victorian salmon fly-tying, which is a whole other kettle of fish. Here the lures are created in accordance with recipes—yes, they are called recipes—calling for exact proportions in a mix of brilliant feathers. The extravagance of these plumes, their colors deeply saturated and flashing like jewels, is the genetic record of the striving of male birds to outdo one another in attracting the females, who though comparatively drab are worth the effort, since they will lay and tend the eggs and hatchlings, thus increasing the odds that the paternal genes will make it into future generations.

The elaborate recipes for salmon fly-tying were created during the Victorian age, the height of British imperialism, when the feathers of exotic birds from far-reaching corners of the empire could be shipped back to the mother country. Most of the feathers went into women's hats, which sported, according to the fashion dictates of the day, elaborate plumage, sending the price of feathers soaring. The white egret, with showy feathers belonging to both males and females and easily hunted, was driven almost out of existence, its feathers worth four times as much as gold, ounce for ounce. The costliest loss of valuables aboard the *Titanic* lay in the boxes of feathers that went down with the ship.

But it wasn't only the haute couture of wealthy women that created the demand for the showiest of feathers.[1] Wealthy men, too, played a part, indulging in the extravagant recipes for salmon fly-tying, given such names as the Britannia, the Champion, the Durham Ranger, the Black Ranger, the Infallible, the Sherbrook, and the Jock Scott. The Jock Scott, for example, uses the feathers of five different species: a golden pheasant (a striking combination of gold and red); a toucan (an iridescent deep blue and vivid yellow); a guinea fowl (spotted with white dots on velvety black feathers); a peacock (shimmering sapphire blue, with an emerald "eye" pattern on its train); and a jungle cock (vivid amber and black-and-white-patterned neck feathers). These glories of nature are assembled by the fly-tyer with elegance and precision.[2]

Do you think the salmon respond to the artistry? Such utilitarian considerations are irrelevant. These creations

THE CARTOGRAPHY OF THE MATTERING MAP, PART ONE

aren't intended for fish. Rather they are works of art, to be appreciated by humans. It was, for much of the twentieth century, a dying art, until the internet resuscitated it, posting photos of the classic lures and original recipes. Enthusiasts gathered on such websites as ClassicFlyTying.com, meeting in person for competitions as they cultivated their own little region of the mattering map. Here are a couple of examples of the kinds of comments posted on the website. "There's something to a fly tied with the old materials," writes one resident of this mattering region, to which another responds, "I've met this something. I'm haunted by it constantly now. It's like a drug. Nothing else matters. Nothing else compares. When it touches my fingers, I feel the history. I'm taken back to a time when fish were as big as logs, fresh from the sea. Reds, yellows, and shades of blues, their texture and color have that power to push you to do your best. There's nothing else that compares to that power." Note the existentially charged emotions contained in these words, indicating that classic salmon fly-tying is, at least for some, no mere hobby but rather a mattering project. In the vast intricacy of the mattering map, among the artistic heroic strivers, there is a small region that is theirs. And so are there a myriad of such narrowly defined regions, too numerous to enumerate, each devoted to an interest or talent powerful enough to serve as a response to the mattering instinct.

Edwin Rist was not only a resident of this particular mattering region but had been recognized as one of its rising young stars. The editor of *Fly Tyer* magazine had hailed him in 2005 as the "future of fly-tying." Almost every mattering region has its heroes, and Rist was determined to be a hero in his. But Rist wasn't rich, and the feathers are prohibitively costly, especially since many of the recipes call for birds that are now extinct or endangered, which makes their feathers not only pricey but illegal, requiring cash outlays in the thousands. As soon as any of the feathers called for in the recipes were listed for sale on eBay, they were snatched up by wealthy fly-tyers. There is a black market for obtaining these feathers, and the passion is such that crimes have been committed by residents of the region.

Which brings us back to the night of June 9, 2009. Ever since Rist had arrived in England to study music, his mattering compass had relentlessly pointed northwest toward Tring, with its renowned ornithological collection. This indeed is why he'd decided to study at the English conservatory. The museum then held about 750,000 bird skins, representing 95 percent of known living species. Many of its specimens had been donated by none other than Alfred Russel Wallace, the man who might have been known as the father of natural selection had not Charles Darwin beaten him to publication. In fact, Wallace's letter to Darwin laying out the outlines of his theory, allegedly scrawled in a fevered dream while he was suffering from the malaria he'd contracted in New Guinea, probably goaded the cautious Darwin into finally publishing *On the Origin of Species* in 1859. There were handwritten notes that Wallace had penned attached to the specimens stored in those metal filing cabinets in the Tring museum, which made them not just scientifically but historically valuable.

But scientific and historical values were extrinsic to the values embedded in Rist's mattering region. Untutored in cat burglary, he suffered several mishaps in breaking into the museum, despite months of preparation. He dropped his glass cutter into a ravine and had to smash a window with a rock, thus setting off a burglar alarm that somehow didn't bring any guard running. And once in the presence of the drawers upon drawers of feathered treasures, Rist lost track of time in a kind of plumose swoon, missing the last Midland train back to London and having to wait on the platform until morning. Still, he had the presence of mind to cram his suitcase with 299 bird skins that were worth close to a million dollars. Unlike the feathers Rist had seen before, which had been sold and resold and were the worse for wear, these were pristine.

He had gone mostly for the male trogons (iridescent greens and blues on their back, bright red or yellow underparts) and quetzals (shimmering green and deep red plumage) from Central and South America, as well as Australasian bowerbirds (varying in their vibrant colors and patterns, ranging from glossy blues to vibrant goldens), Indian roller crows (vivid blue and turquoise), and birds of paradise (almost surreal plumage, ranging from lustrous yellows and reds to nacreous purples and blues), which Alfred Russel Wallace had brought back from New Guinea. Now he would never want for the precious materials needed to bring his visions of perfection to completion.

It was months before the theft was discovered by the museum. Meanwhile, the embarrassment of his riches allowed Rist to sell some of his haul on the black market, where it was snatched up by those who must have known its provenance. Notices put up on the site asking that the feathers be returned to the museum were constantly removed. When the mattering instinct is at stake, even upright citizens can find justifications for flicking away scruples. Detectives were eventually able to track down Rist. Pleading Asperger's syndrome, he was given a slap on the wrist by the judge. The bulk of the feathers have yet to be recovered.

A MEANINGFUL LIFE

The number of regions on the mattering map is vast, and our closest connections with others to whom we are not biologically related are frequently with those who share our region—unless, that is, our region is such as to make us intrinsically competitive with fellow residents. Individualist mattering competitors, a type to be examined in the next chapter, are likely to feel connected, if at all, only to members of their own family and their acolytes—in other words, people they can view as extensions of themselves—rather than those with whom they share their mattering region, whom they regard as mattering rivals. But more often, our co-regionists, being the people who share our vision of what life is meant to be about, are among those we regard as in our lives to whom we wish especially to matter. To quote a cliché particularly apt to a chapter that began with Rist's feather heist, birds of a feather flock together. Our mentors, if we have them, as well as our mentees, if we have them, might well be among the flock.

Some mattering regions teem with billions, as, for example, those demarcated by major religions; others are mid-sized, such as the one inhabited by those pursuing fame for fame's sake; and some are tiny—the Monacos, Maltas, and Seychelles of the mattering map—such as the regions inhabited by Victorian salmon fly-tyers, sommeliers, pickup artists, body builders, trainspotters, Civil War reenactors, and analytic philosophers.

Does it seem disrespectful—even sacrilegious—to put a person who sees the meaning of their life in terms of cultivating their relationship with God on the same level, existentially speaking, with a bodybuilder or a pickup artist? But existentially speaking, they *are* on the same level—the mattering instinct channeled into mattering projects that, despite their high costs in energy, become essential for resisting the entropic transformation from within. Our mattering projects, ongoing for as long as they continue to minister to our mattering instinct, are what give our lives a sense of coherence, allowing our lives to make sense to us. They also give us a sense of purpose, yielding us the impetus to push on into our future.

Some contemporary psychologists have tackled topics related to those of this book, distinguishing meaningfulness, coherence, purpose, and mattering.[3] Their work establishes correlations between the feeling of a meaningful life, largely treated in such psychological literature as the summum bonum, and feelings of coherence, purpose, and mattering. That is, the experimenters have determined that the subjective feeling of leading a meaningful life is correlated with the subjective feelings of having coherence, purpose, and a sense of mattering. They have arrived at their conclusions by presenting questionnaires that propose propositions to which the subjects must assent or dissent in varying degrees—for example, "Even considering how big the universe is, I can say my life matters" (mattering); "I have a good sense of what I am trying to accomplish in my life" (purpose); and "I can make sense of the things that happen in my life" (coherence). The psychologists then statistically correlated these subjective responses with how subjectively meaningful the respondents reported their lives to be. The researchers found that mattering—which is to say the *subjective feeling of mattering*—is most strongly correlated with the subjective feeling of leading a meaningful life.

This result, exactly what we would predict, doesn't take us very far into understanding ourselves, since it entirely leaves out the substratum that generates these correlations between subjective feelings, which are all that these questionnaires can get at. It leaves out the mattering instinct that lies at our core and is intent on *objective* mattering, rather than the subjective feeling of mattering. As we saw in chapter three, the mattering instinct is itself explained by way of our evolved capacity for self-reflection that propels us to seek a justification for our own self-mattering, transforming us into the values-seeking creatures that we are. The mattering instinct is the motivation for the long-term projects that, as long as they are doing their job for us, provide our lives with a subjective sense of coherence, purpose, and mattering. To feel that we are living a meaningful life is to feel no more and no less than that we have a mattering project that is satisfactorily ministering to our mattering instinct, which, together with our sense of connectedness, promotes life satisfaction. The subjective correlations these experimenters have established don't reveal the motivational cause that underlies them, the longing within us that isn't after the feeling of mattering—we're born to feel that!—but rather objective mattering. We are such that no subjective feeling can be our summum bonum. Again, when it comes to our mattering, we are staunch realists. We don't want a simulation of mattering. We want mattering.

A thought experiment devised by the philosopher Robert Nozick gets to the heart of why the kind of correlations

158

between subjective feelings—the feelings of meaningfulness, of mattering, of coherence, of purpose—don't answer the question at the very core of our humanness.[4] Imagine a day in the distant future when neuroscientists have invented an "experience machine." You pick the kind of experience that gives you the maximal sense of meaningfulness, describing it in detail to the technicians. Maybe you're a writer who longs to produce a great work of literature, or an athlete who lives to test your physical endurance, or a romantic wanting to be merged with the perfect lover in a continuous high of fevered passion, or a God seeker who wants to feel enveloped in God's loving presence, or a parent who lives to see their child flourishing. You then step into the experience machine, the technicians attach electrodes to your brain, and there you remain for the rest of your life, as subjectively eudaimonic as you can be. (If you're worried that the eudaimonia of the experiences may diminish with repetition, you can decide in advance to interrupt the process after a certain interval with a different virtual life.) While you're in the machine, you won't know that you're in it: The virtual life will present as your one true life. You'll be blissing out on your subjective feelings—feelings of meaningfulness, mattering, coherence, and purpose. Would you, asks Nozick, opt to plug in? Both he and I suspect that you would not, not for all the subjective sense of meaningfulness in the world. That's because these subjective feelings are not what we want from our one and only life. Implicit in the distancing from ourselves that our self-reflection yields is the longing to live a life that *objectively* matters, rather than *subjectively feeling that it does.* As becomes the dignity of the *Homo iustificans*, we'll opt to strive and struggle toward life satisfaction. We want to actively *pursue* our lives rather than passively suffer them, regardless of how pleasurable that passive suffering might be. Even the hedonist wants to actively be pursuing their life of pleasure, to plan their pleasures, deepen and prolong their pleasures, overcome the obstacles to their pleasures, take pride in the achievement of their pleasures.

Admire for a moment the vast creativity and variety our species has poured into the task of responding to the mattering instinct. There seems to be hardly a talent, interest, passion, or persuasion that hasn't been turned into somebody's reason for living and fashioned into their mattering project. A moment of appreciation is due for the creativity by which we set about responding to the added burden of being human. In this sense, all of us can lay claim to creativity. Our being human demands it.

THE CONTINENTS OF THE MATTERING MAP AND A THEORY OF PERSONALITY

Beneath the dizzying array of regions on the mattering map there are patterns to be discerned, deriving from the four overarching mattering strategies we employ in striving to satisfy our mattering instinct. These are social mattering, heroic mattering, competitive mattering, and transcendent mattering. We may employ more than one of these strategies, of course, depending on the circumstances, but typically one of them prevails in us. Depending on which one prevails we can be thought of as *socializers, heroic strivers, competitors,* or *transcenders.*

Continuing the metaphor of the mattering map, these four mattering types can be thought of as inhabiting four different mattering continents, each one subdivided into many regions.

And as it is on the geographical map, so too on the mattering map communication between continents can be difficult. In particular, the mother of all mattering questions—*Do I matter?*—is heard differently from continent to continent, a phenomenon I've experienced repeatedly in the decades that I've been discussing mattering with others. Socializers hear the mother question as: Do I matter to others? Heroic strivers hear it as: Can I achieve a standard of excellence in my chosen area? Competitors hear it as: Do I matter more than others? And transcenders hear it as: Do I matter to the spiritual presence that exists beyond, or that permeates throughout, the spatio-temporal realm?

There are theories in the psychology of personality that shed some light on our continental divides—in particular, a theory that is associated with David McClelland, who was a professor of psychology at Harvard for thirty years, beginning in 1956, and was a continuation of ideas first proposed by Henry A. Murray, who was associated with Harvard from 1928 until his retirement in 1962. The McClelland-Murray theory sorts us out into three personality types, depending on which of three needs, present to some degree in all of us, is most dominant: power, affiliation, or achievement. The need for power (N-Pow) motivates a person to be in competitive relationships with others, aiming for influence and dominance; the need for affiliation (N-Aff) motivates a person to be in noncompetitive relationships with others, aiming for alliances and intimacy; and the need for achievement (N-Ach) motivates a person to cultivate excellence in themselves. "What should be involved in the achievement motive is doing something better for its own sake, for the intense satisfaction of doing something better," wrote McClelland, making it clear that it's not recognition from others that's key to this need.[5]

There are obvious connections between these personality types and three of my four mattering types. It's not surprising that we would bring the motivational structure of our personality to bear in responding to the mattering instinct. The one mattering type that doesn't have a match with any of McClelland's three categories, transcenders, accommodates all three types of personalities, resulting in fundamentally different types of transcenders: transcenders who are N-Pows, N-Affs, or N-Achs. We'll explore transcenders more closely in the next chapter, The Cartography of the Mattering Map, Part Two: The Transcendent and the Competitive.

We'll begin with the socializers, since this seems to be what most people identify themselves as being.

MATTERING TO OTHERS: INTIMACY AND NON-INTIMACY SOCIALIZERS

We all want to matter to others—that is, to have people whom we regard as in our lives and to whom we need to feel that we especially matter. We need to feel that they are prepared to give us special attention whether we deserve it or not, and that they are attentive to the characteristics that make us the unique individuals that we are. This core desire of ours is what constitutes our need for connectedness, one of the two cornerstones of our humanness, which comes to us by way of our being the gregarious creatures that we are, evolved from gregarious species. However, our need for connectedness doesn't mean that we are all socializers—that is, those who strive to satisfy the mattering instinct by mattering to others.

Some socializers seek their mattering by mattering to the very same people who satisfy their need for connectedness. Others seek it by mattering to people outside their circle of connectedness. We can call the first "intimacy socializers" and the second "non-intimacy socializers."

Examples of intimacy socializers are those who seek their mattering in terms of their relationship with their family members—perhaps specifically with their children, as some child-centric parents discussed in the previous chapter do—or those who seek their mattering in terms of their romantic relationships. The mattering projects of such socializers revolve around cultivating the kind of intimacy they require from the people in their lives to whom they look to satisfy their mattering instinct. For the intimacy socializer, the two cornerstones of humanness are collapsed into one. There's an old song from the 1940s whose title and lyrics express the mattering conviction of intimacy socializers: "You're nobody till somebody loves you."

A former brilliant student of mine dramatically presented to me just such a merging of the two cornerstones into one. "Julie" was enrolled in a PhD program and doing wonderful work when she fell in love with one of her professors and came to me to explain why, with her lover's encouragement, she was dropping out of graduate school. The way that she could most effectively impact the academic field that she had originally planned to pursue, she told me, was in helping him, whom she judged to be more brilliant and original than she. They married, she went on to help him write his articles and books—he always generously acknowledged her—mothered four brilliant and successful children, and has never appeared to regret her choice. I had been forthcoming with my objections to her decision, worried that so promising a mind would live to regret subsuming itself under the mind of another. But her mattering project appears to have worked out well for her, at least so far as I can tell. She appears to be flourishing, feeling satisfied in both her connectedness and her sense of mattering.

To seek the satisfaction of the mattering instinct in our connections with others with whom we are intimately bonded—our family, lovers, friends, colleagues, community members—seems to many people the most salubrious path to satisfying the mattering instinct, wholesome enough to inspire a Hallmark card:

When I see the look in your eyes as I draw near
I know that I matter so long as you care.

But intimacy comes in many varieties, and the intimacy that intimacy socializers seek is not always wholesome. For some, it leads to a creepier version of the Hallmark card:

When I see the look in your eyes as I draw near
I know that I matter so long as you fear.

Why bring up such perversions among intimacy socializers? The answer is to better understand those who baffle us and sometimes menace us. As wholesome as intimacy socializers might sound, some of them are dangerous.

Here, too, I have a story that lies close to my heart, of another young woman and her romantic relationship with a man who lavished her with such an abundance of attention as to be all-consuming. Every quality she most hoped was true of her—her creativity, her capacity for love—was affirmed in his extravagant attention, just as she reciprocally affirmed those qualities in him. He even kept a notebook in which he jotted down her most adorably quirky utterances. (She is adorably quirky.) It was the headiest of romances, almost from the moment that the two met cute, the kind of romance that reconfigures the world for a lover, with all that doesn't pertain to the relationship existing outside and only the two lovers pressed up close within. And the headiness didn't taper off, as romantic headiness tends to do, but rather preserved itself intact for seven intense years, at which point most of her other relationships had withered away. And so it was that she fell asleep one night, as secure in the overwhelming love of this man as she'd ever been—in fact, they had recently been discussing having a child—and awoke at dawn to his arriving home from she knew not where and announcing that he was leaving her that day. There was another romantic relationship he owed it to himself to explore, he explained, and seemed surprised that she was having trouble grasping his explanation.

What had happened to her has a name—love bombing— and occurs when a person acts out the performance of ardent love to gain control over another, often working to isolate them from other relationships. Though some abusive intimacy socializers stay put for life, love bombers typically do not, but must continue to prove to themselves their power to captivate a person, leaving a trail of emotional devastation behind. Both the control over the other and the devastation they leave behind feed their sense of mattering, and they are driven to repeat the seduction and abandonment again and again. Sure enough, this young woman later discovered that her own romance had been at the expense of another young woman, who likewise had been abruptly informed that there was another romantic relationship that he owed it to himself to explore. Doom visits some in the shape of the perfect lover.

In some sense, such intimacy relationships resemble cults—a binary cult consisting of a leader and a follower, though the follower is not likely to realize that they are a follower until the relationship is over.

It can be tricky to collapse the two cornerstones of our humanness into one, placing stress on even a genuinely loving relationship. Advice columns showcase this kind of stress. For example, consider this query to Carolyn Hax, who writes for *The Washington Post*.

My mother-in-law is a dear, sweet woman and very attached to our daughter, "Kristie." They ride horses together—my in-laws bought her a horse and maintain it and everything. Actually, they've both been unbelievably generous to our children and to us.

Kristie will be starting college this fall and my mother-in-law is distraught. She had encouraged Kristie to go to the small, nearby college she went to, but Kristie is eager to try her wings and chose a college almost a thousand miles away.

Now my mother-in-law is looking to buy a condo in the same town as Kristie's university and stay there during the school year. She's saying this way they can still ride together and it will be "good for Kristie since she won't gain weight or feel lonely." My father-in-law is furious, my husband is just saying let her do it, she'll get sick of it really soon, and Kristie is in tears to me because she doesn't want to be followed to college but won't tell her grandmother no for fear of hurting her feelings.

She is looking to me to solve this problem.

On one hand I think this is a good chance for Kristie to learn how to set boundaries. On the other, maybe she's too young for this kind of fight? I also feel bad for my mother-in-law. She isn't close to our son, she has no job or hobbies other than riding, she doesn't have many friends, her husband still works a demanding job, and so in a way I understand, even though on the surface it's crazy. What should I do?   —Anonymous.[6]

This, of course, is an extreme situation, as Hax's opening lines indicate: "Anonymous: I'm typing this around my jaw, which is on my keyboard." Still, extreme situations hold within them a general truth. The more important a relationship is to us—and what could be more important than a relationship to which we look not only for connectedness but also to satisfy the mattering instinct?—the more difficult it is to recognize the autonomous reality of the other person. "Love," remarked Iris Murdoch, "is the extremely difficult realization that something other than oneself is real." Which isn't to say that intimacy socializers are necessarily getting their lives wrong, but only that they are not necessarily getting their lives right, any more than any of us can be assured of our getting our lives right. Special challenges attend every region of the mattering map, even those devoted to relationships of love.

What about non-intimacy socializers? I've mentioned love bombers as akin to charismatic cult leaders, to whom their followers typically look in seeking to satisfy the mattering instinct. It isn't necessary that the cult leader even know of the follower's existence for the mattering instinct to feel satisfied.

The term *charisma* originated in ancient Greece. Charis was one of the three attendants of Aphrodite, goddess of beauty and erotic love. Within Christianity, charisma came to mean the God-given gift of grace. What we now call charisma retains something of this numinous quality, a sense that the charismatic person is endowed with a special grace that places them on an exalted plane of mattering. Charisma also still retains something of the erotic charge that the ancient Greeks had recognized.

There are those who have a charismatic quality felt by others but who have no intention of creating a cult of personality around themselves. But there are people who do create such a cult, marshaling their charisma to attract followers who will see the solution of their life in the charismatic leader. The cult leaders themselves are overwhelmingly individualist mattering competitors—to be examined in the next chapter—who must convince themselves that they matter more than all others do, and that is what they set about convincing their followers is true. They may employ spirituality or politics to do so, or sometimes a powerful amalgam of the two. Such people can present a disruptive force in society. Even within democracies, they play havoc with the assumption that people vote according to their self-interest—most especially their economic self-interest. But the mattering instinct overpowers self-interest narrowly defined. In a society in which there is a sharp divide between the mattering haves and the mattering have-nots, a charismatic person can provide a sense of trickle-down mattering to the mattering have-nots.

L. Ron Hubbard, the founder of the Church of Scientology, made his followers feel infused with his own mattering. The second of his wives, Sara Northrup, remarked on this aspect of Hubbard's power: "He would hold hands with them and try to talk them into these phony memories. He would concentrate on them, and they loved it. They were so excited about someone who would just pay this much attention to them."[7] Not just any someone, of course, but a uniquely special someone, inhabiting, in the eyes of his followers, an exalted plane of mattering, haloed round with the grace of charisma. To receive attention—even contrived attention—from such a special one is validating. To grant the charismatic person your unquestioning trust is to enter into what is experienced as a kind of relationship—whether the leader knows of your existence or not—with their metaphysically enhanced existence in which you can, by your fealty, share. Simply to receive their truth is to feel a bond. And in addition to the intimacy, whether real or imagined, with the cult leader, there is the community of the cult itself. Sharing the special truth that emanates from the leader provides a sense of connectedness and mutual respect, recognizing one another as the only people who get it. It's us—the chosen ones—against everybody else. Almost all cults, whether spiritual or secular, involve a Big Lie dictated by the leader that goes against all of the evidence. To affirm belief in the Big Lie is to pledge allegiance to the leader—the more outrageous the lie, the greater one's loyalty.[8] As one researcher into cults like QAnon writes, "For them, the allure is less about what it makes them think than how it makes them feel."[9] That's always the way when the mattering instinct is in play. And what cultists feel, first and foremost, is that they matter in a way that had been lacking before. The words of Angela Rubino, the Georgia woman who dived into dumpsters to gather proof that the 2020 election had been stolen, are to the point. "This can't be what life is, that you get up and go to work and come home. That as humans, we're nothing."[10]

The lure of cults within a society is correlated with how many of its people need convincing that they're not nothing. A charismatic leader who creates a movement that supplies both trickle-down mattering and connectedness induces what is needed for a sense of flourishing. Trying to dislodge the cult's power by raising practical considerations—even when the cult is political—is as futile as casting shadows in the dark. Epistemological moralizing—citing facts and figures produced by the traditionally accepted norms of rationality—is futile. Such schoolmarmish scoldings are ineffective against cult followers. Cult leaders, addressing themselves directly to their followers' mattering instinct, will convince them to ignore the usual norms of justification: You cannot trust what your family and friends tell you. You cannot trust what the so-called experts tell you. You cannot trust what mainstream media tells you. You cannot trust what the schools tell you. You cannot trust what the government tells you; that is, unless the charismatic leader becomes the government. The longing that provides the allure of cults is existential, and the existential always trumps the rational.

There are thousands of cults, religious and political, currently in the US, most of which function beneath the radar, though a select few soar visibly above it. A cult doesn't cease being a cult even when a majority of people become its followers. To repeat a truth stated in the introduction: Longing on a large scale is what makes history, and of no longing is this truer than the longing to matter.

"I'M GONNA LIVE FOREVER, BABY, REMEMBER MY NAME"[11]

The last group of non-intimacy socializers I want to consider are fame seekers. They too want to matter to others—to multitudes of others, the vast majority of them strangers. As the satirical writer H. L. Mencken put it, "A celebrity is one who is known to many persons he is glad he doesn't know."

The reason that fame is a way to minister to the mattering instinct is obvious. What the mattering instinct is about is trying to prove to ourselves that we are deserving of all the attention that we can't help paying ourselves. And what better proof can there be for concluding that we are deserving of our own attention than the attention others pay to us—which in the case of the famous is a great deal. The attention rendered by the fans to a celebrity can be like the attention of a lover to the beloved, every detail imbued with significance.[12] Daniel Radcliffe has a phobia of cucumbers! Jennifer Lawrence has six toes on her left foot! Channing Tatum used to be a stripper! The fact that the attention givers are strangers, and so can't individually matter to the attention recipient, is compensated for by their sheer numbers. "When I see all these people screaming and chanting and holding those signs that they made just for me, my eyes light up, and my whole body just lifts, and I just feel in another state. I feel like I'm floating on air. It's the most incredible feeling, and I've always wanted it," said Christina Aguilera, a singer who was described at the height of her fame as "the voice of a generation." And to quote the voice of an earlier generation, the singer Joan Baez, "The easiest kind of relationship for me is with ten thousand people. The hardest is with one."

Sometimes fame seekers are those whom you might mistakenly identify as heroic strivers. In her memoir, *In the Shadow of Fame: A Memoir by the Daughter of Erik H. Erikson*, Sue Erikson Bloland relates that her father, the eminent psychoanalyst—he coined the phrase "identity crisis"—had been consumed with the need for fame: "Fame did not simply come to him because he was an extraordinarily brilliant thinker and writer, which he certainly was. But from early childhood on I was aware that his drive to achieve recognition was monumental." Erikson's book, *Childhood and Society*, catapulted him into celebrity. He had dared, with his emphasis on issues of self-identity and ego formation, to take on the hegemony of Freud. "During these years, and for many years to come, my relationship with my parents was untroubled on the surface," writes Erikson Bloland of her parents. "But there was never any question about the highest priority in their lives, which was Dad's career and his still-growing fame." In her description, both her mother and father shared the joint mattering project of building the fame of Erik Erikson.

There is evidence that the striving for fame has become an increasingly common response to the mattering instinct. One contributing factor is how much easier it now is to attain some degree of fame, with social media offering new avenues for attracting the mass attention of strangers. You may appear on TikTok adorably bopping your head while lip-synching to a song by a British rapper—as the twenty-three-year-old Bella Poarch did in 2020—and find yourself going viral. She accumulated over 10 million followers in six days.

Data gathered by Clapit, a social media network, in collaboration with Gov.com, found that one out of four of millennials (born between 1981 and 1996) would choose to quit their job if they could become famous. One in nine millennials would forgo marriage for fame; one in six would forgo children. One in twelve would detach themselves from family, and one in fourteen would break up with their significant other.

Some forms of fame seeking can be deadly. There are people who film themselves doing insanely dangerous stunts that are then posted to the internet—so many that there is a Wikipedia entry for "List of selfie-related injuries and deaths."

More tragic still are those who, in seeking to appease the mattering instinct, are driven to random acts of violence, wreaking violence on innocent others. How do we know that the mattering instinct motivates these atrocities? The perpetrators tell us. It's become almost protocol for them to produce a manifesto, written or filmed, often sent to the media to be released almost simultaneously with the horror—itself an act intended to win mass attention. If there is anything that these manifestos make manifest, it is the toxicity of the mattering instinct left entirely unappeased. All of their words ring with the fury toward a world that has left them feeling like nobody. "I am somebody, I exist! You'll see, you'll see!" is the underlying theme. The shooter who went back to the high school in Parkland, Florida, from which he had been expelled the year before, is typical. He posted three videos before he killed seventeen people, both students and teachers. In just over two minutes of video, he mentioned four times that his name was going to be remembered. "From the wrath of my power they will know who I am." "With the power of my AR, you'll all know who I am." "You will all see. You will all know who my name is." "Location is Stoneman Douglas in Parkland, Florida. It's gonna be a big event. And when you see me on the news, you'll all know who I am."

In between the first and second quotes, there was this: "I am nothing. I am no one."

So much must go wrong in a person's life for such acts of wanton destruction to result. Examine these lives and you find that both of the cornerstones of human flourishing have gone disastrously unmet. These horrific acts are often labeled "senseless" but that's inaccurate. Their sense is glaringly clear: "You have made me feel, every moment of my life, that I don't matter, but I will show you how much I do. If you survive me at all, then your life will be forever bifurcated into two—the time before I made myself known to you and the time after." Described as monsters who exist outside the realm of human motivation, they are laying bare, in their privation, our deepest motivations.

"TO LIVE IN ACCORDANCE WITH THE BEST THING IN US": HEROIC STRIVERS

Most of the individuals who have been mentioned so far have been heroic strivers: the scientists Isaac Newton, Albert Einstein, and Ludwig Boltzmann; the poet John Berryman; the philosophers Jean-Paul Sartre and Ludwig Wittgenstein; the psychologists David McClelland, Sigmund Freud, and William James; the basketball player Michael Jordan; the diarist Alice James; the Victorian salmon fly-tyers Edwin Rist. And lastly, Aristotle, who deserves a special place, since he was not only a heroic striver, but also gave us perhaps the best statement of what it is to be one: "We must not follow those who advise us, being men, to think of human things, and, being mortal, of mortal things, but must, so far as we can, make ourselves immortal by straining every nerve to live in accordance with the best thing in us." McClelland also captures the heroic striver in defining the need for achievement: "What should be involved in the achievement motive is doing something better for its own sake, for the intense satisfaction of doing something better."

The striving of a heroic striver need not be seen as heroic in the eyes of most. What's necessary is that it be seen as heroic in the eyes of the strivers themselves. For them their mattering project not only strains their individual capacities, demanding discipline and perseverance, but is devoted to something that they believe supremely matters. Often, they view what most matters to them in terms of such abstract values as goodness, truth, beauty, courage, or strength. For example, though others may view the project of a Victorian salmon fly-tyers as a waste of time, effort, and money, for a person like Edwin Rist, his is a life devoted to the pursuit of ineffable beauty, all the more treasured for being appreciated by so few.

All of the heroic strivers mentioned so far have been famous, to the extent that I can tell you about their lives even though I've never met them. Even Edwin Rist had a book written about him.[13] But neither fame nor the desire for fame is, in itself, a motivation for heroic strivers, though they may welcome it as confirmation that they have indeed met the standards of excellence that alone satisfy their mattering instinct. In certain regions occupied by heroic strivers, perhaps most particularly the arts, it can be hard to judge whether one's work is as good as one might think it is, and fame and acclaim can, at least for some, help to quell the doubts. And then too heroic strivers might enjoy the perks of fame, because people treat the famous as if they really do matter more. They treat them better. The actor Kevin Bacon confessed to *Vanity Fair* that he had long fantasized about what it would be like to walk anonymously through the world without being besieged by people begging to take a selfie with him, because "I'm not complaining, but I have a face that's pretty recognized." He outfitted himself with fake teeth, a prosthetic nose, and glasses, and went to an LA shopping mall teeming with tourists. His disguise worked, but his delight in anonymity quickly fizzled. "People were kind of pushing past me, not being nice. Nobody said, 'I love you.' I had to wait in line to, I don't know, buy a fucking coffee or whatever. I was like, this sucks. I want to go back to being famous."[14]

Other heroic strivers spurn fame as sullying their mattering project. The British alpinist Tom Livingstone only accepted the Piolet d'Or, or Golden Axe, alpine climbing's highest award, because his two coclimbers wanted him to. But he wrote on his website that he didn't like the way the award "plays on my ego . . . If you really want to say 'nice one,' then I would humbly accept your comment. But a more appropriate word would be 'jebise,' which is Slovenian humour, and a greeting between good friends. It's said with a smile. It means, 'Hey, fuck you!'"

I can imagine the Russian mathematician Grigori Perelman appreciating the attitude behind *jebise*. Perelman, who solved one of the most difficult and important of mathematical problems, the Poincaré conjecture, which had proved to be unprovable for over a hundred years, spurned the Fields Medal, which is the mathematical equivalent of the Nobel

Prize, and also the Clay Mathematical Institute's Millennium Prize, which comes with a million dollars. "I don't want to be on display like an animal in a zoo," he explained. "My activity and my persona have no interest for society."

But then Livingstone and Perelman, though no Kevin Bacon, are famous enough for me to have read what they had to say about not wanting to be famous. So let me tell you about a heroic striver who made sure that he and fame would never intersect.

Scott Harney came from a tough working-class Irish neighborhood in Charlestown, across the Charles River from downtown Boston. Despite recent gentrification, the Boston accent remains thick in Charlestown, and when Scott entered Harvard as a freshman, the first of his high school to do so, he self-consciously erased all signatures of class from his speech.

At Harvard, Scott studied poetry and was among the few who gained admittance to the small workshop taught by Robert Lowell. Prospective students had to submit a writing sample and be handpicked by Lowell for the privilege. There could be no greater measure of the distance Scott had traveled in his short but momentous trip from Charlestown to Cambridge than his studying with Robert Lowell. Besides being one of the celebrated poets of his generation, Lowell was the scion of a Boston Brahmin family so distinguished, at least in one region of the mattering map, as to have inspired the old Boston toast:

And this is good old Boston,
The home of the bean and the cod,
Where Lowells talk only to Cabots,
And Cabots talk only to God.

After graduating, Scott took a series of jobs, including as an aide in MacLean Hospital, the psychiatric facility disguised as a prosperous New England prep school, where many of Boston's Brahmins, including Robert Lowell, have periodically retreated to reconnect with sanity. Eventually Scott became a paralegal. All his jobs were meant to give him the freedom to work on his poetry. But after one rejection too many he made the decision not to send his poems out into the world. One early poem of his had been published in the *Somerville Community News*, but after that no more poetry appeared. "If you have to be sure don't write," as John Berryman had told the young William Merwin. Scott had gotten the message and had apparently given up writing.

I had come to know Scott through my friend Megan Marshall. She and Scott had met as undergraduates at Harvard, when both had intended to devote their lives to poetry. They had become lovers, though eventually they'd split and ended up marrying others. Megan, though she gave up on a life of poetry, remained in the literary world. Eventually—thirty years of eventually to be exact—Megan and Scott found their way back to one another.

Megan's career as a writer flourished in her new relationship, and Scott basked in her late-arriving success. She got pieces placed in *The New Yorker* and won a Pulitzer Prize for her biography of the nineteenth-century transcendentalist Margaret Fuller (who had been no mean heroic striver herself). I remember once chatting with Scott at a reception following one of Megan's readings. He told me, with unwonted emotion stirring his polished voice, of the first time he had seen Megan's name printed in *The New Yorker*. The two crownlike *M*'s standing regal on the page, he said. It was as if her name had been preordained to be set in that font. I remember thinking that this was the most intimate glimpse I'd had of him. It was as if his own forsaken literary love had been resuscitated in his lover's success. He made me think back on my brilliant student who had submerged her own intellectual ambitions into those of her husband.

At our gatherings in and around Cambridge, Scott was a benevolent if unassuming presence, a large and handsome man, rarely holding the floor. There were so many floor holders among us. A master of silence, he sometimes allowed a flash of sly humor. At one dinner party, a writer who had recently broken into bestsellerdom was brag-complaining about how tiresome it was to be read by everybody, to which Scott responded, "If it's any consolation, I haven't read you." His tone was so ingenuous, his smile so amiably open, that the writer had stared in confusion, trying to discern whether she'd just been put down or not.

Having known the earlier Scott in all his promise, and aware that he spent time at his computer on evenings and weekends working over drafts, Megan sometimes suggested that he perhaps join a writing group or enroll in a low-residency MFA program. But he silenced her in his disarming way: "Megan, maybe the thing I'm best at is loving you."

One beautiful spring day, Megan returned home from a literary conference in Manhattan to find Scott lying in their bed, dead. He had been diagnosed with mantle cell lymphoma soon after they had moved in together twelve years earlier. He'd been cured of the cancer, but one of the courses of chemotherapy had left him with fatal congestive heart failure.

When Megan abandoned her marriage she'd left a sprawling Victorian for a cramped apartment. She'd had to discard a great number of possessions, though the grand piano came along with her, squeezed into the living room that she had taken over as her workspace. After Scott moved in, he had asked her if he might use the empty bottom shelf of one of her bookcases to store some notebooks. She'd never looked at what he'd piled there—after all, it was his private property— but after his death she did. And there they were, the many poems he'd been working on, in revision after revision, some of them going back to the Lowell workshop. She found still more on his computer in their storage space in the basement, where she also found a file crammed with rejection slips from the contests and journals to which he'd long ago submitted poems, preserved like the dried flowers from a faithless lover. These talismans of failure had arrived fairly regularly through the late 1970s and early '80s, and included a 1982 postcard that had come from the judges of the Grolier Poetry Prize. The Grolier Poetry Book Shop in Cambridge is exclusively devoted to poetry, and back in 1976 it had established a prize that came with publication. The postcard read, "If your name is not one of the above, we hope you will enter your manuscript again next year." That was the last entry in his file of rejections.

The many revisions of the poems—Megan calls the originals "seed pearls"—show the meticulous reach toward complexity and subtlety that Scott had pursued throughout the decades. You have to admire his self-restraint when Megan had gently suggested how he might perhaps join a writing group or enroll in a low-residency writing program.

For Scott to keep pouring his energy into his writing he had needed to eliminate all the emotions involved in submitting his poetry to those in a position to judge it—those I call the mattering adjudicators, who decide who is a success or failure in a mattering region, who is even permitted to claim residency there. Not all mattering regions have adjudicators, but many do, and Scott, having been dismissed by them one time too many, dismissed the dismissers. Throughout his good-natured silence, he had been in dialogue with the art form to which he dedicated himself and with the poets he revered.

Megan selected from among the discovered poems—an old girlfriend of his sent her more—and a year after his death a publishing house in Cambridge published *The Blood of San Gennaro*, adorned with glowing blurbs from established poets.

Perhaps Scott had intentionally left his poems where he knew Megan would find them, trusting that she would do for his poetry what he hadn't the heart to do, to send these pieces of his living self out into the world where others would decree whether they were good enough. Or did postmortem publication come to matter as little to him as antemortem publication had? Did his devotion to poetry outlive his hope of ever having his work read by others? Had he contented himself with that prospect, too, as he secretly and ceaselessly perfected his lines?

Perhaps this last possibility seems strange to you, to the point of incomprehension. Keats wrote that "heard melodies are sweet but those unheard are sweeter," but what composer is indifferent to whether his scores will ever be performed, and what heroic striver of a poet struggles endlessly with the exact cadence of a line never hoping for others to savor it? And yet Scott Harney had never breathed a word of the efforts he was pouring into his art, as he strived to live in accordance with the best thing in him.

THE MORAL HEROIC STRIVER

As it was for Scott Harney, so it is for many heroic strivers, finding in their perfecting of themselves the mattering project that makes their lives worth living. Their mattering project might make them a film buff, a gardener, a drag queen, or an adept in Tantric sex. It might set them on the unending path of being well-roundedly educated, of gaining fluency in many languages, becoming a gourmet cook, improving their golf, their yoga practice, their knife throwing, their moral character.

This last possibility—striving after moral improvement—leads us to yet a different type of heroic striver. We've looked at intellectual, artistic, and athletic strivers, but not yet at moral strivers—more commonly known as saints.

Let me introduce you to a man known as Baba Amte, a moral heroic striver who devoted himself to restoring the dignity of the most reviled among us, those infected with the bacterium *Mycobacterium leprae*.

The World Health Organization now discourages the use of the word *leper*. Do we call tuberculosis patients tuberculosians, cancer patients cancerites? Why, in the case of leprosy, do we strip a person down to their disease? The reason may be historical. Victims of leprosy have long been regarded as not only physically but morally putrid, a homily against sin written in the visible corruptions of the body. "Unclean is he, alone shall he stay, outside of the camp is his dwelling-place," declares Leviticus (13:45–46).

Baba Amte was born Murlidhar Devidas Amte, the first child of a wealthy Brahmin family in India. His mother affectionately called him Baba, which means father or saintly old man, and the nickname stuck. Not that the boy displayed any inclinations toward saintliness. He was full of high spirits and defiance, much given to testing limits. Rather than playing with other Brahmin children, he preferred the freer ways of the children of his family's servants, even though they were Dalit—those considered "untouchable." In his culture, this counted as not just disobedience but impiety. But even though his father beat him whenever he was caught with these playmates, Amte continued to socialize with them, and, even more scandalously, to eat with their families. This was in a household where even allowing the shadow of a Dalit to fall on your person was forbidden.

His adoring mother protected him as best she could, often sneaking him into a back door of the house and defending him to his father. It was through her, Baba Amte later said, that "the seeds of rebellion entered my veins."[15]

Despite "the seeds of rebellion," he hardly spurned the privileges that came with his high birth but, as he matured, reveled in them. He wore bespoke suits, made by a tailor he shared with the British governor of the district, and cultivated a taste for expensive sports cars. Never one for moderation—he kept a cheetah as a pet—he was so passionate about film as to sometimes watch three in a day. He'd buy two tickets so that he could drape his feet comfortably over the empty seat and would order meals to be delivered between shows. For a time, he played with the possibility of becoming a film actor himself, drawn to the kind of epic life played out on the big screen.

But his enthusiasms didn't make him an aesthetic effete. He was also a person of action, rushing toward danger. He volunteered when there were natural disasters, took up wrestling and boxing, and when he went into the forest to hunt big game, he didn't retreat to the safety of a blind but faced the animals head on, though the killing of animals is forbidden by Hinduism. Amte always had little use for religion.

Drama and danger were his element, as much as pleasure and privilege. And always there was within him a raging sense of justice, calling forth his heroic action. Once, when traveling by train, he witnessed a group of British soldiers behaving lewdly toward a young bride. The groom, not daring to stand up to them, had locked himself in the bathroom. Amte singlehandedly fought off the soldiers and then, when the train reached the station, demanded an inquiry from the commanding officer. Gandhi heard about the incident and dubbed him *Abhay Sadhak*, or fearless seeker of truth. This fit his own conception of himself precisely.

His father's ambition for him was to be a lawyer. The son balked at so humdrum a profession, so the father bought him a green Singer Roadster upholstered in panther skin as an inducement. Amte finished law school and became a criminal defender, but it was work he regarded with contempt. A client would admit that he had committed rape, and Amte was expected to obtain an acquittal and then go out with the rapist to celebrate. In disgust he left the prestigious law firm and set up a practice with a so-called lower-caste colleague and began union organizing among the Dalit workers, the street sweepers and ragpickers. He was told by them that he couldn't possibly understand their lives, and he heard their words as a direct challenge—the one thing in life he could never refuse. For nine months he woke at 3 a.m. to join the workers for four hours of labor before arriving at his law office, carrying wastes away as they did, in a basket balanced on his head. For three months he cleaned forty latrines a day.

Despite his radically non-Brahmin eccentricities, Amte was still considered an eligible bachelor, and his parents were approached by potential in-laws. But Amte knew that the kind of epic life he craved couldn't be consistent with marriage to any of these parentally approved girls. To guard himself from importunate prospective in-laws, he became a *sadhu*, donning the saffron robes of an ascetic and mendicant, who, in renouncing all worldly ties, also takes a vow of celibacy. Still radically irreligious, Amte adopted this tactic for removing himself from the marriage market.

As a monk, he allowed his hair and beard to grow into matted strands and took up the beggar's bowl. Although he found that he had no talent for emptying his mind in meditation, he experienced the deprivations of a monk's life as invigorating.

On a return visit to his family, he accompanied a friend to the home of the friend's bride-to-be for a ceremony that would finalize the engagement. While there he noticed that the youngest sister of the house was behaving strangely. She had crept away from the festivities and was helping one of the servants with the laundry. Hers was an aristocratic family of Sanskrit scholars, orthodox in their Hinduism, which made her behavior toward the servant even more aberrant. He immediately intuited that this might be the girl for him. Following up his intuition with discreet but rigorous inquiries, he learned the girl was indeed an eccentric, flouting, as he did, the Brahmin attitudes toward the Dalit. The conclusion of his investigation was that he decided to stop being a *sadhu*.

Her name was Indu, and Amte sent her a love poem. She hardly knew how to respond to a gesture that managed to violate so many taboos. She was a shy and sheltered girl. She consulted her family who, scandalized, forbade her to have anything to do with the lunatic who, still with matted hair streaming down his back, dared to send a respectable girl a love poem.

The love poem from a monk was bad enough. What made it worse was that he hadn't even proposed marriage! Eventually he did, and the two married, the groom swathed in bandages, having fought off a knife-wielding thief who had broken into a silk shop owned by his bride's family. He had almost lost an eye in the battle, again a reason her family had urged her, until the very last minute, to renounce marriage to a lunatic who might turn out to be half-blind.

Amte's character was as outsize as any swashbuckling adventurer. He might have climbed Mount Everest, or become a soldier of fortune or a revolutionary leader on the model of Che Guevara. Instead, he became a saint. How did the transformation transpire?

He was walking home late one night in a driving rain when he spotted what looked like a pile of rags in a ditch by the side of the road. It turned out to be a naked man, in the last stage of leprosy. "A rotting mass of human flesh," Baba Amte recalled. "With two holes in place of a nose, without traces of fingers or toes, with worms and sores where there should have been eyes. A living corpse."[16]

Terrified and disgusted, he fled. It was a natural reaction, but did not sit well with Amte. "I have never been frightened of anything. Because I fought British tommies to save the honour of an Indian lady, Gandhiji called me *'Abhay Sadhak.'*

When the sweepers of Warora challenged me to clean the latrines, I did so; but the same person quivered in fright when he saw the living corpse."[17]

Unable to reconcile his terrified revulsion with his heroic conception of himself, Amte forced himself to return that night to cover Tulshiram, the dying man, with a jute sack and to stay with him through his death agony. But for weeks afterward his initial cowardly reaction tormented him, lengthening into an existential crisis that endured for six months. The solution to his crisis finally occurred to him. To restore himself to himself he would restore the dignity of those afflicted with leprosy. Here was a mattering project to match the heroic dimensions of his personality.

He volunteered at Gandhi's leper clinic, cleaning out ulcers, giving injections, cutting away gangrened flesh; and in the work he felt his confidence returning. But being Amte, he needed more. He devoted himself to studying leprosy. One doctor explained to him that, because leprosy can't be transmitted to animals, the experimentation that might lead to a cure had been severely hampered. Amte thought about this problem for several days and then offered himself as an experimental subject and was injected with the bacillus. As it happened, he carried natural immunity. Researchers have since discovered that about 95 percent of us have natural immunity, but nobody knew that at the time.

Even after a cure (the drug dapsone) was discovered, those whose faces and bodies had been devastated by the disease, though no longer contagious, were still the objects of opprobrium. In some villages, they were burned alive. Amte, who had been traveling the country dispensing dapsone, decided to create his own community. He applied to the state of Madhya Pradesh for land, and in 1951 was given fifty acres of arid wilderness. When he first inspected the plot, he reported to his wife, whom he had respectfully dubbed Sadhana, that it was "outcast land for outcast people."[18] Together with six leprosy patients, a lame cow, four dogs to protect them from the surrounding wild animals, and their two baby boys, Vikas and Pakash, the family relocated.

There was little food, and the nearest source of water was more than a mile away. The first order of business was to dig a well. It was May when they arrived and 115°F in the shade. It took them six weeks of unrelenting digging until they found water thirty feet down. They built two crude shelters of sticks and mud, one for themselves, the other for the leprosy patients.

Deadly snakes and scorpions and rats were everywhere, invading the huts, most especially when it rained. Leprosy is a disease of the nervous system, and the leprosy patients would sometimes awaken to discover that rats had eaten their insensate flesh while they slept. Tigers came in the night and carried off the guard dogs, one by one, fortunately leaving the two human babies in their beds. Baba Amte named their community Anandwan, literally Forest of Joyfulness.

He didn't spare his sons from the heroic standards he applied to himself. They had no toys and amused themselves by playing with scorpions. Once, when Prakash was six, Baba Amte heard a tiger roaring close to the well and asked the boy, who had also heard it, to go and draw a bucket of water. When the child returned with the task accomplished, Baba Amte was so overcome with his version of fatherly pride that he couldn't help giving Prakash a pat on the back.

Soon a steady stream of the sufferers of leprosy was coming to the wilderness community seeking *ashraya*, or shelter. Their family members would have nothing to do with them, since they themselves would be regarded as outcasts, unable to find friends or marriage partners, were the terrible secret to become known. More dormitories were built, more land cleared for crops.

It was fundamental to Baba Amte's vision of the community that the sufferers would not be regarded as sufferers but rather as useful members of society. Let them lose their limbs, he said, but not their dignity. If a person had lost seven fingers, that still left them with three, and much could be accomplished with three. He admired the great humanitarian Albert Schweizer but could not concur with the practice of consigning those with leprosy to bed. Baba Amte had instead sent them to build dormitories and raise crops, using modern techniques of agronomy.

They farmed, they built, they wove and worked the machinery. The lengths to which he drove everybody—his wife, his sons, his patients—matched the dimensions of his own extraordinary will. But it got results, and Anandwan became a success. He had wanted his community to be self-sufficient and so it became. In just two years, the only items they needed to import were sugar, oil, and salt.

As soon as his community was no longer struggling against impossible odds, Baba Amte had to find himself new impossible odds. He created a yearly cultural festival, bringing his passions for dance and music and theater to Anandwan. He designed a theater, which he and his patients then built, and staged plays that lasted until four in the morning. Outsiders were invited to attend the performances. Wrote one admiring visitor, the playwright P. L. Deshpande, "Usually people avoid looking at leprosy patients. Here Baba Amte is putting them on stage for all to see."[19]

Baba Amte's next project was to establish a school for the blind at Anandwan, building a dormitory so that children could come from far away. A school for the deaf soon followed. And then, after he and Sadhana found a little girl abandoned on the roadside, they created an orphanage. At some point a home for the abandoned elderly was also erected on the grounds. And not one among the participants in Anandwan was spared the obligations of contributing their labor to the community. The elderly could teach others. They could plant and tend the gardens that beautified the grounds. Nobody, said Baba Amte, should be deprived of beauty. A visitor mentioned that the roses of Anandwan have an unusual fragrance. "Of course, they do," responded Baba Amte. "They have been irrigated by the tears of the blind, the deaf, and the orphaned children who tend them."[20]

The term *saint* is often wreathed round with religiosity, but in using the term to mean a moral heroic striver, no religious connotations should be understood.[21] Baba Amte, who remained throughout his life an avowed atheist, is an exemplar of sainthood without religion. He had so little regard for religion that he wouldn't allow priests into his home! There are no religious expressions in Anandwan, no temples, no shrines. "The ultimate truth of this era is 'Food is God,'" said Baba Amte. "I got acquainted with the God enshrined in the bellies of the poor and peeping out from their eyes."[22]

A man whose excesses engendered contradictions, Baba Amte was occasionally accused of being not a saint but a tyrant. He had the perfectionist's intolerance for mistakes. No detail escaped his notice, whether in the care of the patients, the curriculum of the schools, the techniques in the fields, or the methods in the workshops. He was fanatical about book-keeping and would spend hours making sure that every rupee had been accounted for. If Sadhana oversalted the food, he would put down the fork and refuse to take another bite.

A saint? Baba Amte himself vehemently rejected the halo. He had taken up leprosy work, he insisted, "not to help anyone but to overcome that fear in my life. That it worked out well for others was a by-product. But the fact is I did it to overcome fear."[23] Clearly, there is more to it than Baba Amte admitted. Influencing his choice of a mattering project was the capacious-ness of his compassion and the roiling sense of justice that had him rebelling since childhood against Brahmin taboos discrim-inating against classes of people in terms of claims of intrinsic mattering. All of these elements had to have been operating to produce a life story that so exemplifies the moral heroic striver.

There can be no easy explanation for how a person ends up exactly where they do on the mattering map. Even if our personality structure, as revealed by a theory like that of Murray and McClelland, explains how we end up on the con-tinent of the socializers, the heroic strivers, or the competi-tors, still there is the question of how our tendency toward socializing, heroic striving, or competition gets expressed, determining which region on the continent we inhabit and the mattering project we pursue. Our culture, temperament, talents, and interests come into play, as well as autobiograph-ical accidents, such as Baba Amte's encounter with Tulshiram on that rainy night. Had Baba Amte not run into Tulshiram, would some other happenstance have been bound to occur, sooner or later, to provoke a person with just his combination of heroic striving, defiance, compassion, and sense of justice to undertake a moral mattering project commensurate with his nature—perhaps not devoted to the victims of leprosy but equally as daunting?

I was describing Baba Amte's life to a friend, an intimacy socializer who identifies her mattering project with the nurturing of her family. She stopped me when I got to the part about Baba Amte sending his son to the well while a tiger lurked near, so horrified that she refused to accept that anything about him was laudable.

"Don't you see that he was only interested in aggrandizing himself? What you're calling a saint, I call a raging egoist!"

She was not only angry about the story but angry at me, hearing in my admiration for Baba Amte the implication that her own mattering project didn't really matter.

The collision of randomness with all the nuances of talent, temperament, history, culture, and autobiography explodes into the kaleidoscopic choices we make in responding to our shared mattering instinct and scatters us across the wide expanse of the mattering map. But there seems nothing random—there *can* seem nothing random—about the values we embrace in our location there, since these are the values we use in justifying ourselves to ourselves. If they are as arbitrary as our own identity, then how can they save us from our own arbitrary self-mattering?

We are, in being creatures longing to matter, unavoidably value laden, with values unavoidably differing. The clash of values engendered by the mattering instinct sets us up against one another. Is no common ground possible for the normative creatures that we are?

And we've yet considered only two out of the four mattering continents. There are many more clashes to come.

CHAPTER 6

THE CARTOGRAPHY OF THE MATTERING MAP, PART TWO: THE TRANSCENDENT AND THE COMPETITIVE

Short of lunacy, there is no greater sense of mattering than that experienced by transcenders.

Transcenders, like socializers, seek their mattering in *mattering to*. Only the "who" to whom they seek to matter isn't any other human or group of humans. Rather it's a *transcendent presence* believed to ground the being of all that is true in both the physical and moral spheres. A transcender's sense of mattering is grounded in a vision of a metaphysically fortified cosmos, conceived of as numinous, shot through with emanations of unlimited power, knowledge, justice, and—at least in some versions—mercy.

The transcendent presence might be conceived along conventionally religious lines. In the words of the psalmist: "The heavens declare the glory of God, and the firmament shows His handiwork. Day unto day utters speech, and night unto night reveals knowledge" (Psalm 19). Or the transcendent presence might be conceived in less religiously conventional terms: "The universe is programmed to support your happiness, but not at some up-and-down, here-and-gone level. It's programmed to support your deep, abiding, fully actualized joy," in the words of Marianne Williamson, an influential voice among those who identify as SBNR (spiritual but not religious),[1] who received national attention when, in 2019, she garnered enough support for her candidacy for president of the United States to participate in the first two Democratic primary debates.[2]

So far as the mattering instinct is concerned, the difference between the psalmist and Marianne Williamson is less significant than the similarity. The all-important fact for any transcender is that the source of human mattering is embedded in the metaphysical grounding of all reality. Our own mattering is assured by our relationship to the transcendent presence whose own mattering is undeniable: For how could that which is responsible for all of existence not matter?[3] The crux of human mattering, for the transcender, lies in the attitude of extrahuman reality. It cares about us.

To experience as a transcender is to experience the cosmos with a heady fusion of awe and intimacy. The cosmos, while being an awe-inspiring *more*, is also domesticated: You feel at home in it. It was meant for you. The fusion can give rise to emotions that characterize the best of human relationships— overwhelming love and gratitude. In the language of the philosopher Martin Buber, the cosmos becomes a Thou rather than an It. And although the Thou exceeds your full knowledge, you yourself are fully seen and known by It: "You have searched me and know me. There is not a word on my tongue but that Thou, oh Lord, know it well" (Psalm 139). Such transparency before transcendence can inspire fear, as the psalmist continues: "Surely darkness will conceal me, night will provide me with cover. But darkness is not dark for Thou. Night is as light as day; darkness and light are the same."

But even though there is no hiding, you can never doubt how much you matter—*cosmically* matter, seen and known and, in many traditions, judged. The cosmos, in being a metaphysically fortified *more*, also renders the transcender a something *more*. Your life, which can't help meaning all the world to you, means something in the largest sense possible. You yourself, so fragile and tenuous, are implicated in the answer to the most profound of all metaphysical questions: Why is there something rather than nothing? That which answers the question purposefully created you.

Since the subjective *feeling* of mattering is closely linked with the subjective *feeling* of meaningfulness, which is, in turn, linked with the subjective feeling of life satisfaction, the onslaught of psychological research demonstrating that the religious and the spiritual self-report higher levels of life satisfaction is hardly surprising. (Actually, the SBNR have an edge here, since they're not as prone to the negativity of guilt.[4]) Sometimes this research is hawked as a reason to become a transcender, as if metaphysics could be sold to us, like membership in a health club.

The transempirical nature of claims about a transcendent presence leaves ample room for faith to fill in the details. And faith, in turn, leaves ample room for a wide divergence of opinions about the nature of the transcendent presence that grounds reality and what it may want from us in the way of recognition and reverence.

Here is yet another reason to be wary of those selling wholesale transcendence as a boost to life satisfaction. Faith, being exquisitely sensitive to the longings of the faithful, comes in many persuasions. I recall a tweet I saw back in 2014, in the triumphant days of Isis and Abu Bakr al-Baghdadi's declared caliphate. It was written by a young man who had left his native England to fight for Islam's ultimate triumph in the caliphate, and it testified to the exultant boost in his life satisfaction: "I used to spend my days stacking shirts in Primark. Now POTUS trembles at my existence."

The very transcendence that renders the belief of transcenders so powerful a confirmation of their own mattering comes at a steep epistemic price. The epistemic uncertainty contained in the mattering instinct itself—we can't know that we objectively matter even as we can't help longing that we do—is mirrored in the transcender's response to the mattering instinct. The transcender can't know that their version of the cosmos is true even though they can't help longing that it is.

In this sense, all transcenders, whether the psalmist, the jihad fighter, or Marianne Williamson, are alike in being cosmic petitioners. Their mattering is premised on reality's conforming to their vision of it. Doubters can be cosmic petitioners, believing that their mattering can be validated only by reality's containing their version of a transcendent presence, but are unsure of whether it does. Transcenders are cosmic petitioners who have sufficiently vanquished their doubts.

The continent of the transcenders, with its powerful fusion of awe and intimacy, isn't a foreign land to me. This is where I was born and raised. I know what it's like to turn to God many times every day—in the blessing for waking up each morning—"I give thanks to you, living and eternal King, for you have returned my soul within me with compassion"— for every variety of food you eat, for putting on new clothes, for experiencing the beauties of nature—a rainbow, a lightning storm, my mother's rose garden in full bloom: "Blessed are You, Lord our God, King of the universe, who has such things in His world." I recited the blessing for receiving good news—"Blessed are You, Lord our God, King of the universe, who is good and does good"—and also the blessing for receiving bad news—"Blessed are You, Lord our God, King of the universe, the true Judge."

To be a transcender is to believe that your personal existence has a role to play in the narrative of eternity. You would not be at all unless you had a role to play in the drama of all of existence. There is no greater mattering that you can conceive for yourself, short of imagining that you are yourself a transcendent being existing on an exalted plane beyond other mortals—in other words, short of lunacy. Compared to transcendent mattering, any other sense of mattering limps far behind, which again explains why psychologists keep producing data showing that the religious and spiritual report comparatively higher levels of life satisfaction.

Is it any wonder then that, given the mattering instinct, the continent of the transcenders powerfully attracts us? If the cosmos were designed so as to best minister to the longing that defines us, then surely it would be the cosmos that transcenders, in all their differences, believe it to be: such as to confer cosmic mattering on us. Forget the philosophers' arguments for God's existence—the cosmological argument (arguing for God as the necessary first cause); the teleological argument (arguing that the design and order of the universe entails an intelligent designer); the ontological argument (arguing that God's existence is entailed by his definition); the moral argument (arguing for God as the necessary grounding of morality). Arguments for God are like arguments for why you love your children. They are arguments that are concocted after the fact—the fact being how well belief in a transcendent presence ministers to the longing to matter. This ministering doesn't show that transcenders have it wrong—but nor does it show that they have it right.

THE LONGING OF A COSMIC PETITIONER

"When I consider the short duration of my life, swallowed up in the eternity before and after, the little space that I occupy, and even that which I see, engulfed in the infinite immensity of spaces of which I know nothing and which know nothing of me, I am terrified, and am amazed that I am here rather than there, for there is no reason why here rather than there, why now rather than then."[5]

These are the words of a most extraordinary cosmic petitioner.

Blaise Pascal, a Frenchman born in 1623, was a polymath who made historical contributions to many fields—mathematics, physics, theology, philosophy—in addition to being one of the greatest literary stylists in history. The writer François-René de Chateaubriand called him an *effrayant génie*—a scary genius.

Still, his intellectual contributions might have been far greater. It was not only that Pascal died at the age of thirty-nine, after a lifetime of physical frailty that was exacerbated by the penances he inflicted on his body. It was also that his religiosity made him forsake his talents. "When I was a child, I spoke as a child, I understood as a child, I thought as a child; but when I became a man, I put away childish things," according to 1 Corinthians. Pascal put away his worldly genius as a childish thing.

Here is what he had achieved before then: proving as a small child and entirely on his own many of the theorems of Euclid; proving what is known in projective geometry as Pascal's theorem, also known as the hexagrammum mysticum theorem; discovering the basic laws of atmospheric pressure; inventing the first calculating machine, known as the Pascaline; and laying down the foundations of modern probability theory (in collaboration with another French mathematical mastermind, Pierre de Fermat), in answer to a question Pascal had been asked by the French gambler and nobleman Chevalier de Méré concerning how to split up the pot of winnings when a game is interrupted. The problem is now famously known as the problem of points.[6]

Such intellectual interests were set aside after Pascal underwent what is called his second conversion, which convinced him that there *was* a reason why here rather than there and now rather than then.

Sometimes my fellow atheists suggest that transcenders must not be very bright to fall for specious arguments for God's existence, most of which simply plug "God" into the most glaring gaps in our knowledge. But my fellow atheists are ignoring the role of the mattering instinct in spiritual life. And the life of Blaise Pascal is a stunning rebuke to the patronizing view that transcenders must be lacking in intelligence.

For a long time Pascal was a questioning cosmic petitioner, suffering in his doubt. His long years of terror came to an end only with the mystical experience that suffused him with the certainty that the infinite immensity of spaces knew him intimately. To have such a firsthand experience of being transcendently known is the essence of mysticism. Pascal wrote down impressionistic notes of his mystical experience on a scrap of paper, which he then had sewn inside a secret pocket lying close to his heart and which was discovered only after his death:

The year of grace 1654

Monday, 23 November, feast of St. Clement, pope and martyr, and others in the martyrology.

Vigil of St. Chrysogonus, martyr, and others.

From about half past ten at night until about half past midnight,

FIRE.

God of Abraham, God of Isaac, God of Jacob, not of the philosophers and of the learned. Certitude. Certitude. Feeling. Joy. Peace. GOD of Jesus Christ,

My GOD and your GOD. Your GOD will be my God.

Forgetfulness of the world and of everything, except GOD.

He is only found by the ways taught in the Gospel. Grandeur of the human soul. Righteous Father, the world has not known you, but I have known you.

Joy, joy, joy, tears of joy. I have departed from him.

They have forsaken me, the fount of living water.

My God, will you leave me? Let me not be separated from him forever. This is eternal life, that they know you, the one true God, and the one that you sent, Jesus Christ. Jesus Christ. Jesus Christ. I left him. I fled him, renounced, crucified.

Let me never be separated from him. He is only kept securely by the ways taught in the Gospel: Renunciation, total and sweet. Complete submission to Jesus Christ and to my director. Eternally in joy for a day's exercise on earth. May I not forget your words. Amen.[7]

After his night of revelatory incandescence, Pascal withdrew into the exclusivity of religious enthusiasm. He became a Jansenist, a form of Catholicism that had been condemned by Pope Innocent X as heretical. Jansenism stressed God's justice over God's mercy, holding that only the few are saved. Pascal devoted his eristic genius to fiercely arguing the side of the Jansenists against the Jesuits on whether grace requires conversion. The fierceness of his bodily mortifications increased with the fierceness of his rhetoric. He would not eat fruit, because its taste was too sensuous. He wore a cincture of nails that he drove into his flesh at the slightest thought of vanity. He is reported to have said, "Sickness is the natural state of Christians." His last coherent words were said to be "May God never abandon me."

"His great gifts were bestowed on the wrong person," writes Eric Temple Bell in barely veiled disgust, in his classic book, *Men of Mathematics*. Bell, himself a mathematician who had been born in Scotland though he lived most of his life in the US, gives off a strong whiff of the Scottish Enlightenment in the chapter he devotes to Pascal. He is at a loss to understand how someone so mathematically gifted could have flicked those gifts away as so much dust. Still, though Pascal allowed his mathematical talents to lie fallow for roughly a fifth of his short life, he provided enough material for Bell to devote an entire chapter to him. Not even Bell, disgusted as he might have been over Pascal's squandered potential, would dare suggest that the scary genius was not very bright.

For a cosmic petitioner like Blaise Pascal, there is either transcendent mattering or no mattering at all.

THE PSYCHOLOGY OF TRANSCENDERS

Karl Jaspers, an existentialist philosopher of the mid-twentieth century, was the first to observe that the major religious traditions still extant had their origins in roughly the same period, which lasted roughly from 800 to 200 BCE and which also saw the beginnings of Western philosophy. Jaspers christened this period the "Axial Age."[8]

The idea behind the christening was that humanity had made a critical turn, as if on an axis, so that the focus of attention had shifted, from the toil of scraping out a daily existence to reflections on what made that existence worth the effort. From the Far East of China and India, and westward to Persia and all around the Mediterranean, including east to the Judean Hills, and into Europe by way of the ancient Greeks, attention turned on its axis toward the kinds of self-reflective questions we continue to ask ourselves. Is there something I must do, something I must be, in order not to be as naught? The apex of this normative ferment was the sixth century BCE, which saw such thinkers as Confucius (c. 551–479 BCE), Laozi (Lao Tzu) (birth date debated but traditionally dated in the sixth century), Mahavira (Vardhamana) (c. 599–527 BCE), Siddhartha Gautama (Buddha) (c. 563–483 BCE), the Greek mystical philosopher Pythagoras (c. 570–495 BCE), and the Hebrew prophets Jeremiah (c. 650–570 BCE) and the Second Isaiah (Deutero-Isaiah).[9]

It's no coincidence that all the areas that participated in the Axial Age were highly organized and relatively stable—supporting coinage, a standing army, and a literate and scholarly class, as well as enjoying the highest contemporary caloric intake. As Bertolt Brecht put it, "Grub first, then ethics."[10] When the basic requirements for sustaining life are chancy—requirements for food, shelter, safety, and the like that we share with other creatures—then all thoughts about pursuing lives that matter are submerged. All attention is fixed on the biological drive to survive, for both ourselves and our kin. But as soon as we no longer have to think continuously about how we might live to see another dawn, we begin to reflect on what the struggle for existence is about, and the mattering instinct surfaces into consciousness.

The overwhelming response of the Axial Age was to turn people into transcenders, with some of the religions continuing to so powerfully respond to the mattering instinct that there is a throughline reaching from the Axial Age to today—with multiple modifications along the way. The Abrahamic monotheistic response, for example, underwent major transitions that gave us Judaism, Christianity, and Islam, which then underwent their own divisions. Christianity, for example, which represents the majority of transcenders (roughly 30 percent), experienced several historical splits: the Great Schism of 1054 that divided Christianity into the Roman Catholic Church in the West and the Eastern Orthodox Church in the East, primarily over issues of papal authority and theological differences; the Protestant Reformation of the sixteenth century, initiated by figures like Martin Luther and John Calvin, again over issues of papal authority, as well as accusations of mercenary corruptions, which split Protestants from Catholics, and further split Protestants into Lutherans and Calvinists; and the English Reformation of the sixteenth century, which led to the establishment of the Church of England when King Henry VIII broke away from the Roman Catholic Church over issues of marital annulment and papal authority. There were further Protestant splits over time, leading to the creation of new denominations, such as Baptists, Methodists, and Pentecostals, each with distinct beliefs and practices. Modifications have continued to come, so that, among Christians today, there are a staggering 45,000 denominations worldwide.[11] The throughline reaching from the Axial Age to now doesn't entail stasis in the religious life of humanity.

There was another response to the shift in attention of the Axial Age. It was secular rather than religious and is associated with ancient Greece and its philosophers. Ancient Greece had a religion, of course, featuring the lusty, unreliable gods and goddesses of Mount Olympus. But the philosophers ignored those gods in responding to the longing to matter. This was the beginning of secular moral philosophy, at least in the Western world, set forth in human rather than theological terms, with philosophers like Socrates, Plato, and Aristotle relying on reason in their search for the values that alone, they argued, make life worth living. But though the philosophers relied on human reason and not received religion for their view of what matters in living a life that matters—Plato going so far as to argue that a powerful tyrant who could get away with doing whatever he desired was not living a life any one of us should envy[12]—they too, like the religious thinkers of the Axial Age, were united in the search for the values by which we *Homo iustificans* could justify ourselves to ourselves.

For much of our history, the bulk of humankind have

been transcenders, with societies organized around religious institutions, and religious leaders holding significant power. You didn't inquire as to *why* someone was a transcender, since everybody was. The primary way of identifying oneself was given by one's religious affiliation. The secular approach inaugurated by the Greek philosophers was halted as religiosity overtook the world with its fusion of awe and intimacy. The great philosophers of this period were also religious thinkers. But following the great Christian-on-Christian religious wars of the sixteenth and seventeenth centuries, Western philosophers like John Locke took a critical look at religious excesses, deploring "enthusiasm"—from the Greek *enthousiasmos*, derived from *entheos*, meaning "having a god within." "The odd opinions and extravagant actions that men are led into by enthusiasm," wrote Locke, "provide a sufficient warning against it; but many men ignore the warning, and once they have started to think they are receiving immediate revelation—illumination without search, and certainty without proof or examination—it is hard to cure them of this. That is because their love of something extraordinary, the sense of ease and triumph they get from having an access to knowledge that is superior to the natural access that most people have, is soothing to their laziness, ignorance, and vanity. Reason is lost on them; they are above it, they think."[13] It sounds as if Locke had something like the mattering instinct in mind in explaining the appeal of religious enthusiasm.

The purely secular approach to moral philosophy that had been initiated in ancient Greece was taken up once again by Baruch Spinoza, born the same year as John Locke, 1632, though he died far sooner. Just as he was the first thinker of the modern age who refused a religious identification, so his

Ethics is the first book of the modern age to systematically work out a secular response to the longing to matter. Spinoza's magnum opus, a book so dangerous it could only be published after his death, in 1677, was universally denounced as the devil's work, but it was nonetheless read. The authorities made sure that it was read, since, to rise in both the academic and clerical ranks, candidates had to have their refutations of the heretic in place. So many anti-Spinoza tracts were published that a *Catalogus Scriptorium Anti-Spinozanorum* was printed in Leipzig in the eighteenth century. But some who confronted Spinoza's reasonings found them creditable and even inspiring. Responsibility for the European Enlightenment doesn't belong solely to Spinoza's influence, but he undoubtedly played a significant role, with many of the Enlightenment's leading lights, including Hegel and Goethe, acknowledging his influence on them. Goethe claimed that for years he never left the house without a copy of Spinoza's *Ethics* tucked in his pocket and christened Spinoza "our secular saint."

As there is a throughline from the Axial Age to the world's religions that still claim a majority of the world's population, so there is a throughline from the Axial Age to the secularism that has continued to grow since the Enlightenment. Countries where a significant majority of people identify as secular rather than religious include Sweden, Denmark, Norway, Japan, Vietnam, the Netherlands, France, and Estonia. In the United States, the group known as the "nones," meaning that they don't affiliate with any religion, is now the most rapidly expanding cohort, having grown from 2 percent in 1948 to 28 percent in 2024.[14]

I say all this about the secular worldview not to single it out as superior to a transcender's point of view. This book is about describing the differences represented on the mattering map the better to understand one another, not prescribing any one location over another. There are, in my opinion, all too many such prescriptions. But given the increasing expansion of the secular point of view, it now makes sense to ask, as it didn't in former religion-dominated eras, why some among us are transcenders. Is there some type of personality that corresponds to seeking mattering in cosmic terms? For in speaking of transcenders, I'm not speaking of those who simply check off the appropriate box on a questionnaire and dutifully go to the appropriate house of worship and perform other rituals as their family and community require for reasons of conventionality and convenience. I'm speaking of those who are cosmic petitioners, seeing their mattering as being either cosmic or nothing, and who are persuaded it is cosmic. Life would be far less worth living for them if they believed any differently. There's a difference between the performatively religious and transcenders.

The Murray-McClelland theory of personality, which sorts us by whether we most need affiliation and intimacy (N-Aff), achievement (N-Ach), or dominance and power (N-Pow), may offer some help in understanding socializers, heroic strivers, and competitors: We bring the motivational structure of our individual personality to the existential task that our mattering instinct demands of us. But what about transcenders? There's no evidence that seeking transcendent mattering corresponds to a particular type of motivational personality. Instead, among transcenders there are N-Affs, N-Achs, and N-Pows, and they bring their personality type to their choice of a mattering project. An N-Aff might find their project in communal work, perhaps becoming clergy and ministering to their flock. One evangelical Christian with whom I was once acquainted saw herself doing God's work as a psychiatric nurse "ministering to the bruised and the broken, which I suppose, in one way or another, we all are." An N-Ach, like Pascal, might devote themselves to theological exegesis or to the purification of their soul. An N-Ach might even turn their artistic project into an expression of their religiosity, as Johann Sebastian Bach did. Of the roughly one thousand pieces of music Bach produced, three quarters were written for worship, and all his compositions except his last, which was left unfinished, ended with the Latin words *Soli Deo Gloria*—"To God alone, the glory."

And then there are religious N-Pows, whose mattering projects are often devoted to overpowering those who disagree with them. The striving to overpower may take the form of disputations, whether written or oral. The creepiest onstage experience I've ever had was with a professional Christian apologist who stooped so low as to quote my husband to me, citing his words out of context, so that they meant exactly the opposite of what my husband had intended them to mean, but used by the apologist to convey to the audience that I was contradicting my spouse—which, truth be told, has been known to happen, though not in this case. Although this was creepy, it's nothing compared to the violence that can transpire when the personality of the N-Pow joins itself to religious conviction.

Perhaps these three types of religious personalities are also associated with different types of reasons that draw people to the continent of the transcenders, with N-Affs reveling in their sense of affiliation and intimacy with the divine presence they sense in the cosmos, as well as wanting to share the solace that they themselves feel in their faith with others, N-Achs craving an absolute standard of excellence and the validation of an absolute mattering adjudicator, and N-Pows wanting assurance that, being on the right side, they will triumph in the end. But this is all airy speculation, in the absence of sound empirical evidence. And in the end, perhaps no reason beyond the obvious one is needed. The great motivating force behind being a transcender is that nothing, short of lunacy, can so expansively fulfill the longing to matter as the sense of cosmic mattering.

INTOLERANCE

Transcenders are often accused by non-transcenders of intolerance, intent on foisting their own response to the mattering instinct on everyone. They might speak in the name of established religion, preaching to you that you need their version of a transcendent presence, even if you personally feel no such need—as in "You were made by God and for God, and until you understand that, life will never make sense," a statement made by Rick Warren, an evangelical Protestant pastor, who gave the invocation at President Obama's first presidential inauguration (though that wasn't the occasion for his making this statement). Or they might speak in more generally spiritual terms, rather than according to a doctrinal religion, but still laying claim to a view of what your life ought to be about—as in "The last end of man, the ultimate reason for human existence, is unitive knowledge of the divine Ground." This comes from the writer Aldous Huxley, perhaps most famous now for his dystopian novel *Brave New World*. But in the 1960s, he was something of a cultural icon, an exponent of what came to be called psychedelic mysticism.

For transcenders, whether conventionally religious or

SBNR, the Mattering Is Out There, in a metaphysically fortified cosmos in which we are all situated, whether we acknowledge it or not. How then could a transcender, believing their viewpoint to be backed up by nothing less than the cosmos itself, fail to believe that their own response to the mattering instinct ought to be everybody's response? The slide from *is* to *ought* seems irresistible. How could transcenders not regard inhabitants of other regions of the mattering map as tragically—perhaps even sinfully—mistaken? Intolerance seems entailed by their metaphysics and not to try to convince others can seem like unkindness.

Here are two points to consider regarding the intolerance of the transcender. The first involves a distinction. For some transcenders, the transcendent mattering is believed to fall on us all. Call such transcenders inclusionary. Pope Francis, for example, declared in 2013, during a homily in the chapel of the Domus Santa Marta residence in Vatican City, "The Lord has redeemed all of us, all of us, with the Blood of Christ. All of us: not just Catholics. Everyone! 'Father, even the atheists?' Even the atheists. Everyone!" The statement made headlines around the world, "Holy Father says even atheists can go to heaven!" The headlines were appropriate, since exclusionary transcenders—those who think inhabitants of other regions of the mattering map are damned—are more characteristic of Christianity. In fact, spokesmen for the Vatican felt called upon to qualify the pope's statement. "People who know the Catholic Church cannot be saved if they refuse to enter or remain in her," said Father Thomas Rosica.

Though inclusionary transcenders may believe that those who reject their metaphysics are tragically mistaken, the difference, in both attitude and action, between inclusionary and exclusionary transcenders is great, and when people think of the worst that religion can do—crusades, jihads, inquisitions, holy wars—they're thinking of exclusionary transcenders. (A hypothesis yet to be tested: There is a correlation between transcenders who are N-Pows and exclusionary religious viewpoints.)

The second point is that transcenders aren't the only ones who execute the slide from *is* to *ought*—that is, from "this is what most matters to me, if I'm to matter" to "this is what ought to matter to everyone, if they're to matter." Call this the urge to universalize. It's an urge that isn't restricted to the continent of the transcenders but is widespread all across the mattering map. I'll discuss the urge to universalize in chapter eight, Getting Mattering Right, but here are some universalizing declarations from non-transcenders to give you an idea of what I'm talking about.

> "You gotta have style. It helps you get down the stairs. It helps you get up in the morning. It's a way of life. Without it, you're nobody."
> —Diana Vreeland, editor in chief of *Vogue*[15]

> "The only way to achieve cosmic significance, in this otherwise small finite life, is to devote your life to knowing the cosmos itself. And this is exactly what science allows you." —Max Tegmark, cosmologist[16]

> "It is not the goal of grand alpinism to face peril but it is one of the tests one must undergo to deserve the joy of rising for an instant above the state of crawling grubs."
> —Lionel Terray, mountaineer[17]

"One doesn't want to read badly any more than live badly, since time will not relent. I don't know that we owe God or nature a death, but nature will collect anyway, and we certainly owe mediocrity nothing, whatever collectivity it purports to advance or at least represent."
—Harold Bloom, literary critic[18]

"It's a perfectly fine choice to never become a parent, but there is absolutely no chance that your life will be as full or meaningful, or that you will learn as many essential truths about existence, as you would if you had kids. Because when it comes down to it, there are certain truths about life that you literally cannot know until you've become a parent. The list of those truths could go on forever (no, it really could), but the core truth behind all of it is about what human life is about, how we relate to each other, how to care for each other, and the tiny moments that, in the end, are what we do all this other shit to support."
—Sarah Larson, mother of two, among other things[19]

"The effort to understand the universe is one of the very few things that lifts human life a little above the level of farce and gives it some of the grace of tragedy."
—Steven Weinberg, Nobel Prize–winning physicist[20]

"The greatest thing a human soul ever does in this world is to see something and tell what it saw in a plain way. To see clearly is poetry, prophesy, and religion, all in one."
—John Ruskin, art critic[21]

"If you've never risked everything, even your sanity, for the chance of merging yourself, body and soul, with another in romantic bliss, then I hate to say it, but you haven't lived."

—my best friend in my twenties, who has risked everything many times over now

"The purpose of life is to conjecture and prove."

—Paul Erdős, mathematician[22]

"We as human beings are unique in that we can ask questions of our grander environment. It's what makes us great. And societies that don't do that die."

—Margaret Geller, astrophysicist mapping the universe[23]

"Sex is one of the nine reasons for reincarnation. The other eight don't matter."

—Henry Miller, novelist, whose works, regarded as pornography, were banned in the US until 1961[24]

"There is no reason to be alive if you can't do a deadlift."

—Jón Páll Sigmarsson, strongman[25]

"It does not matter that only a few in each generation will grasp and achieve the full reality of man's proper stature—and that the rest will betray it. It is those few that move the world and give life its meaning—and it is those few that I have always sought to address. The rest are no concern of mine."

—Ayn Rand, novelist, founder of objectivism[26]

"Life's most persistent and urgent question is: What are you doing for others?"
—Martin Luther King Jr., pastor of the Ebenezer Baptist Church in Atlanta, Georgia, civil rights activist, Nobel Peace Prize laureate[27]

"Be a yardstick of quality. Some people aren't used to an environment where excellence is expected."
—Steve Jobs, tech designer[28]

"People who move through nature without closely observing it are just taking up space."
—birdwatcher I randomly met in Beech Forest, Provincetown, Massachusetts

"For the sommeliers, sensory scholars, wine makers, connoisseurs, and collectors I met, to taste better is to live better, and to know ourselves more deeply. And I saw that tasting better had to begin with the most complex edible of all: wine."
—Bianca Bosker, journalist[29]

"The satisfactions of manifesting oneself concretely in the world through manual competence have been known to make a man quiet and easy. They seem to relieve him of the felt need to offer chattering *interpretations* of himself to vindicate his worth. He can simply point: the building stands, the car now runs, the lights are on."
—Matthew B. Crawford, motorcycle mechanic and author[30]

"I teach you the superman, because humanity can only pursue one goal: the creation of a superior man of superior culture."   —Frederick Nietzsche, philosopher[31]

"We die. That may be the meaning of life. But we do language. That may be the measure of our lives."
—Toni Morrison, Nobel Prize–winning novelist[32]

As you can see, there's a strong correlation between what the universalizer does with their life, in accordance with their own talents and interests, and the content of their universalizing declaration. The cosmologist doesn't opine that without a sense of fashion, you're nobody, and the "parenting is meaning" mom doesn't maintain that you've got no reason to be alive if you can't do a deadlift. You don't have to ground your mattering on a metaphysically fortified view of reality to give in to the urge to universalize. The seed of intolerance is implanted in the faulty logic to which our longing to matter inclines us. We'll look at this logic and how it goes wrong in chapter eight, Getting Mattering Right.

THE AMBIGUITY OF TRANSCENDENCE

Transcendence and *transcendent* are slippery words which can come to the aid of sloppy inferences. I've been using them in their ontological sense—as carrying a claim about what exists. To make a claim about transcendence in this sense is to claim that the empirical world of space and time, the world that we study through science, doesn't exhaust all that there is. There is a transcendent realm of existence, spiritual in nature, that exists beyond space, time, and all the laws of nature. This is the ontological claim of the transcenders on which they ground their mattering.

But the words are also used to describe a kind of unusual experience and so are also used in a psychological sense. A feature of such experiences is the suspension of the incessant self-referentiality that typically accompanies our experience, no matter what else we are paying attention to. As was discussed in chapter two, self-referentiality is usually an aspect of our normal attention and closely connected with the explanation for why creatures evolved the adaptation of attention in the first place, which is to be able to respond to the changeable aspects of their surroundings that could help in their efforts to persist and flourish—*food!*—or hinder them in those same efforts—*fire! flooding! predator! pandemonium!* In our evolved human consciousness, self-referentiality functions so centrally that when it is interrupted, then so is our sense of time's passage. Lose track of yourself for some interval, and you lose track of time's passing. Being in the flow—so involved in an activity that you lose sense of yourself and of time's passage—is usually a positive experience. But we rarely "metaphysicalize" it—that is, see it as revelatory of a transempirical reality. And that's because, even as we lose track of ourselves when in the flow, we recognize that it's our own activity and agency that lie behind the experience and are not inclined to spread this subjectivity out onto reality.

But it's different when what is riveting our attention isn't connected with our own activity and agency—isn't connected with ourselves. Not connected with ourselves? Why then would we be so riveted? What has the power to concentrate our disinterested attention? There is only one such thing, and it is beauty. This is a point made by Plato, who in general saw little to admire in humans, but for our disinterested love of beauty. He regarded our capacity to be enchanted by beauty as perhaps our most redeeming trait.

Plato was right. Beauty has the power to disinterestedly stun us out of self-referentiality. We even call beautiful things and people *stunning*. It might be the beauty of one another, of art, of nature that stuns us out of our incessant self-referentiality and stills the psychological flow of time, creating the experience of transcendence. One acquaintance told me he experiences transcendence only during Mahler's Third Symphony, as conducted by Leonard Bernstein. It might even be a piece of intellectual work. Mathematics has the power, for those so inclined, to stun with beauty. But most commonly it's nature, putting on one of its sublime displays: a nighttime sky ablaze with stars; a snow-capped mountain ascending into the ethereal swirl; the sun setting over the ocean, the sky a liquid fire poured out over the molten glass of the sea. Stunned by beauty, we forget ourselves and fall headlong into timelessness.

This feeling of timelessness—the *tick tick tick* of our inner clock temporarily halted—is not the same as eternity, but it can feel within calling distance of eternity. And the silencing of the incessant *here I am, here I am, here I am* is not the same as merging one's very identity with infinitude, but it can feel within touching distance of infinitude. Experiences of beauty at their most sublime can blur the distinction between the two senses of *transcendent*, psychological and ontological. And when they do, when we overlay such experiences with ontic significance, we are apt to call these sublimest experiences mystical, revelatory, esoteric, sacred.

The writer Alan Lightman describes such an experience he had one night, returning to the remote island in Maine where he summers. "It was a moonless night, and quiet. The only sound I could hear was the soft churning of the engine of my boat. Far from the distracting lights of the mainland, the sky vibrated with stars. Taking a chance, I turned off my running lights, and it got even darker. Then I turned off my engine. I lay down in the boat and looked up. A very dark sky seen from the ocean is a mystical experience. After a few moments my world had dissolved into the star-littered sky. The boat disappeared. My body disappeared. . . . I felt connected not only to the stars but to all of nature, and to the entire cosmos. I felt a merging with something far larger than myself, a grand and eternal unity, a hint of something absolute. After a time, I sat up and started the engine. I had no idea how long I'd been lying there looking up."[33]

I don't know in what sense Lightman was using the word *mystical*, whether he was endowing it with ontic significance. Some among us—cosmic petitioners aching to answer the mattering instinct by way of transcendence—slip from the psychologically transcendent to the ontologically transcendent, while others, even if just as susceptible to the power of sublime beauty, do not. The divergence in reacting to these experiences of the sublime isn't due to cognitive infirmity, as is sometimes suggested by the more disputatious among my fellow non-transcenders. Nor is it due to moral infirmity, as is sometimes suggested by the more disputatious among transcenders. Rather, the divergence is best understood by reference to the longing to matter, and how, in interacting with all the factors that make us the individuals that we are, it emerges so radically varied among us, making some among us interpret these experiences in a way that answers to the longing to matter, and others content to value them as only the marvelous experiences that they are, rather than portals into otherworldly absolutes.

Though it's only in our species, characterized as we are by the mattering instinct, that experiences of beauty might come to be labeled mystical, we are nevertheless not the only species susceptible to beauty. And here I offer one of my own most transcendent experiences.

I had been hiking on the Cape of Good Hope, the rocky promontory in South Africa that reaches out into the Atlantic Ocean, not far from where it meets the Indian Ocean. The place is also known for its chacma baboons, who can be daringly obstreperous once they learn to associate humans with food. After several hours of hiking, high on a cliff and thinking myself alone, I suddenly noticed below, perched on the cliff, a cluster of five baboons staring out into the ocean in preternatural stillness. It was their rapt attention that drew my own attention to the sight, as if they were silently gesturing outward to the sea, where a rainbow was rising majestically out of the water. It was eerily beautiful, and the transfixed baboons seemed to think so too. In fact, it was sharing the sight with them, feeling that we might even be crossing the interspecies divide to experience the same awed reverence for nature, that pushed my own experience from the beautiful into the sublime.

Though I was no more apt than the baboons to overlay this experience with metaphysical significance, I'll remember its transcendence for as long as I have the power to remember.

TO MATTER MORE THAN OTHERS: COMPETITORS

Mattering competitors regard mattering as a zero-sum game. Their sense of mattering is intrinsically comparative. For them, mattering means mattering more than others. To the extent that they matter, others must matter less, and perceiving others to matter more than they is experienced as a violation. For them, mattering can't help but be adversarial; it's them against others. Competitors may see other *individuals* as rivals (individualist competitors) or other *groups* as rivals (group competitors). We'll consider the individualist competitors first.

Competitiveness is a personality trait that, like other such traits, exists on a spectrum. People at the low end are never inclined to compete, while at the high end, the hypercompetitive feel the need to strenuously compete in any context that allows for competition. To fall at the high end of competitiveness is not necessarily to be a mattering competitor. It's an empirical hypothesis whether those who are hypercompetitive are more inclined to be mattering competitors. Even an established correlation wouldn't determine the direction of the causality. Perhaps a person's hypercompetitiveness is the cause of their being a mattering competitor, with their tendency to see competitiveness in every context making it natural that they would see it in the context of mattering. Or perhaps it's the other way round. It's how they experience the mattering instinct as zero-sum that made them the hypercompetitive people that they are. Donald Trump appears to be such a person. In a rare moment of public self-reflection, explaining why, during the 2024 presidential campaign, he wasn't able to heed his advisors and focus on policies rather than on personal attacks, he confessed that he feels such overwhelming animosity toward anyone who opposes him that he can't refrain from belittling and insulting them even if it politically costs him.[34]

Contemporary psychologists have identified three strains of competitiveness. There is "competing to win" (CW), where the aim is "dominating and suppressing others." Such competitors need to crush their rivals. There is "competing to surpass" (CS), where the aim is to do better than others, to excel over them. And there is "competing to develop" (CD), where the aim is actualizing your own potential. CDs are essentially competing against themselves.[35]

You may find the wording here misleading, as I do—in particular, the conflation of "competing to win" with dominating and suppressing others. Almost all athletes—indeed almost all who engage in certain games, from basketball to poker to the *League of Legends* video game—are competing to win. That's the nature of many games.[36] And if a person's mattering project involves such a game, they are existentially committed to competing to win. Their game is no mere game. But this doesn't mean that their dominant aim is to crush others. "Competing to win" seems the wrong phrase for those whose competitiveness is the assertion of power over others. Perhaps they should be labeled CP, the *P* standing for *power*, or even CC, the second *C* standing for *crushing*. But to be consistent with the psychological literature, I'll stick to their labels.

Some athletes are clearly CWs. "When I fight someone I want to break his will. I want to take his manhood. I want to rip out his heart and show it to him." This from the boxer

Mike Tyson.[37] But then athletes in physical contact sports tend to be more aggressive, so here's a statement from the chess player Bobby Fischer. Asked in an interview when the greatest pleasure happens during a game of chess, he responded, "The greatest pleasure? When I break a man's ego."[38]

Many athletes seem to fit the less aggressive CS or CD category. Sergey Bubka, the Ukrainian pole vaulter, set the world record multiple times during his career in the 1980s and 1990s. His outdoor world record of 6.14 meters, set in 1994, stood for over two decades. Renaud Lavillenie, a French pole vaulter, was inspired by Bubka's achievements and aimed to surpass his legendary record. In 2014, he broke Bubka's indoor world record by clearing 6.16 meters at a meet in Donetsk, Ukraine—incidentally, Bubka's hometown. Bubka was present and congratulated Lavillenie warmly, commenting that records are made to be broken. Whatever Sergey Bubka was, he clearly wasn't a CW.

The basketball player Kobe Bryant made it clear he was a CD, coining the phrase "mamba mentality" to express his attitude toward competitiveness. "To sum up what mamba mentality is, it means to be able to constantly try to be the best version of yourself."[39] And again, "I never tried to prove anything to someone else. I wanted to prove something to myself."[40] And one more: "Each moment of my life I was dreaming of how great I could be and continued working hard. Each time I closed my eyes I could see me shining bright like a sun."[41] These are not only the words of a CD. They're the words of a heroic striver, and that's the continent on which Kobe Bryant belonged.

How do these three strains of competitiveness link up with being a mattering competitor? All of these professional competitors had mattering projects that committed them to winning, but that didn't necessarily make them people who regard mattering in zero-sum terms. Sergey Bubka clearly wasn't a mattering competitor. Nor was Kobe Bryant. Heroic strivers, like Bryant, are focused on their own excellence. They might compare themselves to others who surpass them, but not with the attitude that these others are diminishing their mattering, but rather to assess their own level of excellence, or perhaps learn from and be inspired by them. Again Kobe Bryant: "I would see something I liked in person or on film, go practice it immediately, practice it more the next day, and then go out and use it. By the time I reached the league, I had a short learning curve. I could see something, download it, and have it down pat."[42] Heroic strivers, unlike mattering competitors, don't experience the superiority of others as loss and pain. It doesn't diminish their sense of flourishing.

It can sometimes be difficult to distinguish between heroic strivers and mattering competitors. Just as heroic strivers, whose mattering project commits them to winning, can be misidentified as mattering competitors, mattering competitors can be misidentified as heroic strivers. I once heard a colleague remark about a celebrated scientist, "He's been happy in his life for only fifteen minutes, when he learned he'd won the Nobel Prize. Then he remembered that other people had them too." This comment lays bare the difference between a heroic striver and a person for whom mattering has to mean mattering *more*. It also lays bare the difficulties of being a mattering competitor. One can never rest on one's laurels, not even Nobel laurels. Or as a famous quote puts it, "It's not enough to win. Others must lose."

And there are more difficulties. Individualist competitors

are almost always looking either up, to those whose superior mattering makes them feel diminished, or down, to those who aren't worthy competitors and so are contemptuously dismissed. These options aren't conducive to feeling close with others, exposing mattering competitors to loneliness.[43] The one exception, at least for some individualist competitors, is family members, whom they regard as extensions of themselves and sometimes acolytes. This may not be altogether healthy for those family members and acolytes—which brings me to another of the downsides associated with individualist competitors, the difficulties of engaging with them. When the need to matter more than others is the response to the mattering instinct, it raises the likelihood of off-putting behavior that ranges from one-upmanship and being a sore loser to the more serious offenses of manipulating, lying, cheating, and crying fraud whenever one loses.

Psychologists have studied the correlation between competitiveness and both altruism and Machiavellianism. Altruism, as tested here, is the inclination to make decisions that benefit others when such decisions have no cost or benefit to oneself. This is a low bar. We're not talking about a Baba Amte level of altruism. An example would be letting a neighbor or guest use your Wi-Fi when theirs isn't working or letting somebody with whom you're walking share your ample umbrella during a downpour. People who lack altruism, on the other hand, see no reason to do anything that doesn't benefit them, though they may have learned to perform such actions to avoid negative social reactions. Machiavellianism, as the psychologists define it, is a personality trait characterized by manipulation, exploitation of others, deceit, and a focus on self-interest and personal gain. Psychologists place

Machiavellianism in the "Dark Triad" of personality traits, which also includes narcissism and psychopathy.

Researchers tested how the three strains of competitiveness were correlated with altruism and Machiavellianism. The altruism tested here is qualified as *hypothetical* because the scenarios are played out in the imagination, with no real-life consequences. It's typically measured by resource allocation games that have participants imagine being given some resource (money or points) and asked how they would divide this resource between themselves and one or more other parties. People who rate low on hypothetical altruism are unwilling, even with nothing at stake, to allocate in ways that wouldn't benefit them. This lowers the bar of altruism still further.

Participants are often asked to explain the reasoning behind their allocation decisions. These self-reports confirm that the motivations behind high hypothetical altruism are empathy, fairness, and acknowledging social norms.

Machiavellianism, on the other hand, is usually measured by the Machiavellianism Questionnaire, known as MACH IV, consisting of twenty statements with which the participant can rate their agreement, such as "It is wise to always flatter important people," "Never tell people the real reason you are doing something unless telling them would benefit you," and "All in all, it is better to be humble and honest, than to be important and dishonest."

The researchers found that being a CW, intent on crushing others, is negatively correlated with hypothetical altruism and positively correlated with Machiavellianism; being a CS, intent on surpassing others, was not statistically correlated with hypothetical altruism and was positively correlated with Machiavellianism; and being a CD, intent on self-development, was statistically correlated with neither hypothetical altruism nor Machiavellianism.[44]

What these results suggest is that being a CW is highly correlated with being a mattering competitor, prone to see others as existential adversaries. Why would you do anything that benefits them, even hypothetically? And why wouldn't you take advantage of them if you could get away with it? The CS, on the other hand, who places a high premium on winning, isn't as prone to see others as existential adversaries, as indicated by their being neither positively nor negatively correlated with hypothetical altruism, though their other-directed competitiveness inclines them to take advantage of others. It would take further testing to tease out how being a CS is correlated, if at all, with competitive mattering. The situation as regards the CD is the clearest of all. The CD's correlation with competitive mattering is null, because the CD is a heroic striver.

GROUP COMPETITIVENESS

Individualist competitors need to convince themselves of their superior mattering over other individuals. Group competitors, in contrast, base their mattering on belonging to a group they deem to matter over other groups.

One of the most revelatory statements of group competitive mattering I've encountered belonged to a five-year-old. The child was crying as she watched the Black family next door moving away. "Now," she said, "there is no one that we are better than."[45] At five years old, she was old enough to have imbibed the ambient group prejudice and young enough to be blunt about it.

Race, religion, gender, class, wealth, ethnicity, and nationality provide common ways of drawing lines of claimed superiority around a group, but there are others. The mattering group might be based on occupation—nobody matters as much as we scientists, as we artists, as we techies, as we business leaders, as we academics, as we political insiders do. The group might be based on a trait like attractiveness, fitness, social circle, political orientation, or cultural choice, such as being vegan or green. For some people, it's the family into which they were born. A person needn't possess a last name like Romanov, Grimaldi, or Mountbatten-Windsor to feel themselves born into majestic mattering. Some families possess a mattering mythology that makes them disdainful of anybody not so fortunate as to be related to them. The mythology might be based on one prominent family member, no matter how far removed, or on nothing at all.

People can have a notion of their group's superior mattering without turning it into their mattering project. The circumstances under which such notions get transformed into mattering projects often, though not always, involve rivalry with another group, especially when the other group appears to be making gains. Just as individualist competitors regard mattering as a zero-sum game among individuals, so group competitors regard mattering as a zero-sum game among groups. Any gains enjoyed by a rival group—those Blacks, those women, those gays, those Jews, those Asians, those immigrants—are *ipso facto* regarded as a loss for them. The possibility of mattering's being a positive sum among groups is as foreign to their viewpoint as the possibility of mattering's being a positive sum is to individualist competitors. And since group competitors, like individualist competitors, assume that others share their outlook, they assume that the gaining rival groups, on whom they had before looked down, are now looking down on them. For them, the mattering order has been turned on its head, which might prompt them to take up a mattering project devoted to putting the mattering order back to rights as they conceive it.

Unlike individualist competitors, group competitors don't regard other individuals as slotted into the binary of being either mattering rivals or not mattering. They're prepared to share their perceived superior mattering with those within the group. In this respect, they escape one of the significant downsides of being an individualist competitor, the loneliness of not being able to satisfy the core need for connectedness. They feel bonded with those in their group. This is especially true for those who have transformed their group competitiveness into their mattering project. They are tight with those who share their purpose of putting what they take to be the natural mattering order back to rights.

Their mattering projects can create severe problems for those outside their mattering group who are their targets—obviously, since creating problems for these outsiders is the purpose of their mattering projects, with tactics including trolling and harassment, restricting legal rights, and, in the worst cases, violence, deportation, ethnic cleansing, and genocide. Genocide was the mattering project to which the Nazis wholeheartedly committed themselves during World War II, to the point of allowing it to take precedence over strategic military considerations. The Nazis diverted crucial resources, including trains, fuel, and manpower, from the war effort to support the logistics of transporting Jews to extermination camps. This was particularly evident in the deportation of Jews from Hungary in 1944 even as the Soviet Army was advancing. Observations from individuals and documents of the time, such as the diary of Joseph Goebbels, indicate that Nazi leaders equated their success in exterminating Jews with their personal and ideological victories, regardless of the war situation.

That genocide can become the mattering project of people's lives, the means of convincing themselves that their lives are meaningful, is a brutal reminder to bracket the reverential attitude called forth by claims of subjective meaningfulness. Meaningfulness is a word that often gets imbued with suggestions of loftiness, morality, and even sanctity. Subjective meaningfulness is but a feeling, and despite its exalted tone, it can accommodate the worst of which we're capable. Those psychologists who research subjective feelings of meaningfulness, treating it as, in itself, the summum bonum, often let the sacralizing creep in. But that's a confusion, and we know that it's a confusion, because our mattering instinct makes us staunch realists. We judge that some people are getting mattering wrong, that their mattering projects are way off the mark, perhaps even immoral, no matter how exalted they feel about it, and we desperately don't want to be among them. We want to get our mattering right.

And that's what the next two chapters are about—about getting our mattering wrong or right.

CHAPTER 7

GETTING MATTERING WRONG

Some people struggle, as we saw that William James had struggled, to decide on a mattering project that, channeling the mattering instinct, can carry them forward.

I've known students who have been caught in this struggle, suspended in the stagnation of what the philosopher Walter Kaufmann called decidophobia—the mortal dread of making the decisions that give shape to one's life. Often multitalented, they are able to see the drawbacks of every mattering project to which they might possibly commit themselves. Often, they will go on to graduate studies, jumping through the hoops of getting a PhD, but only as a means of putting off the decision of where they will focus their energy and talents. And if the struggle goes on too long, then, like William James, they fall into misery, their creative life force so dissipated that almost every decision, no matter how insignificant, defeats them.

Is it the fear of failure that keeps them from choosing? All I can tell them is that not to choose is also to choose, and to choose badly. No one can foresee how things will turn out once you go forward in life. Yes, you might fail, as all of us might, and at any point. But not to go forward is to *guarantee* failure.

WHEN OUR MATTERING PROJECTS FAIL US

For others, it's entirely opposite. They have been given a passion that seems to deliver them from the burden of choice. They feel they were born to do this thing that they do and are prepared to give themselves entirely to it, unable to imagine an alternative life. Glenn Kurtz, a friend of mine, could tell you that this can be both a blessing and a curse.

Glenn's passion for music emerged when he was eight years old. Probably any instrument that fell into his hands would have inspired him, but a school of guitar had just opened up in his neighborhood on Long Island, and the guitar became Glenn's destiny. At first, he devoted himself to folk music and then to rock and then jazz. Unusually gifted, he was invited to play with Dizzy Gillespie on *The Merv Griffin Show* when he was just a teenager. At seventeen, he attended a solo performance by the great Andrés Segovia, and from then on it was classical guitar for him.

He recognized that classical guitar has its downsides. For one thing, the instrument, unlike the violin and cello, lacks an extensive repertoire. For another, there is no chance of being hired permanently by an orchestra, as there is for a violinist, violist, or cellist. But a passion is a passion, and Glenn was prepared to give his all to his.

He met with early success—admitted to the prestigious New England Conservatory of Music and winning competitions. After graduating, Glenn moved to Vienna, which offered more opportunities for solo performance. Music, as he told an interviewer, "is a very competitive business especially for something like classical guitar, which is a solo instrument and so it doesn't afford opportunities for an orchestra. They say you really have one career path—as a performer. And the thing that most classic guitarists tend to do, when they don't end up as performers, is play at weddings."[1]

That binary—concert soloist or wedding performer—was a harsh reality. After years of not getting where he had dreamed of getting, Glenn felt his hope and ambition draining away. He would not be the artist he had practiced day and night to be. And with that acknowledgment, his greatest love became his torment. He could barely abide listening to music, especially classical music. "When I quit, the underside of my practice, everything I didn't want, everything I dreaded, finally broke loose: the anger and bitterness and rage, the fear that I wasn't good enough, that without music I was nothing," as he wrote in his memoir, *Practicing: A Musician's Return to Music.*

Glenn overcame the crisis by giving up music and transforming himself into a writer and scholar, getting his PhD in German and comparative literature and publishing books. And once he made this transformation, then slowly he was able to find his way back to practicing the guitar, with his sense of mattering no longer entangled with it. He could approach music in the same way many of us approach pursuits that, not channeling our mattering instinct, aren't existentially charged. We may paint, play chess, rock climb, master the art of French cooking—the sheer pleasure of mastery motivating our efforts. The philosopher John Rawls formulated what he called the Aristotelian Principle: "Other things equal, human beings enjoy the exercise of their realized capacities (their innate or trained abilities), and this enjoyment increases the more the capacity is realized, or the greater its complexity."[2] Life would be a dreary affair without the Aristotelian Principle—if the only motive for mastery was mattering. Not all our efforts at excellence are charged with existential urgency—except for the most hypercompetitive of individualist competitors, who, to preserve their sense of mattering, must convince themselves they are doing better than everybody else at everything they do.

Eventually, Glenn transformed his relationship with music into a source of pleasure, if no longer a source of mattering—pleasure precisely because it was no longer a source of mattering. It took time for the transformation to take place, much as with a romance that ended in heartbreak. You may eventually remember what originally attracted you to the person who had once consumed you. You may even become good friends with them, distancing yourself from the pain you thought you would never outlive. That is what Glenn did with music. He became good friends with it.

The first requirement of a mattering project, the very reason that you embarked on it, is that it respond to your longing to matter sufficiently well as to quell the existential doubts that are inconsistent with your flourishing. A mattering project that doesn't mute the repetition of the mother of all mattering questions is a mattering project that is going wrong. When it becomes apparent that your project—once you locate it, which can be a task in itself—is more harming you than helping you, and that the disastrous ratio may continue indefinitely, it's time for a rethink. Emigration is difficult, no less on the mattering map than on the geographical map, and it takes a leap of courage and hope to relocate on either. The fact that our mattering projects, unlike our other projects, are ongoing, never reaching a natural conclusion—I'll complete the writing of this book, but I'll never complete the mattering project that has me writing this book—doesn't mean that we can't decide to conclude them. We can decide, as Glenn decided, to seek mattering elsewhere.

I recently wrote to Glenn, asking him to reflect on his life in terms of the idea of a mattering project. Here is his answer:

> I've thought about the question you're asking a great deal in the years since I wrote—or started to write—*Practicing*. The practice and performance of music had been the center of my life, certainly my mattering project as you define it, and then, when I quit, it was just absent. Now, so many years later, I play music only intermittently, and I listen to live or recorded music often but not continuously. Still, there's always, always music playing in my head. In that sense, music remains completely present for me. But it does not shape my life the way I think you're describing in the idea of a mattering project.
>
> I would say this: The process of writing *Practicing* made me a writer. Somehow, the ground shifted for me, and the commitment, the attentiveness, the ambition and irritability of pursuing music as a goal (longing for that ideal), transferred to writing. Maybe not transferred, but metamorphosed, because I feel a continuity now, even though, when I quit music, it certainly felt as if I had died. Or maybe, better, it felt as if my love had died. Writing *Practicing* taught me to love—that is, to

give myself to a life project—again. But it's not the same love. I bring my broken heart with me to writing. That love is older, wounded, more circumspect (in good and bad ways). I still mourn for music. But my love for writing is sustainable, while my love for music, apparently, was not. It could not survive the collapse of my ideal, whereas my ideal of writing collapses all the time, and still I keep going.[3]

To have a mattering project that keeps collapsing and yet keeps you going—your love for it sustaining itself, and so you, despite inevitable disappointments and frustrations along the way: This is a requirement of a satisfactory mattering project. As Aristotle pointed out, we aren't striving after happiness but rather something deeper, something that can sustain disappointments and frustrations as long as it quells our existential doubts. It's when our mattering project amplifies, rather than subdues, those doubts that the time has come to consider emigrating from your mattering region.

It's tricky to know the right moment to give up on a mattering project, especially if your mattering project came to you as a passion, making it seem like it chose you rather than that you chose it. You may think, If only I give it more time, things could turn around. You may remember the good times, the incomparable highs, as in a romantic relationship that you know you ought to quit but can't. You may fall victim to the fallacy of sunk costs: I've already sunk so much time and effort into this project that if I give it up now, it will all be for naught. But trying to recover sunk costs is fallacious, like crying over spilled milk, seriously so when it's your own flourishing that's at stake.

So what to do? There's obviously no one-size-fits-all answer to the question. It's a good idea with all serious problems to gain a wider perspective. And what can be more serious than the faltering of a project that's meant to channel your mattering instinct and give you the impetus to carry yourself into your future? Sometimes the widening comes from talking it over with others, whether they're trusted friends, experts in the field, or therapists.

It can also be useful to reflect on the fact that, even if your mattering project came to you as a passion, passions can, as Glenn Kurtz put it, metamorphose. In romantic love, a pernicious myth is that each of us has an "other half," the one and only person who can "complete us." Plato, strangely enough, seems to have originated the myth by creating it for a speech he had the comic poet Aristophanes deliver in the *Symposium*. Just as it hampers a person romantically to believe that there is some one person out there who alone can "complete you," so it can hamper us to believe there is only one project that can channel our longing to matter.

Another stumbling block: Sometimes people get it into their heads that there's one region of the mattering map that represents the highest pinnacle of human achievement. I've heard it claimed about art, literature, physics, music, mathematics, philosophy. Interestingly, the areas for which I've heard it claimed are also those about which there is general consensus that high achievement isn't simply a matter of self-discipline, drive, and grit but also requires an inborn brilliance that can't be acquired. You either have it or you don't. To have such a belief about an area and to be floundering in it brings grief. Would the griever believe me if I told them that their pinnacle premise is mistaken? Almost certainly not.

They must convince themselves of its falsity, though I have a few things to say in the next chapter that might help. But even if they continue to believe that this region that isn't promoting their well-being is where the highest specimens of humanity reside, do they also believe that only the highest specimens of humanity truly matter? Is their thinking as binary as the cosmic petitioner who believes it's either cosmic mattering or no mattering? Do they see the situation as their either standing on the pinnacle of humanity or not mattering? That's an assessment that calls for reexamination.

A few people with whom I've discussed mattering over the years have expressed the following dilemma: They have a mattering project they're pursuing that "answers to their soul," but the contemporary narrowing of mattering to power, wealth, and status leaves them feeling nevertheless that they don't matter. Again, this is a dilemma for which there seems no general answer, though what I have to say in the next chapter might offer some help. In some sense, people facing this dilemma are fortunate. It shows that they at least *have* a soul.

MATTERING ADJUDICATORS

The mattering region that Glenn Kurtz left when he gave up his musical mattering project is one that includes mattering adjudicators. The mattering adjudicators had given him a thumbs-up in getting into the elite conservatory, but once he graduated, he was getting a string of thumbs-down.

The gesture of thumbs-up or -down dates back to the Romans and their gladiatorial fights. After one gladiator had subdued another, the crowd of spectators voted with their thumbs as to whether the gladiator would be finished off or reprieved. The turn of a thumb was literally life and death. With mattering adjudicators, it can only feel like that.

Many regions of the mattering map feature mattering adjudicators. For socializers, their mattering adjudicators are other people. Depending on their region, it may be their romantic partner or their family or community members; if they're fame seekers, their matter adjudicator is everybody. A celebrity writer I know took offence at a party when she introduced herself by name to somebody, and he asked her what she did. "This conversation is over," she announced, turning on her heel and striding off, leaving the poor man bewildered. For transcenders, especially those of the exclusionist sort, the mattering adjudicator is their version of a transcendent presence. The story of Martin Luther presents a fascinating case study of what doubts regarding God's attitude toward oneself can wreak in a believer's psyche and, at least in Luther's particular case, in the history of Christendom. As a young man, Luther suffered acute episodes he called *Anfechtungen*—terror and despair at the thought that God would momentarily be judging him and finding him failing. How could one know that all one's piety would be judged adequate in the eyes of one's mattering adjudicator, aka God? Luther eventually found the cure for his *Anfechtungen* in his famous "justification by faith." We needn't worry about failing in our pious efforts, since nothing we do makes any difference. Our fate is predestined by God, and our salvation is manifest in the conviction of our salvation.

And then there are heroic strivers. Not all heroic strivers live in regions that include mattering adjudicators. Some compete in games, where the rankings are determined objectively, free of adjudicators. A professional poker player told me he knows his exact ranking, as determined by the Global Poker Index, which ranks players based on their performances in tournaments over the preceding three years. Its formula considers the buy-in amount, the number of entrants, the player's finishing position, and the age of the event (with more weight given to recent results). There's peace of mind in knowing exactly where you stand, he told me. Many sports are judged by the clock, dispensing with adjudicators. Ethical heroic strivers, such as Baba Amte, also aren't subjected to mattering adjudicators. Their acts of moral striving are confirmations in themselves.

But many heroic strivers are subject to adjudicators—the admissions officers, coaches, professors, supervisors, referees, editors, curators, connoisseurs, critics, bosses, talent agents, reviewers, etc., whose thumbs declare you a success or failure. They may determine whether you're even allowed to pursue your project at all. It would be interesting to test whether adjudicator-free heroic strivers experience more life satisfaction than those of us who are constantly subjected to their evaluations—mere mortals, as we constantly remind ourselves, who are so often mistaken.

And it's true that mattering adjudicators down through the ages have made colossal mistakes. In sports, the high jumper Dick Fosbury's unconventional technique was ridiculed by coaches and critics as the "Fosbury Flop," believed to have no chance of succeeding in competition. Fosbury won the gold medal at the 1968 Olympics using his innovative technique, which has since become standard. In the 1970s, Swedish tennis player Björn Borg's use of a two-handed backhand was unconventional and initially questioned by traditionalists. His success, including five consecutive Wimbledon titles, validated the technique—personally dear to me and now commonly used among professionals.

The arts supply so many examples of mistaken mattering adjudicators that it's hard to know which to choose as examples. The Beatles were originally turned down by Decca Records, whose spokesperson opined that "guitar groups are on the way out" and "the Beatles have no future in show business." In visual arts, we recall the annual French Salon, sponsored by the French government and the Academy of Fine Arts, which for centuries was touted as exhibiting the best of contemporary French art. A medal from the Salon was a guarantee of a successful artistic career, with winners granted commissions by the French government and sought out to do portraits both public and private. In 1863 none other than Édouard Manet had his painting *Luncheon on the Grass*—now celebrated as an early example of Impressionism—rejected by the show and displayed instead in the Salon des Refusés, organized by him and other artists, alongside pieces by other such "refusés" as Gustave Courbet, Paul Cézanne, and James McNeill Whistler.

Even the sciences, with the more objective standards of data and evidence imposed by mattering adjudicators, offer examples of people wrongfully dismissed. Ludwig Boltzmann, as we saw in chapter two, was one such person. So too was another citizen of the Austro-Hungarian empire, the physician Ignaz Semmelweis, the father of infection control. While working at the Vienna General Hospital in the mid-nineteenth century, Semmelweis noticed that women giving birth in the ward attended by doctors and medical students had a much higher rate of deadly puerperal fever (childbed fever) compared to those attended by midwives. The concept of a germ had not yet been formulated, and in its absence Semmelweis theorized that medical attendants, who often came to examine patients in the maternity ward straight from the autopsy room, were transferring some unknown "cadaverous particles." He advocated for handwashing and antiseptic procedures, setting up a large basin of chlorinated lime solution for attending physicians to use. And when doctors used it, there was a spectacular decrease in the number of dying mothers. But his ideas were vehemently rejected, and even ridiculed, by the majority of doctors. They clung, instead, to the miasma theory of disease, attributing the high rates of puerperal deaths to the "bad air" of cities, which not coincidentally were where doctors had taken over the delivery of babies, rather than the midwives who served in rural areas. It was an emotional issue, as much for the opposing doctors as for Semmelweis. The angry ridicule of his professional peers took a toll on his mental well-being. He became increasingly combative and irritable in defending his views. Eventually he displayed signs of severe distress and depression. He was lured to a mental asylum under the pretext of a consultation, only to be forcibly committed against his will. Only two weeks after his commitment, at the age of forty-seven, he died of septicemia, possibly from a wound on his hand that became infected.

Why were the doctors so lined up against Semmelweis, refusing to accept the evidence he had produced by having doctors wash their hands—evidence measured in women's lives saved? You would think such evidence would have mattered to the doctors. And that is the very point. It did matter, so very much that they refused to accept it, because accepting it would have meant that they themselves were the agents of death. Sometimes it's the mattering adjudicator's own mattering that's on the line, and when it is, things often don't go well for those they are adjudicating.

In this context, consider prejudice, including the soft prejudice of which people may be unaware as operating in themselves. When it's aspirants to their own mattering region against whom they hold the prejudice, they can be expected to tilt toward dismissing their aspirations. Intellectual, artistic, and athletic heroic strivers who were, for example, women, have historically had a harder time persuading the mattering adjudicators. The story of Trudy Ederle, the first woman to successfully swim the English Channel, which is presented in the movie *Young Woman and the Sea*, shows her male mattering adjudicators doing all they could to make sure she failed, as if their own athletic accomplishments would be diminished if a woman could replicate them.

It's interesting to observe the prejudice in those who most glorify reason. No greater advocate for the life of reason ever existed than Baruch Spinoza, who made every claim for reason that has ever been made. "Therefore, without intelligence, there is not rational life; and things are only good, in so far as they aid man in his enjoyment of the intellectual life, which is defined by intelligence. Contrariwise, whatsoever things hinder man's perfecting of his reason, and capability to enjoy the rational life, are alone called evil."[4] Spinoza tragically died at forty-four, his ailing lungs further damaged by the means he found to support himself—grinding lenses for optical instruments. He died before finishing his *Political Treatise*, but not before finishing the paragraph in which he excluded women from civic leadership, arguing:

If by nature women were equal to men, and were equally distinguished by force of character and ability, in which human power and therefore human right chiefly consist; surely among nations so many and different some would be found, where both sexes rule alike, and others, where men are ruled by women, and so brought up, that they can make less use of their abilities. And since this is nowhere the case, one may assert with perfect propriety, that women have not by nature equal right with men: but that they necessarily give way to men, and that thus it cannot happen, that both sexes should rule alike, much less that men should be ruled by women.

This, sadly, was Spinoza's last written paragraph.

A hundred years later, in the midst of the European Enlightenment that Spinoza's *Ethics* had seeded, philosophers who marched under the banner of reason continued to explicitly exclude women, as well as people of color. Here are some statements, first on race:

"I am apt to suspect the Negroes to be naturally inferior to the whites. There scarcely ever was a civilized nation of that complexion, nor even any individual eminent either in action or speculation."   —David Hume[5]

"The Negroes of Africa have by nature no feeling that rises above the trifling."   —Immanuel Kant[6]

"Africa . . . is no historical part of the World; it has no movement or development to exhibit."
—Georg Wilhelm Friedrich Hegel[7]

I throw in a bit of casual anti-Semitism from *le bon David* for good measure:

"Where any set of men, scattered over distant nations, maintain a close society or communication together, they acquire a similitude of manners, and have but little in common with the nations amongst whom they live. Thus the Jew in Europe, and the Armenians in the east, have a peculiar character; and the former are as much noted for fraud, as the latter for probity."[8]

And now some statements regarding women:

"The education of women should be relative to men. To please men, to be useful to them, to beget them, to be brought up by them, to be their companions, to make their lives agreeable and sweet—these are the duties of women at all times, and what they should be taught from their infancy."   —Jean-Jacques Rousseau[9]

"Laborious learning or painful pondering, even if a woman should greatly succeed in it, destroy the merits that are proper to her sex, because they make of her an object of cold admiration and weaken the charms with which she exercises her great power over the other sex."
                —Immanuel Kant[10]

"Women can, of course, be educated, but they are not made for the higher sciences, for philosophy, and for certain productions of art which require a universal element."   —Georg Wilhelm Friedrich Hegel[11]

"Women are directly fitted for acting as the nurses and teachers of our childhood by the very fact that they are themselves childish, frivolous, and short-sighted."
—Arthur Schopenhauer[12]

The prejudice of these philosophers presumably didn't consist in literal chauvinism for their own race and sex but from a failure of imagination. They knew of few women or Africans whose achievements impressed them. But for men of their intelligence, willing to see through so many of the questionable opinions of their day, it's surprising that they didn't attribute these observations about women and Africans to their historically contingent circumstances (child-rearing necessity in the case of women, geographic disadvantages in the case of Africa[13]), which, being contingent, shouldn't have been allowed to contaminate judgments of innate inferiority. Toward the end of the eighteenth century and beginning of the nineteenth, philosophers like John Stuart Mill and William Godwin did overcome such prejudices, at least as regards women, by just such explanations. But still the prejudices linger. It was only ten years ago that a prominent philosopher, only a few years older than I, confessed to me that for most of his life he had been convinced that women couldn't do philosophy at the highest level. This philosopher had the benefit, as Spinoza et al. had not, of knowing women philosophers—in fact, supervising their graduate studies—and yet his prejudice persisted. I can only hypothesize that there is a strong tendency to regard one's own mattering project to matter all the more for excluding certain groups of people. This tendency may be even more pronounced in those areas whose practitioners ascribe to the "innate brilliance" view of their area.

Research has found that those academic fields which most prioritize innate brilliance—philosophy, physics, math, and music composition—have the lowest numbers of women and people of color.[14]

The prejudices concerning both race and gender were, of course, far more widespread in the past. We can't begin to estimate how many heroic strivers weren't allowed to pursue mattering projects in the sciences, humanities, arts, technology, industry, politics, architecture, law, medicine, and sports, diminishing our collective achievements, not to speak of their individual lives. We of course can't name most of these people.

But I want to tell you about one such heroic striver, whose name and sobriquet we do in fact know: Scott Joplin, the musician dubbed "the King of Ragtime."

Ragtime music is an African American musical innovation that emerged in the 1890s. One of its defining features is its syncopated rhythm, where the melody plays off-beat notes against a march-like bass line. This gives ragtime its distinctive "ragged" feel. It evolved from earlier forms of African American music, including African rhythms and cakewalks, minstrel songs, work songs, spirituals, and folk tunes. Initially, it was regarded with a mix of curiosity and disdain by mainstream American culture. It was played in dance halls, saloons, vaudeville theaters, amusement parks, juke joints, and brothels, all of which contributed to its sketchy status. The syncopation and rhythmic intricacies of ragtime were perceived as both exciting and debasing by mainstream audiences, and the association with the African American community made it seem morally lax to many.

Ragtime's origins are associated with two cities in Missouri, Sedalia and St. Louis, where Joplin composed his most famous pieces. But to understand his life and the mattering project that consumed it, we have to look beyond ragtime to the wider world in which Joplin struggled as a heroic striver.

Scott Joplin was born just after the Civil War, in 1867 or 1868. His father had been enslaved on a North Carolina plantation. With emancipation, Giles Joplin migrated to Texarkana, on the border of Texas and Arkansas. Many freed slaves headed there, where they formed a community of mostly sharecropping families. The only valuable possessions Giles had to bring with him were the spirituals and work songs that had been sung in the fields and that continued to echo in his head. The Joplin household, which eventually included six children, was alive with music, with banjo and fiddling, singing and harmony filling their evenings.

Scott's mother, who had been born a free woman, cleaned houses for a living. She recognized her secondborn son's unusual responsiveness to music and bartered with the white ladies whose houses she cleaned, offering to work for free on days that they'd let the self-taught Scott practice on their piano. A local music teacher, Julius Weiss, employed by a wealthy family in the town, heard the boy playing and offered him free lessons. Weiss was a Jewish immigrant from Germany who had studied music at the University of Saxony. He instructed Joplin from the ages of eleven to sixteen, teaching him to sight read as well as instilling the principles of harmony and European musical forms, including classical music theory, composition, and opera. Joplin remembered Weiss throughout his life, often crediting him for giving him the foundations that he needed. Later, when Weiss had returned to Europe and was living in straitened circumstances, Joplin sent him continued financial support.

By sixteen, Joplin was singing in a vocal quartet around Texarkana, performing on the piano and the cornet, and giving lessons in the guitar and mandolin. The circumstances of his family, who had always lived at the ragged edge of poverty, became desperate when Giles abandoned them, and soon the baby-faced Scott took to the road to earn his living through music in the segregated world of Jim Crow that had succeeded the short-lived days of Reconstruction.

The expression *Jim Crow* derives from the world of vaudeville. A struggling white performer named Thomas Dartmouth Rice (1808–1860) revived his flagging career with a song-and-dance routine supposedly modeled after a buffoonish slave he named Jim Crow. Rice wasn't the first to don a wooly wig and darken his face with burnt cork and exaggerate his lips with white greasepaint, but it was his Jim Crow that became the most popular version. Audiences roared with laughter, and we might now wonder why. What was so hilarious about a white person darkening their face and pretending to be Black? Humor often involves loss of dignity, which is why so much of it relies on sex, scatology, or slapstick. Those who laughed at Jim Crow performances saw a loss of dignity in a performer presenting himself as Black. It's no accident that the laws that started to be drafted in 1870—a mere five years after the end of the Civil War—were dubbed "Jim Crow." After all, their intent was not only to segregate but to demean—to ensure that Blacks didn't get any ideas about mattering as much as white folks.

In 1893, when Joplin was about twenty-five, he traveled to Chicago and formed a ragtime band in which he arranged the music and played the cornet. The venue was a fair that was grandly entitled the World's Columbian Exposition, also known as the Chicago World's Fair, a celebration of the four hundredth anniversary of Columbus's arrival in America. It was a colossal event, meant to proclaim America's emergence as a world power. The costs had been largely assumed by the United States Congress, and President Grover Cleveland appointed the overseeing board. Women were excluded from the board and, after protesting and lobbying, were given a single pavilion, the Woman's Building, in which to make the case for women's contributions to their country.

Around the gleaming artificial lake that represented the ocean Columbus had crossed, Beaux-Arts buildings and statuary arose. The buildings were faced in white stucco, which yielded the fairgrounds its classic gleam as well as its alternative name, the White City.

The name was doubly apt. A pamphlet protesting the marginalizing of Black Americans, "The Reason Why the Colored American is Not in World's Columbian Exposition," had been put together by Black civil rights leaders, including Frederick Douglass and Ida B. Wells, the muckraking journalist who devoted her life to reporting on the lynchings of Black men on trumped-up charges of sexual violations of white women, for which reporting she was run out of Memphis in 1892.

In keeping with the ideals of civilization, the music performed in the exposition proper, within the gleaming white Court of Honor, were classical pieces played by the newly formed Chicago Symphony Orchestra. Another kind of music was to be heard on the Midway, which stood at some distance from the White City. A carnival atmosphere prevailed there, crowded with food stalls and rides, including the first Ferris wheel, which was the Chicago World's Fair's answer to the recently built Eiffel Tower.

People were displayed as well on the Midway, their designated positions determined by the principles of social Darwinism, a theory popularized by the English thinker Herbert Spencer. It was Spencer, and not Darwin, who coined the phrase "the survival of the fittest," which Spencer applied not only to individuals but to groups, implying that certain groups are more successful due to inherent biological factors. Social Darwinism offered, under the guise of a pseudoscientific explanation, a flawed justification for the kind of prejudice that had survived in the minds of even the European Enlightenment's foremost thinkers.

And it was social Darwinism that provided the educational portion on display among the Midway's rowdy entertainments. At the far end of the strip were the "least evolved" peoples of the world, including Native Americans and the Dahomeans of Africa. (The Dahomeans, also known as the Fon people, are an ethnic group from the Kingdom of Dahomey, which was located in what is present-day Benin in West Africa.) Next came those representing the "half-civilized"—for example, Middle Easterners and Pacific Islanders. And closest to the White City were the Japanese, Chinese, Irish, and Germans— almost there but not quite at the level of the Anglo-Saxons. The *Chicago Tribune* reported that "an opportunity was here afforded to the scientific mind to descend the spiral of evolution, tracing humanity in its highest phases down almost to its animalistic origins." It's easy to translate these observations of "the scientific mind" into the language of mattering.

Scott Joplin played his ragtime music just outside the Midway in the saloons, cafes, and brothels that lined the fair. And the ideals of civilization notwithstanding, the crowds loved Joplin's music. The exposure of Joplin's music to the hordes

Two Dahomeans on display at the World's Columbian Exposition

who visited the fair that year boosted the popularity of ragtime. The Chicago Symphony Orchestra eventually stopped holding its poorly attended concerts, while Joplin was almost as big a hit as Ferris's wheel ride.

A year after the fair, Joplin moved to Sedalia, Missouri, and began to publish his own compositions. He signed a contract with John Stillwell Stark, who had a shop in Sedalia selling musical instruments and who became Joplin's publisher. The contract stipulated that Joplin would receive a 1 percent royalty on all sales of his compositions, with a minimum sales price of twenty-five cents. Eventually, the popularity of his pieces earned him enough to support himself, and he quit performing in honkytonks. But Joplin disapproved of the way his pieces were played by others—too quickly, obscuring their underlying complexity. In the original sheet music, you can find a boxed note reading, "Do not play this piece fast. It is never right to play Ragtime fast," and signed "Composer."

Joplin was a bad manager of his finances, but what doomed him was his mattering project. It was as much sociological and political as musical. What Joplin meant to do with his life was take the music he was creating from out of the Black American experience and integrate it with the transcendent ideals of classical music, which he had first absorbed in his childhood piano lessons with Julius Weiss. His mattering project was to demonstrate, in the music he would create, how much each of these cultures could give to one another, and it was a project that was intimately bound up with the groundbreaking opera he would compose, *Treemonisha*.

Treemonisha wasn't Joplin's first opera. While living in St. Louis he had met Alfred Ernst, the director of the St. Louis Choral Symphony. Ernst praised Joplin in the *St. Louis Post-Dispatch* as "an extraordinary genius," with a deep knowledge of classical music, adding that while he appreciated the talent that made Joplin "the King of Ragtime," he looked forward to Joplin's turning his talents to more serious composition. Joplin needed only this encouragement to begin work on his first opera, *A Guest of Honor*. The plot involved the "shocking" invitation from President Theodore Roosevelt to Booker T. Washington—the educator, author, and orator—to join him and his family for dinner at the White House. Black Americans had, to be sure, been invited to the White House before. Frederick Douglass visited President Abraham Lincoln at the White House several times, most notably during the Civil War. But none had ever been invited for dinner. The event enraged some—segregation being the law of the land—while it exhilarated others.

Joplin filed for copyright for *A Guest of Honor* on February 16, 1903, but he didn't include a copy of the score. He formed the Scott Joplin Ragtime Opera Company to tour the opera. It was performed either in Missouri or Kansas; the record is unclear. But somebody associated with the company stole the box office receipts, and Joplin lacked the funds to pay a boarding house bill. Not only the costumes but the only copy of the opera score were confiscated.

It's painful to imagine what such a loss must have meant to the composer. Yet it didn't stop him. In the early years of the twentieth century, Joplin began work on *Treemonisha*. Set on a plantation outside Texarkana soon after the Civil War, the plot revolves around a young Black woman who becomes the leader of her community, helping to free them from the illiteracy and superstition that were, Joplin believed, the manacles still binding Black Americans after manumission. It's also noteworthy that in making the hero of his opera a young woman Joplin was an early feminist.

Treemonisha is a complicated work that includes an overture, a prelude to the third act, various recitatives, choruses, small ensemble pieces, several arias, and a ballet. It manages to fit into the classical European structure tributes to Black folk music—not only the syncopated rhythms of ragtime, but also the "field hollers," spirituals, fiddle tunes, revival hymns, and African step dances that Joplin had heard as a child, transmitted to him by his once-enslaved father. The blending of these folk elements into the sweep of grand opera was groundbreaking, as *The New York Times* described it in an obituary it belatedly granted to Joplin 102 years after his death.

Sometime between 1904 and 1907, Joplin arrived in New York City, determined to do right by *Treemonisha*, which he continued to perfect over the next four years. Now he put his energy into getting the opera heard or at least published. He took the score to all the music publishing businesses on Manhattan's Tin Pan Alley. He met only with rejection. Worse, he came to believe that a well-connected person who worked on Tin Pan Alley plagiarized the music. This person is reputed to be none other than Irving Berlin, who then worked as an editor at a music publishing house on Tin Pan Alley. Joplin reputedly submitted the score of *Treemonisha* directly to Berlin, who rejected it several months later. The following spring, in 1911, Berlin published "Alexander's Ragtime Band," which was Berlin's first major hit. It catapulted him to national fame and marked the beginning of his prolific and influential career in American music. Joplin complained to his friends that the song's musical verse was taken from the "Marching Onward" section of *Treemonisha*'s "A Real Slow Drag." According to the story, Joplin then altered that section, so that *he* wouldn't be accused of having plagiarized Berlin. Joplin's biographer, Edward Berlin (no relation to Irving Berlin), in his book *King of Ragtime: Scott Joplin and His Era*,[15] concludes that although Joplin no doubt believed he'd been plagiarized, the case against Irving Berlin is not clear-cut, since a creative person like Irving Berlin is sometimes not conscious of his sources. "Things" can just come to them, and it can feel the same whether they are originating it or vaguely remembering it. Still, it's heartbreaking to imagine how Joplin, consistently frustrated in his hopes for his magnum opus, must have felt in believing his opera so violated.

Joplin never found a publisher for *Treemonisha*, much less

backers who would mount a performance. Here was a society that still found something hilarious in white performers blackening their faces to act like buffoons. How could they wrap their heads around an opera—an *opera*—not only composed by a Black man but utilizing elements of Black music to speak to the contemporary climate of Jim Crow?

His resources almost entirely drained, Joplin produced a simplified piano-vocal score and paid for its publication. He sent a copy of the score to the *American Musician and Art Journal*, which wrote a glowing, full-page review calling it an "entirely new phase of musical art . . . and a thoroughly American opera." Encouraged by the review, Joplin set about trying to arrange a performance of the opera but again was unsuccessful. Over the next few years, he announced several full productions, but none materialized. He never witnessed a completely staged performance of his opera.

Scott Joplin was described by his contemporaries as serious, modest, and intensely quiet. He disliked small talk and rarely smiled, though if a topic caught his attention he could speak animatedly. He was generous with his time and prodigious musical knowledge, willing to instruct younger musicians, with whom he sometimes collaborated. He had perfect pitch, and once he'd learned musical notation, was able to compose without any musical instrument other than his voice, which was described as a fine baritone. He lived and breathed music.

In 1915 Joplin arranged and paid for a concert read-through of *Treemonisha* at the Lincoln Theatre in Harlem. There were no costumes, props, or orchestra. An ailing Joplin, his fingers palsied by the syphilis that would kill him, played the piano as the only accompaniment. The performance was a sad one and attracted no critical attention, and Joplin's resilience finally gave way to grief. Two years later, at forty-eight, he was dead, by then almost forgotten. His focus on his opera had prevented him from composing more ragtime pieces, and, in any case, interest in ragtime was waning, eclipsed by the rise of the genre to which it had given birth: jazz. He was buried without a marker in a pauper's grave with two others, a man and a teenage girl. The only score that remains of *Treemonisha* is the piano and vocal one that Joplin had paid for, not the one he'd scored for a full orchestra. Also known to be lost are his first opera, a symphony, a piano concerto, and a musical called *If.*

The 1970s saw a resurgence of interest in Joplin. The classical pianist Joshua Rifkin released an album of Joplin's ragtime pieces on the classical label Nonesuch Records. *Piano Rags* became the first album under the label to sell in the millions. Rifkin treated Joplin's music with respect, unleashing the pathos and the tenderness of the music. He followed all of the composer's directions, including his warning that "it is never right to play Ragtime fast." Harold Schonberg, then the classical music critic at *The New York Times*, wrote a Sunday feature article titled "Scholars, Get Busy on Scott Joplin!" Scholars did, and soon they were declaring Joplin a genius. He was finally getting the thumbs-up from the mattering adjudicators who had always snubbed him. His rag "The Entertainer" was featured in the 1972 film *The Sting*, starring Paul Newman and Robert Redford, and its recording reached number three on the Billboard chart. In 1974, the American Society of Composers, Authors, and Publishers paid for a bronze plaque to mark his grave.

Most importantly, considering Joplin's own heroic striving, *Treemonisha* finally received full productions. Morehouse

1867–1917; Scott Joplin; A pianist and ragtime master who wrote "The Entertainer" and the groundbreaking opera *Treemonisha*. Scott Joplin as described in his *New York Times* "Overlooked" obituary, printed on February 4, 2019.

College, aided by a Rockefeller grant and in collaboration with the Atlanta Symphony Orchestra, mounted an ambitious performance. Thomas J. Anderson, a visiting professor at the college, orchestrated the opera, reconstructing Joplin's intentions as best he could, with the Morehouse Glee Club singing and Morehouse students performing as the dancers. Harold Schonberg, who was there for the opening, reported that the "Real Slow Drag" that ends the opera "is amazing. Harmonically enchanting, full of the tensions of an entire race, rhythmically catching, it refuses to leave the mind. Talk about soul music! The audience tonight went out of its mind after hearing 'A Real Slow Drag.' There were yells, and great smiles of happiness, and curtain call after curtain call."[16]

Since its premiere, the opera has been performed all over the United States, with other composers offering their orchestration. In 1975, it opened on Broadway to critical and popular acclaim, and in 1976, it received a posthumous Pulitzer Prize.

In 2019, *The New York Times* published an obituary series titled "Overlooked," giving heroically striving women and people of color their belated obituaries, one of whom was Scott Joplin.

MORAL DEFECTS OF MATTERING PROJECTS

Even if a mattering project is serving a person's longing to matter reasonably well, their sense of flourishing chugging along in good order, they may nevertheless be wrong in pursuing it. Recall, for example, those intimacy socializers whose sense of mattering comes at the expense of others—love bombers, for example, or others who derive their mattering by depleting the mattering of those who have the misfortune of being in their lives, as friends or lovers, as children or parents, as neighbors or coworkers.

There's a word for when a person's own sense of mattering demands, as the very condition of being fulfilled, the diminished mattering of others; that word is *immoral*. It's immoral whether the diminishment is focused on those with whom the diminisher is personally connected, or, as it is for zero-sum group competitors, focused on a group.

The kind of soft prejudice I referred to in the last section, which can contaminate the adjudication of mattering adjudicators, is different from the hard prejudice a person may utilize to construct their mattering project, giving them their reason to live.

"The Jews are Satan's generals. The fucking Jews call the shots for all the mud people. They fucking control everything, the cops, the government, the media. It's all ZOG: the Zionist Occupational Government. ZOGs everywhere. And most whites have totally fallen for it. Most whites are too fucking blind to realize they're helping set up their own genocide."

The person whose words these are—or once were—is Frank Meeink. He is, of all my friends, the least likely. Having read so many books and research papers about those who derive their mattering from hating some targeted group, I wanted to meet such a person and discuss mattering with them. I wrote to many who were, or once had been, white supremacists, incels, or neo-Nazis, but Frank was the only one who responded. And from our first phone call, he astonished me. (I'll return to the phone call.)

I first learned of Frank from his astonishing memoir, *Autobiography of a Recovering Skinhead: The Frank Meeink Story As Told to Jody M. Roy*, though the most astonishing parts of Frank's story came after it was published in 2017. The words of Frank's I quoted come from the book, which sports a photo of Frank on its cover, face in profile so that you get the full image of the flaming swastika that used to adorn the left side of his neck.[17] His chest was tattooed with the image of Joseph Goebbels, the chief Nazi propagandist, and his knuckles spelled out S-K-I-N-H-E-A-D.

He'd grown up rough in South Philadelphia, exposed to violence not only in his school and on the streets but in his home, where he lived unprotected and in fear, with a drug-addicted mother and her brute of a second husband, who immediately declared Frank his enemy. "You lost the battle the minute I moved in. This is my house now. You're my prisoner of war." Frank was ten years old and had no idea what his stepfather had in mind but soon found out. He was beaten so often and so badly—his stepfather had been trained in boxing in the Navy—that there were times, walking home from school, when he tried to get hit by a car. His stepfather typically addressed him as *retard* and forbade Frank from even eating in his presence, telling Frank's mother that the sight of her "retarded" son ruined his appetite. Not once did Frank's mother defend him. When Frank was fourteen, his stepfather finally threw him out of the house. When Frank showed up at his father's bar, his father took one look at him and said, "Your mother chose dick over you."

Frank was in the eighth grade, and he started going to school in his father's neighborhood. This new school had few white kids, and Frank was routinely beaten up. But he didn't think of it as racial. He thought of the beatings as a gang thing. The Irish and the Italian gangs that Frank had known all his life acted the same. Most of his older relatives, including his father, had been proud gang members. Nevertheless, the brutality of this new situation was intense enough that he just stopped going to school.

It wasn't in the mean streets of Philly but in bucolic Lancaster, Pennsylvania—Amish country—where Frank learned to overcome the fear that had been a constant. The summer after he dropped out of school, he visited his aunt and uncle who had moved, together with their son Shawn, from Philly to Lancaster. Shawn was a bit older than Frank, and Frank had always looked up to him. In Philly, he had been a long-haired skateboarding dude just like Frank was. But Shawn had gone through a change. His room was decorated with two flags, a Confederate battle flag and a black swastika on a red background. And Shawn had shaved his head and wore the combat boots and thin suspenders of a skinhead. The vibes he gave were different, his eyes holding an intensity that impressed Frank as cool. It was the same thing with the skinhead friends Shawn introduced to Frank that summer—none of whom, by the way, were Amish. These neo-Nazi skinheads paid Frank respectful attention, "me being somebody who had actually done battle with the enemy of the white race."

> They knew what to do and say to snag the interest of a fourteen-year-old half-Irish, half-Italian kid from Philly whose real dad was an addict, whose stepdad was an asshole, whose mom was indifferent, whose school was a war zone, and whose only real desire was never to feel like a fucking victim again: they gave a shit about me. The Lancaster County white supremacists talked to me like they cared about what I thought and what I could become. Then they told me I had a destiny. They told me I could become a warrior. They told me all I had to do was look in the mirror and see the truth: I was white and that was all that mattered.

By the end of the summer, Frank had earned the red shoelaces in his combat boots, having shed blood. He was a fourteen-year-old neo-Nazi skinhead, ready to pursue his destiny. "For the first time in my life, I felt like I mattered."

Frank never returned to school. When he got back to Philadelphia, he organized his own violent neo-Nazi group. He describes himself as having been at the center of the rebirth of the neo-Nazi movement in Philadelphia. Frank had charisma and ambition, and his organized forays made even the

Ku Klux Klan nervous. Skinheads were giving the KKK a bad name, and they severed ties with his group. "Getting the boot from the Klan drove our egos over the edge. We were unstoppable after that."

They were so unstoppable that soon Frank had to escape Philly. He headed to the Midwest, where his efforts continued. He even managed, while living in Springfield, Illinois, to get his own neo-Nazi cable network television show, which he cheekily called *The Reich*. Instead of having boring older Aryan men, with their same old rants, his show appealed to younger people, with *SNL*-type skits.

Frank's considerable smarts and drive had made him a force within his brotherhood of the aggrieved. That drive was fueled by a mattering instinct so damaged that only brute power, in its most primitive form, could satisfy it. Or as Frank put it to me, "I was either The Shit or a piece of shit."

Frank's descriptions of the violence his sense of mattering required can be difficult to stomach. Often when he speaks, I find myself thinking of his victims and also thinking that many kids grow up in hideous circumstances, as Frank undoubtedly did, without becoming vicious. Yes, it's all complicated, how the longing to matter emerges in us, and yet I have to say that if Frank didn't now live his life by the remorse he feels, I could never consider him the friend I do.

Eventually, Frank ended up in jail. He'd kidnapped and tortured another teenager he believed was a despised SHARP—a Skinhead Against Racial Prejudice—and recorded it on a camcorder. He sold the camcorder but forgot to delete the recording, and it fell into the hands of the Springfield police. He'd committed a felony and was lucky to get only three years. Although only seventeen, he was incarcerated in an adult jail.

But his reputation had preceded him, and factions of the white supremacy movement in the prison immediately reached out to him. "At least I wasn't gonna get raped."

But the real support that Frank found while in prison came from two Black inmates. Like Frank, they were young, and also like Frank, they were athletes, channeling their energy into basketball and football. More importantly, all three were worried about whether their girlfriends would remain faithful to them while they were inside. They would read the letters their girlfriends had sent them aloud to one another, parsing the phrasing to try to extract some reassurance that the worst wasn't happening. "You don't get more human than a man whose heart's breaking and able to share with another man whose heart's breaking. That's all human." By the time Frank left prison he found that he just couldn't hate a person because of his skin color. He heard his former comrades spouting the same old stereotypes, and they sounded like idiots. However, Frank was still committed to hating Jews, if anything more than ever, since it was the thread that kept him connected to his old brotherhood of the aggrieved.

When Frank got out of prison his prospects were dismal. As an ex-felon and eighth-grade dropout, on parole for aggravated kidnapping and assault with a deadly weapon, sporting a huge swastika on his neck, Frank had trouble finding a job. "These ain't good people skills I was giving off in an interview," Frank told me. "What are people gonna say? Oh, he's got a big swastika on his neck. That looks like management. Yeah man, let's put him in management." He was desperate enough that he took a weekend job with a Jewish high-end antique dealer named (possibly) Keith in upscale Cherry Hill, New Jersey. "The guy was having a sale. He needed some muscle to move his merchandise," he told me. When it came time to be paid, Frank couldn't find the guy. Stands to reason, he thought. The Jew was going to jew him. He'd heard this phrase, *jewing*, since he was a little kid, his older relatives promising that he'd come to understand its meaning soon enough. "Then that bastard showed up and did something even worse than jewing me out of my pay: he blew the living freaking crap out of the one and only stereotype I still had to hold on to. He thanked me for my hard work, paid me a hundred bucks more than the wage he'd promised me, and asked if I wanted to come to work for him full-time."

Keith went on to have a huge impact on Frank, not only in dislodging the final bits of racist ideology from Frank's brain but also improving that brain's self-image. He'd object to Frank's habit of calling himself stupid. One day he almost lost his temper with Frank over it: "Listen hard to what I'm saying. Smart people can fake being dumb, but dumb people can't fake being smart. You just are smart. Get used to it."

The tone with which Frank still quotes these words, almost with awe, is an indication of the effect they had on him. The two of them had been sitting in Keith's truck, and Frank tells me that when he got out of the truck, he was in a daze. Were the words enough to wipe out the damage done in his early years? Of course not. Frank would be the first to tell you about the inner demons he constantly battles. But if ever anybody has set about transforming himself—from racist ideologue to anti-racist activist—it's Frank.

One thing he understands only too well is the appeal of extremism to those who have little else to make them feel they matter, which makes it counterproductive to belittle and humiliate them. "I marched as a skinhead a lot," he told me, "and people would throw stuff at us, bottles, snowballs, whatever. I never ducked a bottle or snowball and thought, 'Hmm, maybe I should change my beliefs here.' When people started to talk to me like I was a fellow human, it changed everything. We have to start talking. It's human beings being human beings among human beings."

A great deal of Frank's current mattering project, devoted to exposing and fighting the ideology that used to define him, has been premised on the importance of these mutually validating human encounters. He's arranged interventions between what he calls "wobbly" neo-Nazis—those who aren't yet diehards—and Holocaust survivors, so that these wobblies can engage with the victims of anti-Semitism as "human beings being human beings among human beings." He was a cofounder of Life After Hate, an organization established by former members of hate groups that works to help people leave extremist movements and support their rehabilitation through programs and support networks. And he used his love of sports to organize and coach a program called Harmony Through Hockey, associated with the Philadelphia Flyers, a team Frank had idolized as a Philly kid, to teach kids from disadvantaged backgrounds—Black, white, Asian—to play together on a team. Why hockey? I asked him. In addition to his love of the sport, "most disadvantaged kids have never been on the ice. So they all start out the same, namely falling on their butts. It's a great equalizer."

Another aspect of Frank's mattering project is more dangerous. It involves police brutality, specifically its connections to white nationalism, something Frank knows about from the years he spent among the Aryan brotherhood. He often heard its leaders exhorting young followers to clean up their act—or at least their look—and join police departments. *Grow your hair out and stop getting so many tattoos. Once you're cops, you're going to get as many mud people convicted of felonies as possible, so that they won't be able to vote. That's the democratic way.*

The first time Frank heard the message was in 1991, when he attended a meeting of the White Student Union at Temple University. He heard the same message repeated in many different settings, from celebrations of Hitler's birthday to Aryan fests. At least three people Frank had known back in the day are now in police departments. "And that's just from my limited experience. Imagine how many altogether there gotta be," he told me. In September of 2020, Frank testified in a House Congressional hearing on white supremacy infiltrating police departments, chaired by Maryland Representative Jamie Raskin. He named names, positions, departments.

Frank had often felt his life threatened, first when his stepfather unleashed the full repertoire of his naval boxing training on Frank's ten-year-old body, and later after he had quit the neo-Nazi movement, whose members don't look kindly on defectors. But the death threats that followed his sworn congressional testimony were of a different order of intimidation, and Frank had to go into hiding for two years. He got himself a rickety boat docked in an out-of-the-way marina. A boat is a great thing to have, in case you ever have to go into hiding, he told me. No address and, should it become necessary, you can escape over the water.

It's a big job Frank has taken on, trying to expose the power of racist ideology—the power it has to wreak havoc on those it deems inferior and also the power it has over those who embrace it as their mattering project. If you ask Frank what can detach them from their project, he'll answer: perspective. "People have to come out of themselves to begin to see what bullshit these ideologies are and why they can feel so right when they're so fucking wrong."

But as Frank's own story demonstrates, the work of gaining perspective is a task that not even someone with all the native talents that Frank possesses can do on his own. Frank needed a Keith to begin the job of gaining perspective and turning his destructive project into a constructive one. For someone whose core psychological longing to matter has gone so brutally unmet, anything and anyone that makes them feel better about themselves will be grabbed at with all their life force. You might as well tell a drowning person not to grab at a lifeline as to tell someone who has habitually felt worthless not to grab hold of a proposed ideology that binds them in a fellowship of aggrievement against a group they can blame. *These mud people, these immigrants, these women, these Jews! They are the ones who are meant to be the losers, not people like us! They're the ones who have taken what is rightfully ours!*

Frank is an unusual person, which is what Keith saw. Keith hadn't been kidding when he told Frank he'd better just get used to the fact of being smart. Frank is wickedly smart. But do people have to be smart—do they have to be in any way unusual—to earn the right to feel that they matter? That's not the way it is in good-enough families, whose job is to make every member, but most especially the kids, feel that they matter as much as anybody else in the family—no more and no less. The family presents the first model to a child of the world at large. And this message—that the child matters no more and no less than others—is a good one with which to face the trials of the greater world—not only for pragmatic reasons but also because it happens to be true. We none of us matter any more or less than any others. We are all equally deserving of attention. For all too many, life feels like being a kid raised in a not-good-enough family.

I don't want to minimize the complex challenges of parenthood, nor overstate the causal connection between how children are raised and their chances of living a flourishing life. Clearly there is causality, and some families all but doom their children to never seeing their way toward a flourishing future—although Frank's story of an exceedingly not-good-enough family is not only a story of the causality between family and flourishing but also of the limits of the causality. Frank, though he struggles, also flourishes. And in contrast to Frank, some people brought up in good-enough families will make a mess of their lives.

The general lesson I draw from Frank's story is that the most pragmatic, not to say moral, thing that we could do for society is create enough mattering to go around, providing for all what ought to have been the birthright of having been born. Frank could use help from all of us in pursuing the mattering project that he's taken on in his later life.

But I still haven't told you about that first phone conversation.

I could hear the laughter of young voices in the background, and I asked Frank whether this wasn't a good time for him. No, it's fine, he said. Yeah, they're my kids, but they're old enough that they don't need constant attention. "Thank Ha-Shem," he said with a little laugh, "I don't have little kids anymore."

Ha-Shem, a Hebrew word which means the Name, is the way observant Jews, the kind that I was raised to be but am no longer, refer to God.

Frank Meeink is now a practicing Jew. It's not just because of what Keith did in helping Frank turn his life around. Frank also discovered that his mother's maternal great-grandmother had been, of all things, Jewish. Given the matrilineal determinant of Jewish identity, this lineage makes Frank halachically (according to Jewish law) 100 percent Jewish. And this fact at first tickled Frank and then did something more, deep in the core of him. It's been incorporated into the mattering project with which he's tried to repair the damage he knows he's done.

I didn't ask him about his use of the term Ha-Shem in that first phone conversation, nor how he knew that I'd know what it meant, since, according to my severely limited sampling, four out of five secular Jews don't know what it means. He'd obviously done a bit of research about me before he agreed to take my call. But his use of the term made me all the more eager to meet him.

The man I meet is shorter and slighter than I'd pictured, his handsome face tracking the hardships he's gone through, which have included alcohol and substance abuse. The tattoos have been removed, only one little bit of discoloring remaining on the knuckles that had once spelled out S-K-I-N-H-E-A-D.

"Yeah," he tells me during that first meeting, "I found out through a beautiful gift from Ha-Shem that Jewishness is in my DNA." That "beautiful gift from Ha-Shem" had been delivered by way of 23AndMe. He'd taken the test after someone told him he "looked Jewish." "I think more Jewish than you," he tells me, laughing.

But the DNA is only a small part of how Frank has come to speak of Ha-Shem, which, by the way, he does a lot. He had used those two years that he'd been hiding out in his boat to study Judaism and to connect with those he now calls his rabbis.

Frank asked me once about my own Jewish faith and observance. We were in an Uber returning from the quirky marina where his waterlogged boat is still docked.

When I come clean to him about my lack of religious belief and observance, he gives me his lopsided grin and tells me that it's all okay, but he hopes I know I'm going to hell. (A joke. Frank doesn't believe in hell.)

Wait a minute, I say, grinning back. You of all people have got to believe in redemption.

"Yeah, you're right," he says. "Me of all people. I gotta believe in redemption even if it ends up killing me."

CHAPTER 8

GETTING MATTERING RIGHT

I first started thinking about the second law of thermodynamics when I was an undergraduate and studying physics. I was entranced by the elegance of Boltzmann's unraveling of the paradox of irreversibility. But what made my interest lifelong was the human dimension I sensed to be lurking in the physics.

When you've been mulling over a set of ideas for as long as I've been, it can seem like the ideas have become absorbed right down to the level of your cells. You might think such absorption would make them easier to express, but my experience has been otherwise. This book has taken me longer to write than any of my other books.

Sometimes people would question me.

Are you working on anything new?

Thank you for asking. I'm working on a book.

What's it about?

Mattering. I think that the longing to matter, which has us striving to prove ourselves deserving of all the attention we have to pay to ourselves just to pursue our lives, is the secret motive of almost everything we do and almost everything we're willing to endure. I think it's the most human, peculiar, and poignant thing about us. And the irony is that the very thing that we have in common is the very thing that most baffles and divides us.

So then you're going to tell us what really matters?

That this was the most frequent response always took me aback. Was it an indication of what people would expect from a book about mattering?

To say what is the thing that most matters in living a life that matters is tantamount to revealing the meaning of life. Is that what I would be expected to deliver in a book about mattering?

If you've gotten this far in the book, then you know that oracularly revealing the meaning of life is not what I've been up to—at least not yet. Instead, I've been intent on explicating how we came to be what we are, creatures of matter who long to matter, and how this longing implicates both the most fundamental law of the science of matter, the law of entropy, and the biological imperative to resist it. Our most human longing, often expressed in the denial that we are mere creatures of matter, is the result of how a creature with our evolved capacity for self-reflection experiences the physical laws that have shaped it. This is what engenders our definitive longing that has us striving to live in a way that justifies, at least in our own case—which is of course the case that most matters to each of us—what biology dictates. This is the extra burden that we take on for ourselves in being human.

I've also been intent on showing the multitude of ways with which we respond to the mattering instinct, as manifested in the vastness of the mattering map, a testament to the human creativity aroused by our longing, and I've identified the four mattering strategies of transcending, socializing, heroic striving, and competing. The application of these strategies, according to such individually variable factors as temperament, talent, interests, passions, influences, and sheer random accidents, results in the mattering projects that propel us into our future. These are the projects that, together with our need for connectedness, go into our assessments of how well our lives are going. And I've looked at the ways in which mattering projects can go seriously wrong, for reasons both personal—they are not conducing to the person's own flourishing—and moral—they aim for the diminished flourishing of targeted others, whether these others are intimates known to the person or whole groups of people.

I hope that this way of looking at our shared motivation, together with the multitude of ways in which the motivation is expressed among us, may provide insight into yourself and others, particularly those who seem most baffling, annoying, and even appalling. We have all been through tough times recently in our world, and as often happens in tough times, instead of turning toward each other, we do the opposite, the divisions on the mattering map demarcating regions of hostility. For me, the framework presented in this book has helped me to keep in mind, even in moments of antipathy, the longing to matter that lives in all others. This is not to excuse everybody, but to better understand them—an antidote against animus.

It is one thing to assert that a mattering project can go wrong, even morally wrong. But it is quite another to say which mattering project is the right one, the one that enshrines the objective meaning of life. In other words, I haven't yet said anything that addresses what people might guess is the point of this book.

But this is the last chapter, and it's entitled Getting Mattering Right. Is this where I yield to the urge to universalize, proclaim my own mattering region as the one that truly matters, and elevate my own mattering project into the very meaning of life? If so, I would follow in the footsteps of many philosophers who extoll the life of contemplative reason as the highest goal. Aristotle was so convinced that contemplative reason is what matters above all else that when it came to describing the unmoved mover, he argued that not only does its existence consist in contemplative reason, but the object of its contemplation must itself be what matters above all else, namely itself. This sounds like the ultimate exercise in recursive mentalizing: God perpetually contemplates God who perpetually contemplates God who perpetually contemplates God . . . *ad infinitum.*

Among the philosophers who universalize and moralize the life of reason is Baruch Spinoza. I've already quoted these words once before, but I'll quote them again: "Therefore without intelligence there is not rational life: and things are only good, in so far as they aid man in his enjoyment of the intellectual life, which is defined by intelligence. Contrariwise, whatsoever things hinder man's perfecting of his reason, and capability to enjoy the rational life, are alone called evil."

There you have it, both the universalizing and the moralizing, in the words of my most beloved of all philosophers, and it once made perfect sense to me. To understand things in the widest sense possible, and so approach ever closer to the best perspective in which to view both yourself and others in a way that might guide your behavior: Isn't this what we all ought to do, what we ought to spend a lifetime doing, since a lifetime is what, at the least, it takes? Shouldn't this constitute the mattering project of us all?

The answer is no. The first requirement of a satisfactory mattering project is that it respond to the individuality of the person whose project it is so as to propel them productively into their future. The result of not finding one's way to such a project is the kind of psychological catastrophe that had the young William James contemplating suicide for months on end and that had his sister Alice greeting the news of a fatal disease with relief. Your mattering project is meant to increase your zest for life, not diminish it, and that inevitably depends on your temperament, talents, interests, passions, and influences. Spinoza's rationalist mattering project, as laid out in his *Ethics*, gave me the boost I had needed to reject the ill-fitting mattering project that my own background had chosen for me. I wrote in a previous book about hearing of Spinoza for the first time at the age of fourteen while I was attending an ultra-Orthodox all-girls high school, and how I responded to it.[1] But Spinoza's approach to life would be anything but invigorating to many others. That's the way it is with universalizing declarations about mattering projects. Which statements you find most stirring is an indication of who you are and want to be. Not only are we different, but we want to be different.

And the world needs us in all our differences. Save me from the impoverished world in which there are no people whose mattering project is playing the drums, or running a successful discount plumbing supply business, or trying to reconcile quantum mechanics with relativity theory, or creating new recipes, or doing all the good for others they possibly can, or analyzing the poetry of Paul Simon's lyrics, or raising joyful, flourishing children, or designing public art installations, or performing the gymnastic feat of the triple-double in floor exercise and the double-double dismount off the balance beam. Spinoza's universalizing now strikes me as just as wrong, and even offensive, as when a transcender preaches that my life will never make sense to me unless I accept their version of a transcendent presence and shape my life accordingly. I'm glad you've found something that appeases your longing to matter, I want to tell them. Now leave me to my own devices in appeasing my own.

The differences among us are such that there are likely always to be transcenders, socializers, heroic strivers, and competitors, with these four types each further expressing themselves in a multitude of ways, so that even those who share the same continent may clash with one another on the necessarily fraught question of how to live a life that matters. The paramount question then is: How do we live together without either wanting to throttle each other or pretending that we are all alike?

THE FLAW IN THE LOGIC OF THE URGE TO UNIVERSALIZE

It's hard to resist the logic underlying the urge to universalize, since it seems to derive from the mattering instinct itself, which has us longing to convince ourselves that we truly and objectively matter. We easily slip into thinking that if our mattering project is indeed grounded on what truly and objectively matters, then it ought to be the grounding of everybody's mattering project. Your stubborn insistence on claiming to live a meaningful life in violation of what *I* take to be necessary for *my* meaningful life can't fail to offend me. In fact, your way of life, so different from mine, itself seems to refute my claim to objectively matter, and so I must devalue and dismiss your attempts to validate your mattering. If you've got it right, then I must have it wrong—the very last thing I want to think. I therefore conclude that you must have it wrong. Intolerance blooms in the soil of our faulty logic.

Where then does the logic go wrong? Its fallacy doesn't lie in its universalizing. To claim objective grounds is necessarily to universalize. Rather the fallacy lies at the *level* at which the logic universalizes. We must locate the level that is at once restrictive enough to objectively distinguish between better and worse ways to satisfy the longing to matter but also expansive enough to accommodate us in all our recalcitrant diversity.

Transcenders seem to have the clear advantage here, at least so far as satisfying the requirement of objectivity. If they're right about their particular version of a metaphysically enhanced reality—a rather large *if*—then it's a reality that we all inhabit, whether we know it or not, and therefore it ought to be on the basis of its objective reality that we seek our objective mattering.

There are, ironically, many versions of metaphysically enhanced realities, which is why transcenders often clash violently with one another. But even given this variety, not all of us are drawn to any one of them in a way that answers, in us, to the longing to matter. Perhaps we are adherents of what philosophers call naturalism, as opposed to supernaturalism, disbelieving in any purely spiritual being that transcends the spatio-temporal realm. Perhaps it's not only because we are skeptical of any of the claims of ontological transcendence, whether religious or spiritual, whether inclusionary or exclusionary. This skepticism was expressed by Bertrand Russell, an atheist, when he was asked what he would say, if, after he died, he discovered that God actually exists. "I will say: I'm terribly sorry, but you didn't give us sufficient evidence." Skepticism may be an aspect of our naturalism, but there is also something else, more positive, a feeling that the ancient Greeks called *thaumazein*: ontological awe. While for some it enhances their life to believe that the cosmos is ultimately inexplicable and can be appreciated only through mysticism and mute wonder, for others it's more awe-inspiring to believe that the cosmos is intelligible, and that our human minds can ultimately explain it.

For devotees of naturalism, the laws of nature are a thing of beauty. The sheer elegance with which these laws subsume a seeming chaos of widely divergent phenomena under their precision can induce a deeply aesthetic sense of reverence, which Einstein described as a "cosmic religious feeling," that arises from contemplating not any transcendent presence—he was firm on this—but rather the order and harmony of the thoroughly natural cosmos. It's a reverence that generates the hope that, as science goes ever deeper into understanding the cosmos, finally the most fundamental and powerful laws will be beheld, laws that explain, as the physicist Stephen Hawking put it, the *fire in the equations*, by which he meant the capacity to explain, at least in principle, not only all phenomena but also why it must be *these* laws, rather than any others, and why it must be *this* cosmos, rather than nothing at all.[2] This is the dream of the "Theory of Everything," and *everything* means everything. We, too, with our vast complexity, which yields the rich diversity that has us dreaming so differently from one another in shaping our lives, must be included in the Theory of Everything—we creatures whose very dreaming can be explained by the laws of nature that have formed us.

It's a beautiful dream for those of us who dream it, a dream that enhances our delight in living in this cosmos, just as feeling purposely created by a transcendent presence enhances the life of a transcender. For those of us inclined toward naturalism, the dream of a Theory of Everything inspires our sense of transcendence—a transcendence *naturalized*.

I wouldn't dream of foisting this dream on those disinclined to dream it. But likewise I wish that the transcenders who dream their own version of transcendence might refrain from foisting their dream on me. We are temperamentally different in our dreaming and should accept our difference with equanimity and perhaps even delight, enjoying the range of creativity with which we confront the longing that makes us human.

BEYOND THE MATTERING MAP

If we're to agree on some objective standards of what it is to lead a good life, then we must find the right level of universalizing—restrictive enough to distinguish between better and worse ways of meeting the longing to matter but expansive enough to accommodate us in all our diversity, which means leaving out appeals to any visions of a metaphysically enhanced reality or any secular but nevertheless exclusionary universalizing declarations, such as those I presented in chapter six.

Can the advantage of the transcenders, in being able to

appeal to reality—that is, their version of a metaphysically enhanced reality—be shared by those of us who can appeal only to the natural cosmos? I think so.

I suggest that the scientific law that occupies "the supreme position among the laws of Nature" can provide the objective grounds for distinguishing between better and worse ways because, like it or not, we all inhabit a reality governed by the law of entropy. That law is as objectively verified as it gets. Implicated in the story of how we came to be the long-ing, striving, tribally divided creatures that we are, the law of entropy can provide objective grounds for distinguishing between better and worse ways of pursuing meaningful lives.

It's not that the law of entropy *dictates* the normative choices that we should make in responding to our mattering instinct. The laws of nature, culminating in the self-reflective brains we have, may have shaped us into the values-seeking creatures that we are, determined to justify ourselves to our-selves, but they can't decide between the conflicting values that range across the mattering map that we *Homo iustificans* inhabit in our diversity. If free will exists anywhere, then it is here, in this decision of how to respond to the longing to matter, the values we embrace in deciding what matters in our creating for ourselves a life we can regard as mattering. No law of nature can dictate our choice—no *is* can entail an *ought*—but a law of nature can suggest a criterion for judging between a multiplicity of bad choices and better ones.

If we are to live together with recognition of the dignity of human life in all its incommensurable meaning-seeking forms, then we need to find an objective standard that we all can accept to distinguish between better and worse ways of responding to the mattering instinct. A person's overall effect on entropy provides such an objective standard. A life well-lived is a life that, while pursuing mattering in a way that accords with an individual's temperament, talents, and interests, joins forces with life in its resistance to entropy.

Life is a ceaseless struggle against entropy. Consciousness, knowledge, reflection, beauty, love, compassion, forgiveness, tolerance, grace, creativity, happiness: They are states of great order that must be wrested, with the expenditure of energy, from the entropic transformation from within.

There are people who, in responding to the mattering instinct, ally themselves with the descent into entropy, increasing the chaos of our world, provoking conflicts and confusion, discontent and despoliation, disease, disaster, and death. They might do this on a grand historical scale—approaching a Hitler, a Stalin, a Pol Pot, a Putin—or on a more local scale, increasing entropy in their immediate proximity, sometimes among the people who are closest to them: their families, friends, lovers, colleagues, and community members. However they do it, they quit the world leaving behind more entropy than there would otherwise have been—disorder and desolation of the planet, disorder and desolation of lives.

At the other end of the spectrum, there are people who ally themselves with the counter-entropic struggle that is life's own struggle, increasing the spread of flourishing, knowledge, love, joyfulness, peace, kindness, comity, beauty—all of which must be hard-won against the dissipation and dissolution that is entailed in the direction of time. The best of our mattering projects are counter-entropic. Everything worth living for must be hard-won local reprieves from the law of entropy.

Though given our inherent diversity, there can be no region of the mattering map that is right for all of us, no one mattering project enshrined as the meaning of life, that doesn't mean that there's no way to judge how well we are living our lives. People's effects on entropy provide the best overarching means I know to assess their lives.

Two sages, from different ethical traditions, had much the same idea.

The first is Hillel the Elder, the Jewish sage who was active from the end of the first century BCE and into the beginning of the first century CE. Born in Babylonia, he moved to Jerusalem to study, becoming one of the scholars, known as the *tannaim*, responsible for writing down the Oral Law recorded in the Mishnah, which became part of the Talmud. His liberal and humanistic interpretative approach contrasts with the more rigid and legalistic approach of his contemporary Shammai, and the two approaches came to be known as the Schools of Hillel and Shammai.

Hillel wrote: "If I am not for myself, then who will be for me? But if I'm only for myself, then what am I? And if not now, when?"

Updating the sage's words with the scientific knowledge gained in the millennia since he lived, we might elaborate his maxims like this:

Since continued life demands continual counter-entropic resistance, my self-mattering is baked into my identity. And yet my capacity for self-reflection compels me to justify my self-mattering by pursuing a mattering project, of which the best choices are as expansively counter-entropic as possible, both for me—since if I'm not for myself, then who will be for me?—and for the world beyond me—since if I'm only for myself, then what am I? And since the passage of time must necessarily increase entropy, then if not now, when?

The second sage is Rumi, the thirteenth-century Islamic scholar, poet, and Sufi mystic. Born in what is now Afghanistan, at the edge of the Persian Empire, Rumi found the people among whom he lived to be spiritually lethargic and choreographed a careful set of motions to awaken the best within them, thus founding the Order of the Whirling Dervishes.

Rumi wrote: "Let the beauty we love be what we do. There are hundreds of ways to kneel and kiss the ground."

ENOUGH MATTERING TO GO AROUND

My husband and I were in a hotel dining room having breakfast when a strange noise interrupted us. Nearby sat a young mother with her two sons. One child was about six, a lively child, full of commentary. It was a treat for him to be staying at a hotel, ordering his breakfast by himself, sounding out the words on the menu, his mother beaming her encouragement. *Sausage* presented a challenge.

The other son was perched in a high chair set up close beside the mother, emitting grunts and squeals, a boy with many disabilities. By his size I judged him to be about four, but it was hard to say. It was his grunts that had interrupted my husband's and my conversation.

The mother was too absorbed in her attention to each of her sons to notice how closely she was now being watched. The child in the high chair required so much from her. She was feeding him, repeatedly touching him, stroking his cheek, his hair, whispering in his ear, returning him to a more comfortable position when he helplessly slipped down in his seat. And all the while she was also attending to her other child, with his many observations and questions, responding to the ripples of excitement that he gave off, laughing along with him, delighting in his delight in a family vacation. Could he swim in the hotel's indoor pool? Could he ride up and down on the elevator all by himself? There was an abundance of grace and beauty in how the mother distributed her attention between her two sons.

On our way out, I stopped to tell her how much I admired her mothering. She asked if we could hug. Her husband was upstairs in a bedroom. He was dying and had wanted one more family vacation. My husband and I hadn't realized that what we were witnessing wasn't only a display of grace and beauty but something more.

It would have been natural for the mother to devote all her attention to the attention-demanding disabled child, with some left over to her dying husband. Yet she managed to muster the full attention required to ensure that the easily forgotten older child felt that he mattered too. The differences in the natural capacities of her two children made no difference to her in what they were owed by the fact of their existence. There could be no question of zero-sum mattering, not even in the cruelest of circumstances. There was a reservoir of mattering to draw on, and that's what she clearly saw.

She had love, of course, to help her see so clearly, but still what she saw—that reservoir of mattering—is the truth. It's the truth that can be universalized. What the mother saw in relation to her sons applies to everybody. There's a reservoir of mattering that is (or should be) enough for all. That's the truth, but only the saints, with their gift for love, can see it as clearly as that mother did for her two sons. We can't be expected to love as the saints love. To command such love is like commanding us to think like Einstein, sing like Callas, fly toward the hoop like Jordan.

We are undeniably different in our natural capacities and dispositions, but that is a difference that makes no difference in terms of mattering. We pay lip service to this truth in speaking of our inherent human dignity, but we don't feel it and we don't act on it. Guilty until proven innocent: worthless unless proven that you're not. We dismiss the existential dimension that makes everybody exquisitely sensitive to indications that they don't matter, ignoring how deeply the hurt cuts into the core. Our concentrated concerns with our own mattering obscure the poignancy all around us. It doesn't help that, in their striving to matter, others often act like such jerks.

What then *can* help? We can't command ourselves to love as the saints love nor command others to stop acting like jerks. But we can try to recalibrate our allocation of status—society's standard for how much an individual matters—in terms of a person's effects on entropy. The manual laborer, the worker in health care management or food production, the primary school teacher, hair stylist, NICU nurse, nanny, gardener, grief counselor, charity worker, speech therapist, community organizer, copyeditor, yoga instructor: All of those who reduce entropy in ways valued by others should be boosted in status.

"Move fast and break things" has long been the motto of Silicon Valley. Presumably, when it was first proposed, it wasn't suggesting that things should be broken for the sake of breaking them, but rather to make room for demonstrably better things. In the context of Silicon Valley, the advice perhaps made some sense, though even there it could be shortsighted. The pleasure of breaking things can discourage the hard work of thinking through consequences. More seriously, the mindset has spread far beyond Silicon Valley, where moving fast and breaking things has become an assertion of raw power. Breaking things, the bigger the better—institutions, conventions, the norms of morality themselves—can maximize the attention that others pay to a person.

"Move fast and break things" is the very negation of how we should act in the face of the law of entropy. As the law tells us, breaking things is easy. It's resisting entropy that's hard. Our way of calibrating status should change accordingly.

JUJU'S MOTHER

Lou Xiaoying was an impoverished woman who earned her living as a scavenger, going through rubbish in search of recyclables—paper, plastic, metal, and glass—to be sold to recycling depots or processing facilities. That was how she found the babies. They had been left in dumpsters, public toilets, garbage heaps, or on the side of the road, a blank sheet of paper placed on top of them. They were overwhelmingly female.

This was under China's strict one-baby policy, implemented in 1980 and lasting until 2016, when the policy was liberalized to two babies per family. If a family could have only one child, they wanted a boy. There were strong traditional reasons for the preference. The Chinese custom is for a daughter to care for her husband's parents, not her own, in their old age. "A daughter is like spilled water," goes the adage.

Over the course of her life, Lou found many babies, some for whom she found homes, others whom she brought home to become her own children. She ended up raising over thirty little girls.

"They were little babies held in arms, and some were not in good health," Juju tells me. Juju is one of the children her mother found while scavenging. She's now in her forties, herself a mother of two children, a daughter and son. She lives in Jinhua, in the eastern Zhejiang province.

My eldest sister was abandoned in the toilet of the hospital. And Jingjing, who is about the same age as me, was picked up under the bridge. I was on the side of the road. It was not adoption. My mother just found us and took us back with her and gave us everything she could. Or else she found families who had no child and would take one. But it was hard to find such families. Nobody wanted girls. It was always girls who had been thrown away.

The older children like me would help Mother to look after the babies. We didn't have cradles. What we did is to remove the handle of the bamboo basket and then spread some straw and rags at the bottom of the basket to make it softer. That's our cradle for babies. We would gently shake the basket and lull the babies to sleep, with both hands taking care of one basket each.

We lived in a public gazebo. On the way to Jinhua City, there is a pavilion every five kilometers for people to rest on their journey. The one where we lived is called Wuli Pavilion. The pavilion is ventilated on all sides, in winter too, and it is very shabby. We spread straw on the ground and then slept wrapped in torn quilts my mother had found. This was our beds. There was no electricity, and we burned firewood. My mother had fashioned her own kind of earthen stove, built with bricks of mud. And when the walls of the pavilion would crumble, my mother would repair it with yellow mud.

My father was also a scavenger, a kind man, a good man. His name was Li Zin. He was the second of my mother's partners. The first had the surname of Liu. I don't know his given name, so I'll call him Father Liu. In those days, there was no marriage registration. They had fled from famine together and come to Jinhua. But then they got separated. My mother was pregnant with his child. It was a snowy day in the wilderness when the man I know as my father met my mother. He took her to the Wuli Pavilion and helped her to give birth. This is my older brother.

When I was young, we had little food to feed the kids. The source of our food was all from begging and the scavenging by my parents. My parents spent countless thoughts and efforts to bring us up. If one day we discovered food like milk powder, it would be a precious treasure to us. My mother and father would always keep the nice food, like milk powder or rice paste or sweet potato porridge, for the children.

When Juju was twelve, Li Zin became sick with stomach cancer. There had been no money to treat it.

People in the nearby army said that they would take my father to see a doctor. After staying in the hospital for a few days, my father passed away. My mother was then the only one left at home with all the children. And she kept finding more. When it became known that my mother was taking in babies, do you know how many children would show up at the gate of our ruined pavilion in one night? Sometimes as many as four children. My mother won't abandon the child again. If there is a child at our door, we will take her in, make her better. My mother knew many remedies. People sometimes said it was a miracle how she could cure such sick babies. We had babies always passing through, but usually there were about seven or eight or nine also living with us. If she had the strength enough to collect garbage, then how could she not recycle something as important as human lives? This is what she said.

How did she have so much love? It's strange because she didn't get it herself when she was a child. I sometimes asked my mother, Where are you from? She said she didn't know for sure. But she knew she was born in the year of the ox.

This would be 1925. From 1927 to 1949, there was a civil war between the Chinese Communist Party and the Chinese Nationalist Party. Lou's parents had both died when she was three or four.

"Life was very hard at that time. Her childhood memories were confused, but what she remembered made her put everything into giving us kids a good life. We were happy. My sister Jingjing and I even got to go to school after we moved to Dongguan."

This move happened when the Wuli Pavilion was requisitioned by the state for the construction of a railway station.

This is when our family became known to the higher authorities. The leader above asked my mother whether she wanted a subsidy or something else. My mother said that she wanted to have a place to live with her children. She was getting old and was afraid that we children will have no place to live in the future. These subsidies wouldn't allow us to afford to buy a house. The leader said that if we didn't need the subsidy, they would build a house for us in a remote place. My mother reasoned that the kind of tile-roofed house must be better than the open pavilion. Then our Dongguan Village Committee helped us move to the present place, and we have been living here until now. My mother was in her seventies when she finally got to live in her own proper home. My father died before this great good luck.

When my mother was eighty-two years old, she brought home a baby boy. This was the last child she found and the only boy who became part of our big family. Our next-door neighbor took my mother to see this boy, found in a dustbin. The neighbor said that a little girl may have given birth to the boy. His weight was only a little more than two Chinese pounds.

A pound avoirdupois, the standard pound used in the US, is a little more than the *catty*, or Chinese pound.

He would have had no chance to survive if not for my mother. He was lucky, as all of us were lucky to be found by my mother. She was old, but she said that she could not ignore the baby and leave him to die in the dustbin. He looked so sweet and helpless, she said. She named him Qilin. It means rare and precious. My little brother is seventeen now, and my mother saw that he went to school. She had no education and couldn't read, so she took great joy in her children knowing how to read. She died at eighty-eight, and this was her dying wish for Qilin. When she had arranged his schooling, she died happy. A happy life, a happy death.

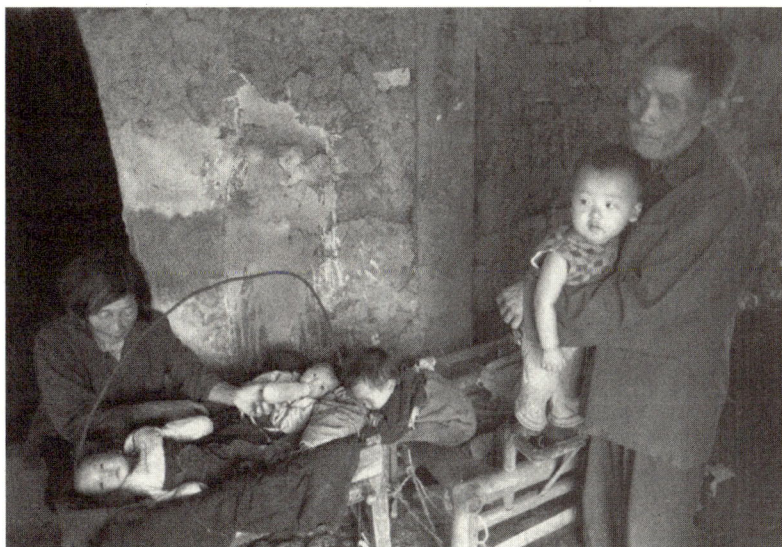

Lou Xiaoying and Li Zin caring for some of their infant girls

She was happy in life? I ask.

"Yes, from the first baby she found in the trash and brought home to raise, she saw that it gave her great happiness. There could be worry to find enough food, to cure the sick babies. But still always happiness surrounding her."

When I ask Juju if she has ever wondered who her birth mother is, she forcefully answers no.

"I had the most wonderful mother that it is possible to have," she manages to say, though my question has brought her to tears. "She gave me everything a child could ever want in this world. I can still feel her love. I will always feel it. This is how it is for every one of those babies who passed through her arms. This is what she leaves behind in the world."[3]

ETHICS

"All things deteriorate over time in the approach to the journey's end, worn out by the ancient span of years," wrote the Roman philosopher Lucretius in the first century BCE.

The second law of thermodynamics predicts that eventually the universe will wear out, when it reaches a state of maximum entropy. Physicists refer to this state as the heat death. There will be no temperature differences to drive thermodynamic processes. All will be lifeless and inert. Stars will have long since exhausted their fuel and burned out, black holes will have dissipated, and all matter will have broken down into its simplest form. The universe will be in a state of complete thermal equilibrium, cold and dark, silent and still.

In the end, entropy will get all of us, all of everything. As Rudolf Clausius, the physicist who coined the term *entropy*, stated, "The entropy of the universe tends to a maximum."

That's physics.

But meanwhile, since seeking our sense of mattering is what we are driven to do, the most peculiar, human, and poignant thing about us, we can seek to matter by resisting entropy in ways as expansive as possible, allying ourselves with life and not with death, with happiness and not with sorrow, with creativity and not with destruction, with knowledge and not with ignorance, with care and not with cruelty, with clarity and not with confusion, with peace and not with turmoil, with beauty and not with ugliness.

That's ethics.

And if not now, when?

ACKNOWLEDGMENTS

I wrote my first book when I was a young assistant professor of philosophy, having just earned my PhD in philosophy of science. It was not what my senior colleagues expected. Not only was it a novel but its point of view was outside the mainstream analytic philosophy in which I'd been rigorously trained and with which I identified. People warned me that I was jeopardizing my nascent philosophical career. They were right, but it was not to be helped. The novel had peremptorily announced itself to me in its opening sentence, the plaintive "I'm often asked what it's like to be married to a genius." I felt I had no choice but to try to find out to whom this first-person sentence, and its attached point of view, belonged. I knew that it wasn't me, which made it exciting. The question that my editor asked me, as to why my smart, funny, sexy protagonist was always on the brink of despair, the question that allowed me to make sense of my character and her story, opened up a new range of questions that I might never have explored otherwise, culminating, now forty years later, in this book. The editor, who was then as young as I, went on to the kind of brilliant career in publishing that might have been predicted from his spot-on question to me. His name is Jonathan Galassi, and I will always be grateful.

I am grateful to Martin Seligman for organizing a three-day workshop in 2018 in San Francisco, to which I was invited to present my ideas about mattering, and I am grateful to all those who participated: Roy Baumeister, Gabriella Kellerman, Andrew Reece, Barry Schwartz, and David Yaden. I don't believe I would have undertaken to write this book without the encouragement that I derived from those three days.

The ideas presented in this book cross boundaries between many domains—physics, evolutionary biology, psychology, philosophy, politics—and I want to thank the experts in these, all of whom are also friends, who commented on sections of previous drafts and sometimes even on whole drafts: Roy Baumeister, Ken Goldberg, Sheldon Goldstein, Glenn Kurtz, Megan Marshall, Clancy Martin, Colin McGinn, Lachlan Morrow, Alec Rosenberg, Tiffany Shlain, and Michael Strevens. Any mistakes that survived their scrutiny are due to my own limitations. Among those with whom I discussed the ideas of the book over the years were Janice Perlman, Barry Skeist, and Andrew Norman, who first suggested the phrase "the mattering instinct." I am also grateful to Tina Bennett for our shared exchanges about mattering early on in my thinking.

Lucy Cleland became my literary agent midstream, amid rough waters, and she got me to the other side. I hadn't realized quite how much I needed her encouragement, insights, and sagacity until, so luckily, they were granted to me. The same can be said for Pete Simon, who is everything I could want in an editor. Every criticism and suggestion he has offered was on the mark. This book is fortunate in having found its wayward way into their hands. Kadiatou Keita was endlessly patient with helping me procure various permissions and with sundry other tasks, and Emily Andrukaitis's work on the book was such as to prompt me to add copyeditor to the list of occupations that ought to be applauded for bringing more order into the world.

My two daughters, Yael Goldstein-Love and Danielle Blau, who have heard me nattering about mattering their entire lives, have not only suffered my obsession but helped to deepen my ideas. Yael insisted that I give connectedness its due, even if it complicated the presentation, and of course she was right.

Steven Pinker, my beloved, read every single draft—and there were many—commenting copiously. For this, as with so much in my life for which I must constantly pinch myself to know that I'm not dreaming, I am unspeakably grateful.

NOTES

INTRODUCTION

1. I'm using the phrase "forms of human life" in much the same way as the philosopher Ludwig Wittgenstein wrote in *Philosophical Investigations* of forms of life as being fundamental to understanding (linguistic) meaning and usage: "What has to be accepted, the given, is—one could say—forms of life."

2. Here is the entire Kant quote, from *Critique of Practical Reason*: "Two things fill the mind with ever new and increasing wonder and awe, the more often and the more steadily we reflect upon them: the starry heaven above me and the moral law within me."

1. THE MOST PECULIAR AND MOST HUMAN THING ABOUT US

1. Charles Darwin, "Self-Attention, Shame, Shyness, Modesty, Blushing," in *The Expression of the Emotions in Man and Animals* (New York: D. Appleton & Company, 1872), 309.

2. In classical Darwinism, the concept of "survival of the fittest" was often interpreted at the level of the organism—meaning that individuals that are better adapted to their environment are more likely to survive and reproduce. Modern Darwinism, informed by advances in genetics, emphasizes that the true unit of natural selection is the gene. This perspective views genes as the primary drivers of evolutionary change, arguing that genes motivate those behaviors and traits that enhance the genes' own propagation across generations.

3. Martha Nussbaum uses the phrase "a recognizably human life" in her work

related to the capabilities approach, which she developed alongside econo-mist Amartya Sen. See her *Women and Human Development: The Capabilities Approach* (Cambridge University Press, 2000), where she outlines the essen-tial capabilities required for a life that can be deemed recognizably human. She numbers them as ten: life; bodily health; bodily integrity; senses, imag-ination, and thought; emotions; practical reason; affiliation; relations with other species; play; and control over one's environment.

4. Some literary critics believe that in his last novel, *Humboldt's Gift*, Saul Bellow based the character of Sewell on Blackmur, known for his dense and sometimes pedantic style of literary criticism. Bellow paints Sewell as the consummate literary snob, a pretentious, self-important, and overly academic figure. Merwin held Blackmur in higher regard, describing him as "the wisest man and the greatest literary intelligence I ever knew." Cather-ine Richardson, "A Poet and Nothing but a Poet," *Princeton Alumni Weekly*, October 13, 2010.

5. INTERVIEWER: "You, along with Lowell, Sylvia Plath, and several oth-ers, have been called a confessional poet. How do you react to that label?" BERRYMAN: "With rage and contempt! Next question." Peter A. Stitt, "John Berryman, The Art of Poetry No. 16," *The Paris Review* 53 (Winter 1972).

6. Jane Howard, "Whiskey and Ink, Whiskey and Ink," *Life*, July 21, 1967.

7. W. S. Merwin, *Migration: New and Selected Poems* (Copper Canyon Press, 2005), 100.

8. See "The Town Crier," *Washington Post*, June 1, 2022. All the quotes from Angela Rubino come from this article.

9. "A person's location on [the Mattering Map] is determined by what mat-ters to him, matters overwhelmingly, the kind of mattering that produces his perceptions of people, of himself and others: of who are the nobodies and who the somebodies, who the deprived and who the gifted, who the better-never-to-have-been-born and who the heroes." Rebecca Goldstein, *The Mind-Body Problem* (Random House, 1983), 22.

10. Bernard Williams, "Persons, Character, and Morality," in *The Identity of Persons*, edited by Amelie Oksenberg Rorty (University of California Press, 1984), 197–216.

11. William James, "Attention," in *Principles of Psychology* (Henry Holt and Company, 1890), 1:403–404.

12. Here is William James's equation for self-esteem:

$$\text{Self-esteem} = \frac{\text{Successes}}{\text{Pretensions}}$$

This means that self-esteem can be increased either by achieving more successes or by lowering one's aspirations or "pretensions." In essence, it's a balance between how well one does in relation to what one aims to achieve. Over the years, I've pondered whether James's elegant equation is sufficient to capture the psychological reality of all of us. For example, some people seem determined to maintain the same level of self-esteem no matter the ratio of their successes to their pretentions—for example, by downgrading their successes almost immediately on achieving them and for no other reason than that they have achieved them.

13. In modern physics, things that are not composed of matter can also take up space. They are called force fields. But there was no scientific notion of fields for many centuries, certainly not at the time of Aristotle. The concept of a field awaited the seventeenth century and Isaac Newton's formulation of the equation for universal gravitation, which was criticized for entailing action at a distance—that is, that a material body could affect the motions of other material bodies without any contact with it. In the eighteenth century, Michael Faraday, a self-taught scientist, formulated the notion of a magnetic field, and later in the century, James Clerk Maxwell unified electricity and magnetism with his equations for electromagnetic fields. In the twentieth century, Albert Einstein interpreted space-time as a field, and Erwin Schrödinger, in formulating the equation that governs the wave function of a quantum mechanical system, discovered the quantum field. The history of physics is not only the history of our discovering truths about matter, and about space and time, but also about fields. All of which is to say that you can't equate occupying space with being made of matter.

14. I argued this point in my PhD dissertation: "Reduction, Realism and the Mind" (Princeton University, 1976).

15. Erwin Schrödinger, "What Is Life? The Physical Aspect of the Living Cell," in *What Is Life and Other Scientific Essays* (Doubleday, 1944, 1956). Based on lectures delivered under the auspices of the Dublin Institute for Advanced Studies at Trinity College, Dublin, in February 1943.

16. Robert Sapolsky, "Dude, Where's My Frontal Cortex?" *Nautilus*, June 25, 2014.

17. See Judith H. Langlois et al., "Infant Preferences for Attractive Faces: Rudiments of a Stereotype," *Developmental Psychology* 23, no. 3 (May 1987): 363–69.

18. See Faraz Farzin, Chuan Hou, and Anthony M. Norcia, "Piecing It Together: Infants' Neural Responses to Face and Object Structure," *Journal of Vision* 12, no. 13 (December 2012). Also Elinor McKone, Kate Crookes, and Nancy Kanwisher, "The Cognitive and Neural Development of Face Recognition in Humans," in *The Cognitive Neurosciences*, 4th ed., ed. Michael S. Gazzaniga (MIT Press, 2009), 467–82.

19. See T. A. Walden, T. A. Ogan, "The Development of Social Referencing," *Journal of Child Development* 59, no. 5 (October 1988): 1230–40.

20. Runnan Cao, Chujun Lin, Nicholas J. Brandmeir, and Shuo Wang, "A Human Single-Neuron Dataset for Face Perception," *Scientific Data* 9, no. 365 (2022).

21. Heinrich Meng and Ernst L. Freud, eds., *Psychoanalysis and Faith: The Letters of Sigmund Freud and Oskar Pfister*, trans. Eric Mosbacher (Hogarth Press and the Institute of Psycho-Analysis, 1963).

2. THE TRANSFORMATION FROM WITHIN

1. René Descartes, *The Philosophical Works of Descartes*, trans. Elizabeth S. Haldane and G. R. T. Ross, vol. 1, *Meditations on First Philosophy* (Cambridge University Press, 1911), 190.
2. Saul Kripke, *Naming and Necessity* (Harvard University Press, 1980).
3. Paul Bloom, *Descartes' Baby: How the Science of Child Development Explains What Makes Us Human* (Basic Books, 2005).
4. Ernst Becker, *The Denial of Death* (The Free Press, 1973). Becker's views gave rise to a theory in psychology called terror management theory, which accepts his premise that our denial of death is the basis of our uniquely human behavior, including the ways in which we cling to our group identifications. Proponents support their theory with some empirical findings. For example, if subjects are questioned about their group identifications in the vicinity of a cemetery, they will express more commitment to their group identification and less tolerance for those who don't share it. However, these findings can just as easily be used to support the mattering theory laid out in the course of this book, since suggestions of death strengthen our longing to matter.
5. See "Annie Hall – 'the horrible and the miserable.' YouTube channel, 0:40, July 13, 2012.
6. "The law that entropy always increases—the second law of thermodynamics—holds, I think, the supreme position among the laws of Nature." Arthur Eddington, *The Nature of the Physical World* (MacMillan, 1928), 74.
7. "A theory is the more impressive the greater the simplicity of its premises is. Therefore, the deep impression which classical thermodynamics made upon me. It is the only physical theory of universal content concerning which I am convinced that within the framework of the applicability of its basic concepts, it will never be overthrown." Quoted in *A Stubbornly Persistent Illusion: The Essential Scientific Works of Albert Einstein*, edited by Stephen Hawking (Running Press, 2007), 353.
8. "Our subjective sense of the direction of time, the psychological arrow of time, is therefore determined within our brain by the thermodynamic arrow of time. Just like a computer, we must remember things in the order in which entropy increases. This makes the second law of thermodynamics almost trivial. Disorder increases with time because we measure time in the direction in which disorder increases. You can't have a safer bet than that!" Stephen Hawking, *A Brief History of Time* (Bantam Press, 1988), 146.
9. George Steiner, *The Death of Tragedy* (Faber and Faber, 1963), 8–9.
10. John Tooby, Leda Cosimides, and H. Clark Barrett, "The Second Law of Thermodynamics Is the First Law of Psychology: Evolutionary Developmental Psychology and the Theory of Tandem, Coordinated Inheritances: Comment on Lickliter and Honeycut (2003)," *Psychological Bulletin* 129, no. 6 (2003): 858–65.
11. It was the American scientist Josiah Willard Gibbs who bestowed the name

statistical mechanics on the new field, to which he too was a major contributor along with Boltzmann, that explained the laws of thermodynamics as consequences of the statistical properties of the ensembles of the possible states of a physical system composed of many particles.

12. See William D. Hamilton, "The Moulding of Senescence by Natural Selection," *Journal of Theoretical Biology* 12, no. 1 (1966): 12–45.

13. These are the species that have passed the so-called mirror test, also known as the mirror self-recognition (MSR) test, developed in 1970 by the psychologist Gordon Gallup Jr. The animal is first given time to become accustomed to a mirror. Initially, it may react as though it is confronting another animal, but over time, it may begin to exhibit different behaviors. After the period of familiarization, the animal is anesthetized or distracted, and a nontoxic, odorless mark or dye is placed on a part of its body that it can't see without the use of a mirror (such as on its forehead). Once the animal regains normal consciousness, it's given access to the mirror again. If the animal uses the mirror to investigate and possibly attempt to remove the mark, it's considered to have shown evidence of self-recognition. For instance, touching the mark or examining it closely indicates that the animal understands the reflection is of itself. If it continues to treat the reflection as another animal or displays no interest in the mark, it may suggest a lack of self-recognition.

14. Gerard Manley Hopkins, *Sermons* (Oxford University Press, 1959), 348–49.

15. There are emotions that are named in some languages and not in others. For example, the Yiddish word *nakhos* means the bursting joyful pride a parent feels in the achievements of their offspring, no matter how ordinary they may seem to others. In Japanese, *mono no aware* is the feeling of joyful sorrow that is blended into our deepest experiences of beauty, knowing as we do that beauty inevitably fades. And then there's ancient Greek's concept of eudaimonia, which means the feeling of flourishing. We'll look more closely at eudaimonia in chapter five.

16. Louis A. Sass and Josef Parnas, "Schizophrenia, Consciousness, and the Self," *Schizophrenia Bulletin* 29, no. 3 (2003): 427–44. See also John Gerald Taylor, "A Neural Model of the Loss of Self in Schizophrenia," *Schizophrenia Bulletin* 37, no. 6 (November 2011): 1229–47.

17. Here is the relevant quote from Hume: "For my part, when I enter most intimately into what I call myself, I always stumble on some particular perception or other, of heat or cold, light or shade, love or hatred, pain or pleasure. I never can catch myself at any time without a perception, and never can observe any thing but the perception. . . . If any one, upon serious and unprejudic'd reflection thinks he has a different notion of himself, I must confess I can reason no longer with him. All I can allow him is, that he may be in the right as well as I, and that we are essentially different in this particular. He may, perhaps, perceive something simple and continu'd, which he calls himself; tho' I am certain there is no such principle in me" (*Treatise on Human Nature*, 1.4.6, "Of personal identity"). Hume believed that all clear concepts can ultimately be traced back to impressions received

either through sensory perception or introspection. Using this theory, he argued that many concepts are actually vacuous, and he is arguing here for the vacuity of the concept of the self.

18. See Baruch Spinoza, *Ethics*, part 2, propositions 7 and 8.

19. The only counterexample I can find to the claim that our conatus is pounded into our identity comes from literature—Herman Melville's short story "Bartleby the Scrivener." The incomprehensibility of the character of Bartleby itself attests to the claim I'm making. Melville was, in fact, a student of Spinoza, as I discuss in "Literary Spinoza," a chapter in *The Oxford Handbook of Spinoza*, ed. Michael Della Rocca (Oxford University Press, 2017). Melville's deep ponderings on Spinoza make me wonder whether Spinoza's theory of conatus inspired Melville to create his character of Bartleby as a counterexample.

20. Her collaborator in the discovery of nuclear fission, Otto Hahn, alone won the 1944 Nobel Prize in Chemistry. Her omission is said to have been the product of both sexism and anti-Semitism. The Nobel committee had failed to take into account the extent to which the Nazis, then in power in Germany, falsified the contributions of German Jewish scientists. See Timothy J. Jorgenson, "Lise Meitner—the Forgotten Woman of Nuclear Fission Who Deserved a Nobel Prize," *The Wire*, February 12, 2019. Also see Marissa Moss, *The Woman Who Split the Atom: The Life of Lise Meitner* (Harry N. Abrams, 2022) and Ruth Lewin Sime, *Lise Meitner: A Life in Physics* (University of California Press, 1966).

21. Lise Meitner, "Ludwig Boltzmann," *Scientific Weekly* 79, no. 3 (September 1954): 140.

22. Boltzmann reported these words of Mach's in his inaugural philosophy lecture. See Ludwig Boltzmann, *Populäre Schriften* (J.A. Barth, 1905), 338. He doesn't say exactly when the words occurred. Walter Höflechner, in *Ludwig Boltzmann: Leben und Briefe* (Akademische Druck und Verkagsanstalt, 1994), argues that the most likely debate was January 1897, when Boltzmann delivered his lecture "On the Question of the Objective Existence of Events in Inanimate Nature." See David Lindley, *Boltzmann's Atom: The Great Debate That Launched a Revolution in Physics* (Free Press, 2001).

23. Lindley, *Boltzmann's Atom*, 99.

24. The bias against probabilistic reasoning also played a role in the rejection of natural selection. Probability pops up in various steps of natural selection, including the probability of random mutations, the probability that random mutations will be beneficial in certain environments, the probability that organisms with adaptive traits in the environment will survive long enough to have their genes replicated into future generations, and the probability that those adaptive traits will lead to the disappearance of variants.

25. Lindley, *Boltzmann's Atom*, 142.

26. And yet Boltzmann had himself essentially understood Brownian motion. In 1896, he indicated in a letter to Zermelo that Brownian motion was a direct consequence of his own theory of molecular motion. He had tossed off the insight, incidentally, in the course of trying once again to explain

why the possibility of fluctuations in entropy's increase doesn't indicate a weakness of statistical mechanics but rather a strength. For some reason, it seemed never to occur to him to work out the details of Brownian motions as Einstein later did. It would hardly have been beyond his scientific capabilities to do so. In fact, Einstein had used Boltzmann's previous work (the standard Maxwell-Boltzmann formula for the distribution of atomic velocities) to arrive at his conclusion. "One can hardly imagine how different Boltzmann's last years might have been if he had taken the trouble to publish even a rough calculation of Brownian motion, instead of letting the idea slip out as an incidental suggestion," writes Lindley, *Boltzmann's Atom*, 213.
27. Lindley, *Boltzmann's Atom*, 214.
28. David Goodstein, *States of Matter* (Dover Publications, 1975), 1.

3. BECOMING HUMAN

1. What part of the brain, exactly, is this? The fusiform gyrus, which is located in the middle of the ventral temporal lobe on the basal surface of the temporal and occipital lobes, is supposed to be where our ability to identify faces is located, but I was unsure whether it was also involved in our identifying our own faces, or if rather another area of the brain is specifically devoted to this task, even though my thesis that our capacity for studying ourselves derives from our capacity to study others would seem to point to the same area of the brain being involved in our recognizing other faces and recognizing our own face. So I wrote with my questions to Jason Mitchell, a Harvard neuroscientist, and here is his answer: "The literature shows that one's own face activates the fusiform gyrus (perhaps even more than unfamiliar faces). As you probably know, there is a technical difference between the fusiform gyrus (FG), which is an anatomical region one could point to on a postmortem brain, versus the fusiform face area (FFA), which is a functionally defined patch of your cortex (or mine) that maximally cares about faces. Most of the studies that have looked at regions that respond to one's own face have not functionally identified the FFA and are limited to reporting that regions of the FG are active for self faces. I'm not sure how relevant this distinction is for your purposes, but I want to point it out that strictly speaking, we don't know if the FFA is active for self faces, although the fact that the FG is active for self faces strongly implies that the FFA is."
2. See Beate Sodian and Susanne Kristen, "Theory of Mind," in *Handbook of Epistemic Cognition*, eds. Jeffrey A. Green, William A. Sandoval, and Ivar Bråten (Routledge, 2016), 68–85.
3. This is the last stanza of his poem "To a Louse, on Seeing One on a Lady's Bonnet at Church." First published in Robert Burns, *Poems, Chiefly in the Scottish Dialect*, 1796, Kilmarnock, Scotland.
4. The famous passage from Jean-Paul Sartre's novel *Nausea* (*La Nausée*), originally published in 1938 by Gallimard, occurs when Sartre's character, Antoine Roquentin, is sitting in the park under a chestnut tree, its knotty roots sinking into the ground, when he has a vision of the utter arbitrari-

ness of all existence, none of it grounded—not the ancient chestnut tree, the park, or Antoine Roquentin himself. "The word absurdity is coming to life under my pen. . . . And without formulating anything clearly, I understood that I had found the key to Existence, the key to my Nauseas, to my own life" (trans. Lloyd Alexander [New Directions, 1949]).

5. In fact, it *is* the drama that he stages in all of his plays.

6. Thomas Nagel, "The Absurd," first published in the *Journal of Philosophy* 68, no. 20 (1971): 720; reprinted in Thomas Nagel, *Mortal Questions* (Cambridge University Press, 1979), 11–23.

7. It's occurred to me that the inclination on the part of some social psychologists to reject any inner processes that don't serve interpersonal functions is itself a manifestation of the mattering instinct within them—the sense of their own mattering swelled by the belief that social psychology explains all of human behavior.

8. For example, since amphibians, reptiles, and mammals are descended from a lobe-finned fish, a strictly genealogical taxonomy might have ray-finned fish in one class and lungfish, amphibians, and mammals in another. As Steven Jay Gould pointed out, if we allowed evolutionary descent alone to determine taxonomy, we'd be classified as a kind of fish! But in a compromise with phenotypic distinctiveness, the Linnean taxonomy puts all the fish in one class and the amphibians, reptiles, and mammals in their own classes. I'm suggesting that a similar phenotypic-similarity respecting taxonomy and overriding evolutionary descent would place humans in their own phylum. See Steven Jay Gould, "A Quahog Is a Quahog," in *The Panda's Thumb: More Reflections in Natural History* (W. W. Norton, 1982).

9. Martha C. Nussbaum, *Justice for Animals: Our Collective Responsibility* (Simon & Schuster, 2023).

10. That all people—and even animals—are presented as vegetarians before Noah's flood is derived from interpretations of the Book of Genesis and is expanded upon in Jewish midrashic and rabbinic literature. It's based primarily on the comparison between God's instructions to humanity before and after the flood—to wit, a comparison between Genesis 1:29–30 and Genesis 9:3–4.

4. LIFE, LIBERTY, AND THE PURSUIT OF EUDAIMONIA

1. See Ephrat Livni, "A Nobel Prize–Winning Psychologist Says Most People Don't Want to Be Happy," *Quartz*, December 21, 2018.

2. See Gretchen Livingston, "They're Waiting Longer, but U.S. Women Today More Likely to Have Children Than a Decade Ago," Pew Research Center, January 18, 2018.

3. See Rozsika Parker, *Torn in Two: The Experience of Maternal Ambivalence* (Virago, 2005).

4. See "Dan Gilbert: Happiness: What Your Mother Didn't Tell You," Pearls of Wisdom YouTube channel, 20:27, January 5, 2021. See also Daniel Gilbert, *Stumbling on Happiness* (Vintage, 2006).

5. Jennifer Glass, Robin W. Simon, and Matthew A. Anderson, "The Parenthood 'Happiness Penalty': The Effects of Social Policies in 22 Countries," *PRC Research Brief* 2, no. 7 (May 2017).

6. Glass et al., "The Parenthood 'Happiness Penalty.'"

7. Claire E. Ashton-James, Kostadin Kushlev, and Elizabeth W. Dunn, "Parents Reap What They Sow: Child-Centrism and Parental Well-Being," *Social Psychological and Personality Science* 4, no. 6 (2013): 635.

8. See Sophie Cetre, Andrew E. Clark, and Claudia Senik, "Happiness and the Parenthood Paradox," Paris School of Economics, September 7, 2015, 3, http://www.parisschoolofeconomics.com/clark-andrew/HappinessandtheParenthoodParadox.pdf.

9. James L. McQuivey, "To Have Kids or Not: Which Decision Do Americans Regret More?" Institute of Family Studies, June 10, 2021.

10. Quoted in Norman Malcolm, *Ludwig Wittgenstein: A Memoir* (Oxford University Press, 1962).

11. See "Bertrand Russell on Ludwig Wittgenstein," Jack Jones YouTube channel, 0:56, April 10, 2012.

12. Malcolm, *Ludwig Wittgenstein*.

13. Malcolm, *Ludwig Wittgenstein*, 30.

14. Ray Monk, *Ludwig Wittgenstein: The Duty of Genius* (Penguin Books, 1990), 577.

15. Ms-183,108[2], Wittgenstein Source, http://www.wittgensteinsource.org/BTE/Ms-183,108[2]_n.

16. William James, *The Varieties of Religious Experience* (Simon & Schuster, 1997), 138.

17. See Cushing Strout, "William James and the Twice-Born Sick Soul," *Daedalus* 97 (1968), 1062–1082.

18. William D. Phelan, "William James at Harvard," *Harvard Crimson*, May 7, 1963, www.thecrimson.com/article/1963/5/7/william-james-at-harvard-pwhat-doctrines/.

19. William James to Henry P. Bowditch, December 29, 1869, in Ralph Barton Perry, *The Thought and Character of William James* (Little, Brown, 1935), 1:320.

20. James Jackson Putnam, "William James," *Atlantic Monthly*, December 1910, www.theatlantic.com/past/docs/issues/96may/nitrous/putnam.htm.

21. James, *The Varieties of Religious Experience*, 304–5.

22. William James, *The Principles of Psychology* (Henry Holt and Company, 1890), 547–48.

23. James, *The Principles of Psychology*, 546–47.

24. William James, "What Is an Emotion?" *Mind* 9, no. 34 (April 1884): 189.

25. William James, *Psychology: The Briefer Course* (Harper Torchbooks, 1961), 306.

26. Dickinson Miller to Henry James (son of William James), August 24, 1917, James Papers, Houghton Library, Harvard University.

27. Remembrance of John Jay Chapman, in Linda Simon, *William James Remembered* (University of Nebraska Press, 1991), 56.

28. William James, notes for "Abnormal Mental States" lectures, 1896, James Papers, Houghton Library, Harvard University.

29. James, *The Varieties of Religious Experience*, 79.

30. It is well-established that women are about twice as likely to develop depression as are men—in the US, Canada, and globally. There are a host of clinical papers aimed at explaining the gender gap. See, for example, Paul R. Albert, "Why Is Depression More Prevalent in Women?" *Journal of Psychiatry and Neuroscience* 40, no. 4 (July 2014): 219–21.

31. Harriet F. Bergmann, "'The Silent University': The Society to Encourage Studies at Home, 1873–1897," *New England Quarterly* 74, no. 3 (September 2001): 447–77.

32. See Susan E. Gunter, *Alice in Jamesland: The Story of Alice Howe Gibbens James* (University of Nebraska Press, 2009).

33. Some scholars do not see innocent teasing on William's part when it came to Alice, but rather unwholesome eroticism. See for example, Howard Feinstein, *Becoming William James* (Cornell University Press, 1984). The sketches William drew of Alice, the sonnets he composed for her, were strikingly erotic.

5. THE CARTOGRAPHY OF THE MATTERING MAP, PART ONE: THE SOCIAL AND THE HEROIC

1. Women, in fact, were eventually responsible for calling a halt to the slaughter of birds. Nearly a thousand women, led by Boston socialite Harriet Hemenway and her cousin Minna Hall, joined in the protest against the fashionable slaughter. Their boycott of the feather trade culminated in the establishment of the Massachusetts Audubon Society, the oldest Audubon Society in the country, and laid the groundwork for the passage of the Migratory Bird Treaty Act of 1918, which prohibited the hunting of protected bird species and forbade interstate bird transport.

2. Timo Kontio, "Jock Scott Step by Step," *Fly Tying Archive*, http://flytyingarchive.com/fly-tying-jock-scott-salmon-fly-step-by-step.

3. See Frank Martela and Michael F. Steger, "The Three Meanings of Meaning in Life: Distinguishing Coherence, Purpose, and Significance," *Journal of Positive Psychology* 11, no. 5 (2016): 531–45.

4. See Robert Nozick, *Anarchy, State, and Utopia* (Basic Books, 1974), 42–45. Nozick's experience machine thought experiment is generally regarded as an argument against hedonism—that is, that pleasure or happiness is the highest good.

5. David McClelland, *Human Motivation* (Cambridge University Press, 1961).

6. See "Carolyn Hax: She's Off to College and Her Grandmother Wants to Tag Along," *Washington Post*, April 20, 2020.

7. Quoted in Lawrence Wright, *Going Clear: Scientology, Hollywood, and the Prison of Belief* (Vintage, 2013), 80.

8. See Rebecca Newberger Goldstein, "Truth Isn't the Problem—We Are," *Wall Street Journal*, March 15, 2018.

9. Jesselyn Cook, *The Quiet Damage: QAnon and the Destruction of the American Family* (Crown, 2024).

10. "The Town Crier," *Washington Post*.

11. This is a lyric of the song "Fame," which was the title song for the movie *Fame*.

12. In the condition known as erotomania or de Clérambault's syndrome, the attention of a fan to a celebrity strays over into the delusion that the two are actually in a romantic relationship.

13. See Kirk Wallace Johnson, *The Feather Thief: Beauty, Obsession, and the Natural History Heist of the Century* (Penguin, 2019).

14. See Julie Miller, "Kevin Bacon Spent a Day as a Regular Person: 'I Was Like, This Sucks,'" *Vanity Fair*, July 3, 2024.

15. Neesha Mirchandani, *Wisdom Song: The Life of Baba Amte* (Roli Books, 2006), 28. Other sources I consulted to learn about Baba Amte are A. K. Gandhi, *Baba Amte* (Prabhat Prakashan, 2016), and Larissa MacFarquar, *Strangers Drowning: Impossible Idealism, Drastic Choices, and the Urge to Help* (Penguin Books, 2016).

16. Mirchandani, *Wisdom Song*, 57.

17. Mirchandani, *Wisdom Song*, 57.

18. Mirchandani, *Wisdom Song*, 65.

19. Mirchandani, *Wisdom Song*, 78.

20. Mirchandani, *Wisdom Song*, 92.

21. In "Moral Saints," the philosopher Susan Wolf defines a moral saint to be "a person whose every action is as morally good as possible." Though her use of the term is, like mine, secular, allowing for nonreligious saints, by her placing such a requirement on every one of the moral saint's actions, rather than on their meaning-making project—leaving no room for the moral saint to perform actions outside of their meaning-making project, as all of us do—she presents a more rigid profile of the moral saint, which aids her conclusion that "moral saintliness does not constitute a model of human well-being toward which it would be particularly rational or good or desirable for a human being to strive." See *Journal of Philosophy* 79, no. 8 (August 1982).

22. Mirchandani, *Wisdom Song*, 28.

23. Mirchandani, *Wisdom Song*, 58.

6. THE CARTOGRAPHY OF THE MATTERING MAP, PART TWO: THE TRANSCENDENT AND THE COMPETITIVE

1. This way of characterizing oneself has become common enough to be used on dating apps.

2. After the second debate, when she accused Donald Trump of harnessing a "dark psychic force of the collectivized hatred," Marianne Williamson was the most googled candidate in forty-nine of the fifty states. Nevertheless, she didn't make it to the third debate.

3. In this sense, arguing for a transcendent presence on the basis of providing

objective grounds for mattering is stronger than arguing for a transcendent presence on the basis of providing objective grounds for morality. The latter claim is vulnerable to what's known as the Euthyphro argument, whereas the former argument isn't. The Euthyphro argument, first put forth by Plato in his dialogue *Euthyphro*, states that either God has a reason for his moral commandments or he doesn't. If he does, then there is an independent reason grounding those commandments that God is merely rubberstamping. And if he has no reason then his commandments are merely arbitrary; they might just as well have been reversed. So God's commandments are either redundant or miss the mark. Either way, goes the argument, God's commandments don't provide a justificatory grounding for morality.

4. See, for example, Zuzana Dankulincova Veselska et al., "Spirituality but Not Religiosity Is Associated with Better Health and Higher Life Satisfaction Among Adolescents," *International Journal of Environmental Research and Public Health* 15, no. 12 (2018): 2781.

5. Blaise Pascal, *Pensées*, trans. A. J. Krailsheimer (Penguin Classics, 1955), Fragment 199.

6. Here's a simplified version of the problem. Two players are engaged in a fair game where they have equal chances of winning each round, and they agree to play until one of them wins a predetermined number of rounds (let's say five rounds). However, the game is interrupted before they can finish, with one player, say Player A, needing only one more win to reach five, and the other player, Player B, needing two more wins. The question is: How should the pot (the stakes to which both players have contributed) be fairly divided, given that the game can't be completed?

7. "Pascal's Memorial," trans. Elizabeth T. Knuth, in Donald Knuth, *Things a Computer Scientist Rarely Talks About* (Center for the Study of Language and Information Publications, 2001), Appendix A.

8. Jaspars first presented the idea of the Axial Age in his book *Vom Ursprung und Ziel der Geshichte*. Translated into English by Michael Bullock, under the title *The Origin and Goal of History* (Yale University Press, 1959).

9. Although traditionally attributed to the prophet Isaiah, modern scholarship often considers the latter parts of the Book of Isaiah (chapters 40–55) to be written by an anonymous prophet during this period, focusing on themes of hope and restoration for Israel.

10. This is said by Mother Courage, also known as Anna Fierling, in Brecht's play *Mother Courage and Her Children*.

11. This figure comes from the Center for the Study of Global Christianity, which estimates that there are more than 200 denominations in the US and around 45,000 globally. See "Frequently Asked Questions," Gordon Conwell, https://www.gordonconwell.edu/center-for-global-christianity/research/quick-facts/.

12. Plato, *Republic*, book 9, especially 571a–580a. Also Plato, *Gorgias*, especially 470e–480a, 507a–509c, and 522e–527e.

13. John Locke, *An Essay Concerning Human Understanding* (Thomas Bassett, 1894), book 4, chapter 19.

14. Jason DeRose, "Religious 'Nones' Are Now the Largest Single Group in the US," NPR, January 24, 2024.

15. "50 Shades (Quotes) of Diana Vreeland," *Into the Gloss*, n.d., https://intothegloss.com/2012/09/50-shades-of-diana-vreeland-best-quotes.

16. Max Tegmark, *Our Mathematical Universe: My Quest for the Ultimate Nature of Reality* (Alfred A. Knopf, 2014), 10.

17. Lionel Terray, *Conquistadors of the Useless*, trans. Geoffrey Sutton (Baton Wicks, 2001), 11.

18. Harold Bloom, introduction to *How to Read and Why* (Scribner, 2000), 27.

19. Sarah Larson, "I Think People Without Kids Have Empty Lives and I'm Not Sorry About It," *Thought Catalog*, May 9, 2024.

20. Steven Weinberg, *The First Three Minutes: A Modern View of the Origin of the Universe* (Basic Books, 1977), 154.

21. John Ruskin, *Modern Painters* (Smith Elder & Co, 1856), 3:329.

22. Paul Hoffman, *The Man Who Loved Only Numbers: The Story of Paul Erdős and the Search for Mathematical Truth* (Hyperion, 1998), 4.

23. "Interview with Margaret Geller," American Physical Society YouTube channel, 6:15, April 9, 2013.

24. Laurence J. Peter, *Peter's Quotations: Ideas for Our Time* (Bantam Books, 1977), 447.

25. This quote was spoken by Jón Páll Sigmarsson during a live competition. It was captured on video during the 1984 World's Strongest Man competitions at the moment when he was preparing to perform a deadlift event. He shouted it with characteristic intensity and showmanship, and it has since become legendary in the strength community.

26. Ayn Rand, introduction to *The Fountainhead*, 25th anniversary edition (New American Library, 1968), xxix.

27. Martin Luther King Jr., *A Gift of Love: Sermons from Strength to Love and Other Preachings*, ed. Coretta Scott King (Beacon Press, 2012), 18.

28. Walter Isaacson, *Steve Jobs* (Simon and Schuster, 2011), 381.

29. Bianca Bosker, *Cork Dork: A Wine-Fueled Adventure Among the Obsessive Sommeliers, Big Bottle Hunter, and Rogue Scientists Who Taught Me to Live for Taste* (Penguin Books, 2017), 5.

30. Mathew B. Crawford, *The World Beyond Your Head: On Becoming an Individual in an Age of Distraction* (Farrar, Straus, and Giroux, 2015), 15.

31. Friedrich Nietzsche, *Thus Spoke Zarathustra: A Book for All and None*, trans. Walter Kaufmann (Modern Library, 1995), 124.

32. Toni Morrison, "Nobel Lecture," December 7, 1993, Nobel Prize, https://www.nobelprize.org/prizes/literature/1993/morrison/lecture.

33. Alan Lightman, *Searching for Stars on an Island in Maine* (Pantheon, 2018), 6.

34. Michael C. Bender and Michael Gold, "Trump's Carefully Scripted Week Kept Veering Off Script," *New York Times*, August 24, 2024.

35. Maoxin Zhang, Björn Andersson, and Fang Wang, "Are Competitive Peo-

ple Less Altruistic and More Manipulative? Association Among Subtypes of Competitiveness, Hypothetical Altruism, and Machiavellianism," *Personality and Individual Differences* 181 (October 2021).

36. A majority of games have rules that dictate how players win. There are, however, some games where there are no winners or losers. An example is the cooperative game *Pandemic*, in which all the players work as a team to stop the spread of diseases and find cures. Success is shared, and the focus is on teamwork and strategy. Many children's games, such as playing house, have no winners or losers.

37. Mike Tyson, interview with *USA Today*, June 24, 2000.

38. Said by Bobby Fischer on *The Dick Cavett Show* in 1971.

39. Kobe Bryant, *The Mamba Mentality: How I Play* (Farrar, Straus, and Giroux, 2018), 8.

40. Kobe Bryant, *Mamba Mentality*, 17.

41. Kobe Bryant, "Dear Basketball," *Players' Tribune*, November 29, 2015, https://projects.theplayerstribune.com/legend-of-kobe-bryant/p/1.

42. Kobe Bryant, *Mamba Mentality*, 48.

43. Ann H. Farrell, Mollie Eriksson, Tracy Vaillancourt, "Brief Report: Social Comparisons, Hypercompetitiveness, and Indirect Aggression: Associations with Loneliness and Mental Health," *Aggressive Behavior* 50, no. 5 (August 2024).

44. Zhang et al., "Are Competitive People Less Altruistic," 111–37.

45. Quoted in Gordon Allport's classic study, *The Nature of Prejudice* (Basic Books, 1979), 323.

7. GETTING MATTERING WRONG

1. "Try, Try Again: A Guitarist's Second Time Around," NPR, August 18, 2007.

2. John Rawls, *A Theory of Justice* (Harvard University Press, 1999), 374.

3. Glenn Kurtz, email to me, March 30, 2022. Permission to quote from Glenn Kurtz.

4. *Ethics*, part 4, appendix, v.

5. David Hume, "Of National Characters," in *Essays: Moral, Political, and Literary*, ed. Eugene F. Miller (Liberty Fund, 1987), 208 (footnote 10 originally published 1753. The footnote did not appear in the first edition, of 1748).

6. Immanuel Kant, *Observations on the Feeling of the Beautiful and Sublime*, trans. John T. Goldthwait (University of California Press, 1960). Original German title: *Beobachtungen über das Gefühl des Schönen und Erhabenen*, 1764.

7. G. W. F. Hegel, *The Philosophy of History*, trans. J. Sibree (Dover Publications, 1965), 99. Original German title: *Vorlesungen über die Philosophie der Geschichten*, 1837.

8. David Hume, "Of National Characters," 208.

NOTES TO PAGES 244-291

9. *Emile, or On Education*, trans. Allan Bloom (Basic Books, 1979), 358. Original French title: *Emile, ou De le'éducation*, 1762.

10. Immanuel Kant, *Anthropology from a Pragmatic Point of View*, trans. Mary J. Gregor (Cambridge University Press, 2006), 78. German title: *Anthropologie in pragmatischer Hinsicht*, 1798. Kant makes anti-African statements in his earlier *Observations on the Feeling of the Beautiful and Sublime* as well, but in the interim years his racial bias is reconsidered, and he rethinks his thoughts on slavery and colonialism, whereas his bias against the capacities suitable for women hardens.

11. G. W. F. Hegel, *Elements of the Philosophy of Right*, trans. H. B. Nisbet, ed. Allen W. Wood (Cambridge University Press, 1991), 156. German title: *Grundlinien der Philosophie des Rechts*, 1821.

12. Arthur Schopenhauer, "On Women," in Schopenhauer, *Essays and Aphorisms*, trans. R. J. Hollingdale (Penguin Books, 1970). German title: "Über die Weiber," in *Parerga und Paralipomena*, vol. 2, 1851.

13. See, for example, Jared Diamond, *Guns, Germs and Steel: The Fates of Human Societies* (Vintage, 1998).

14. Sarah-Jane Leslie, Andrei Cimpian, Meredith Meyer, and Edward Freeland, "Expectations of Brilliance Underlie Gender Distributions Across Academic Disciplines," *Science* 347, no. 6219 (January 16, 2015): 262–65.

15. Edward Berlin, *King of Ragtime: Scott Joplin and His Era* (Oxford University Press, 1994).

16. Harold C. Schonberg, "Music: Treemonisha," *New York Times*, January 30, 1972.

17. Unless I indicate otherwise, all of the quotes from Frank Meeink are from his autobiography (Hawthorne Books, 2010). When quotes are from statements that he made to me in person, I indicate that as well.

8. GETTING MATTERING RIGHT

1. *Betraying Spinoza: The Renegade Jew Who Gave Us Modernity* (Schocken Books, 2006).

2. I'm referring to this quote: "Even if there is only one possible unified theory, it is just a set of rules and equations. What is it that breathes fire into the equations and makes a universe for them to describe? The usual approach of science of constructing a mathematical model cannot answer the question of why there should be a universe for the model to describe. Why does the universe go to all the bother of existing?" Stephen Hawking, *A Brief History of Time* (Bantam, 1988), 190.

3. I am grateful to my friend Liang Schweizer, who served as my go-between and translator in speaking with Zhang Juju, and to Sue (Huafei) Sun and Koyo (Yang) Hu for all their additional help in preparing the transcript. And I am so very grateful to Juju for sharing her mother's story with me and for allowing me to reproduce her precious photograph.

CREDITS

"Berryman" by W.S. Merwin from *Migration*. Copyright © 2005 by W. S. Merwin, used by permission of The Wylie Agency LLC.

"Carolyn Hax: She's Off to College and Her Grandmother Wants to Tag Along," from *The Washington Post*. © 2026 The Washington Post. All rights reserved. Used under license.

IMAGE CREDITS

INDEX

Page references after 296 refer to notes.
Photographs and maps are indicated by *italic* page references.

Eden, banishment from, 98–101
Ederle, Trudy, 242
Ehrenfest, Paul, 81
Einstein, Albert, 69, 79, 80, 119, 174, 278, 284, 299, 300, 303
emotions; *See also specific emotions, e.g.:* happiness
  associated with mattering projects, 21–22
  episodic, 105–8, 111–12
  exercising will over, 137–38
  experienced by parents, 111
  function of, 105
  future projection of, 62–63
  inspired by cosmos, 194–95
  selving and, 64, 66–68
encephalization quotient, 11, 34
energy
  brain's use of, 63
  for failing mattering projects, 94–95
  and neurasthenia, 78–79
  to resist entropy, 57, 59
English Reformation, 204
"Entertainer, The" (song), 256
entropy; *See also* counter-entropic resistance; law of entropy
  attention and, 47–48, 67–68
  calculating system's, 55, 80
  in closed systems, 58
  defined, 50–51
  likelihood of order vs. disorder, 56, 57
  mattering projects that increase, 281, 285–86
  negative, 58
episodic emotions, 105–8, 111–12
equilibrium, 51–52, 54–55, 60
Erdős, Paul, 213
Erikson, Erik, 172
Ernst, Alfred, 252
erotomania, 307
Eternal Sunshine of the Spotless Mind (film), 117
ethics, 292
Euclid, 199

eudaimonia, 104–49, 301
  connectedness and, 109–16
  happiness vs., 104–9
  impact of mattering adjudicators on, 239
  joy derived from, 126
  objective mattering and, 158–60
  parenthood as source of, 109–16
  sense of mattering as source of, 117–26
  subjective feeling of mattering and, 158, 159, 195–96
  for transcenders, 195–96
  for William and Alice James, 126–49
European Enlightenment, 206, 243–45, 250
Euthyphro argument, 308
excellence, xiii
exclusionary transcenders, 210–11, 238
existential crisis, 7–9, 127–33, 187
experience machine, 158–59

failure, fear of, 230–31
faith, xii, 195–96
fame, 133
  for heroic strivers, 120, 174–77
  as motivator, 62–63
  posthumous, 76–77, 181
  socializers who seek, 156, 171–74
family(-ies)
  connectedness in, 37–38, 144–45, 224
  distribution of attention in, 37–38, 131
  good-enough, 37, 267–68
  as group competitors, 227
  of William and Alice James, 147–48
  mattering in relationships within, 163, 166–67
  as mattering project of parents, 286–91
  need for mattering in, 144–45
  reservoir of mattering in, 283–84
Faraday, Michael, 299

mattering projects, 230–92; *See also
specific individuals*
abandoning/changing, 231–37,
264–70
allocating status based on, 285–86
author's, 271–74
best and worst of humanity represented in, 3–4
criminal activity to further, 150–56
dangerous, 164–66, 173
defined, 6
demonstrating objective mattering
with, 94
ethics and, 292
existential dimension of, 22
in face of rejection, 91
factors in determining, 191–92,
273, 275
to fight previous ideology, 264–70
of group competitors, 227–29
of heroic strivers, 118, 177–81
immoral, 96–97, 258–70, 273
impact of mattering adjudicators
on, 237–58
limitations on women's, 142–46
and location on mattering map, 21
moralizing, 274–75
motivation for, 158
objective standard for, 6, 50,
279–83, 293
of parents, 110, 113–14
perfection of oneself in, 177–81
requirements of, 233–35, 275–76
and reservoir of mattering, 283–84
self-mattering in, 68
struggle to choose, 230–31
that increase entropy, 281, 285–86
universalizing, 274–79
variety of, 3–5, 10, 14, 21, 95–96,
160, 218–19, 272–73, 275–76
of violent extremists, 259–65
mattering strategies, 6, 40–41, 160,
273
mattering types, 160–62
competitors, 220–29
heroic strivers, 174–92

mattering adjudicators for, 238–39
on mattering map, 6, 160–62
personality types and, 161–62
socializers, 162–74
transcenders, 193–220
maturity, parental happiness and,
114–15
Maxwell, James Clerk, 299
McClelland, David, 161–62, 174, 175,
191
McClelland–Murray theory of personality, 161–62, 191, 207–9
meaningful lives
correlates of, 157–59
non-Darwinian imperative to pursue, 13–14
subjective meaningfulness, 157–59,
195, 197, 229
Meeink, Frank, 259–70, 311
Meitner, Lise, 72, 302
Melville, Herman, 302
men
depression rates for women vs.,
142, 306
parental happiness for, 112
Mencken, H.L., 171
Mendel, Gregor, 77, 78
Méré, Chevalier de, 199
Merwin, William Stanley "W.S.,"
15–17, 20, 76, 178
miasma theory of disease, 241
Migratory Bird Treaty Act (1918), 306
Mill, John Stuart, 245
millennials, fame seeking by, 173
Mind–Body Problem, The (Goldstein),
xv–xvii, 298
Minsky, Marvin, 63
mirror self-recognition (MSR) test,
86, 301
Mishnah (Talmudic text), 283
mistakes, by mattering adjudicators,
239–42
Mitchell, Jason, 303
Moene, Karl, xvii
Montaigne, Michel de, 87
moral heroic strivers, 182–92, 239

Rebecca Newberger Goldstein grew up in White Plains, New York, the daughter of a cantor who had come to the United States from Ukraine. She graduated Barnard College summa cum laude and went onto Princeton University where she earned her PhD, specializing in philosophy of science. She then returned to Barnard as a professor. It was in her early years teaching there that she found herself, much to her surprise, writing a novel. It was published as *The Mind-Body Problem* and became a bestseller.

Since then, in between teaching philosophy, she's devoted her writing career to both fiction and nonfiction, all of her writing premised on her belief that humans are, at their core, philosophical animals—our philosophical orientations influenced by our characters, and our characters in turn influenced by our philosophical orientations. She has written seven books of fiction, the last of which was *Thirty-Six Arguments for the Existence of God: A Work of Fiction.* Her nonfiction books are *Incompleteness: The Proof and Paradox of Kurt Gödel, Betraying Spinoza: The Renegade Jew Who Gave Us Modernity,* and *Plato at the Googleplex: Why Philosophy Won't Go Away.*

Among her many prizes is a MacArthur "Genius" Award, which declared that "Goldstein's writings emerge as arguments for the belief that fiction in our time may be the best vehicle for involving readers in questions of morality and existence." Another cherished award came when she was given the National Medal of the Humanities from President Obama at a White House ceremony. The citation read "For bringing philosophy into conversation with culture. In scholarship, Dr. Goldstein has elucidated the ideas of Spinoza and Gödel, while in fiction, she deploys wit and drama to help us understand the great human conflict between thought and feeling."